May 7, 2017

Dear Rabbi,

Wishing you joy,
fulfillment & peace
in your rabbinic
career.

Mazal Tov!
The Plaut Family

THROUGH THE SOUND OF MANY VOICES

---·❧·---

*Writings
Contributed on the
Occasion of the
70th Birthday of*
W. GUNTHER PLAUT

EDITED BY JONATHAN V. PLAUT

LESTER
&ORPEN
DENNYS
PUBLISHERS

"God is heard through the sound of many voices."
Midrash Samuel

Canadian Cataloguing in Publication Data
Main entry under title:
Through the sound of many voices: writings contributed on the occasion of the 70th birthday of W. Gunther Plaut

Bibliography: p.
ISBN 0-88619-030-4

1. Judaism–Addresses, essays, lectures.   2. Plaut,
W. Gunther, 1912-   I. Plaut, W. Gunther, 1912-
II. Plaut, Jonathan V.

BM42.T47   296   C82-095186-2

Design Catherine Wilson for Sunkisst Graphics
Production Paula Chabanais Productions
Typesetting Rowsell Typesetting
Printed and bound by T. H. Best Printing Company Ltd.
for
LESTER & ORPEN DENNYS LIMITED
78 SULLIVAN STREET
TORONTO, ONTARIO
CANADA M5T 1C1

CONTENTS

FOREWORD

Reaching the age of three score and ten is an event of biblical proportions. This Festschrift is a tribute to a septuagena-
rian whose creative scholarship and international leadership have brought him in contact with many scholars and
leading personalities, who here join in paying him tribute.

There is no need to dwell at length on the details of my
father's life. Only last year his autobiography, *Unfinished
Business*, was published. Thus, a brief outline will suffice
to draw a broad picture of the man we salute on the occasion of his milestone birthday.

My father was born to a middle-class family in Münster,
Westphalia, in western Germany, not too far from the
Dutch border. His father, Jonas, had come from Hessen, and
now taught at the Jewish teachers' seminary. His mother,
Selma Gumprich, was a native of this small university
town. Shortly after, my grandfather accepted a teaching
position in Berlin, where the family lived until their emigration from Germany during the Hitler years.

My father's childhood was spent during the days of the
First World War. Two of his uncles died as German officers
at Verdun. His school years saw the rise of the Weimar Republic, rampaging inflation, and the growth of antisemitism. My father, however, led a rather sheltered life. His
parents were superintendents of an orphanage in Berlin,
which afforded all those who lived there a splendid degree of
isolation from the turmoil of the outside world. This quie-
tude was shattered when my father went to the university
and became exposed to the political life on campus. He

entered law school in 1930, one of the youngest to enroll. When three years later he took his exams, the Nazis had already come to power. Although he was still able to obtain a doctorate in international law, his legal career was finished.

Grandfather suggested that for the time being he take courses at the rabbinic seminary of which Dr. Leo Baeck was president. In preparation, father studied Hebrew with Abraham Joshua Heschel, and then immersed himself in Jewish law and tradition. He had a good grounding, for he had grown up in the midst of his parents' magnificent library, which had large Jewish components. In the spring of 1935 he received an invitation to study for the rabbinate at the Hebrew Union College in Cincinnati, Ohio, and in the fall he, along with four others, traveled to America to take up a new life. In 1937 he went back to Germany briefly to bring out his brother, Walter, who later also became a rabbi.

My father was always a passionate athlete. In Germany he had been a major-league soccer player and a tournament-tennis competitor. He had traveled to Tel Aviv in 1935 to participate in the Jewish Olympic Games.

He met Elizabeth Strauss in early 1938, and on the tenth of November, not knowing that this was *Kristallnacht*, they were married in Cincinnati—while in Berlin his father was a refugee from the police.

My father's first pulpit was in Chicago, on the west side of the city. He served as an assistant rabbi, which gave him an opportunity to prepare his few sermons carefully and also to spend some time in scholarly pursuits. Already as a rabbinic student he had begun to publish, and now he proceeded to do it at an increasing pace. He became contributing editor in Bible for the *Universal Jewish Encyclopedia* and wrote for various journals. His first contribution to literary life in America was a brief article in the *Atlantic Monthly*.

When America entered the war in 1941, my father was declared an "enemy alien." The day after he received his citizenship papers in 1943, he entered the Chaplains' Corps of the American army and later went overseas as a chaplain with the 104th Infantry Division. He saw combat and was present at the opening of the first concentration camp. He received the Bronze Star for his war service. When in 1946 he left the army, he returned to Chicago, where he became deeply involved in communal life and once again took up his scholarly pursuits.

In 1948 he became rabbi of Mt. Zion Temple in St. Paul, Minnesota, where he served for thirteen years. During that period he began to publish his first books on history and Bible. He became part of the political life of the community and an associate of many who would later make their mark in national politics, among them, Hubert Humphrey, Walter Mondale, Eugene McCarthy, and Orville Freeman. He was asked to serve as the chairman of the Governor's Commission on Ethics in Government. His wide interests led him to take active part in the artistic life of the community. For seven years he was president of the St. Paul Gallery and School of Art (later called the Minnesota Museum of Art), participated in the growing World Federalist Movement, and his weekly television and radio programs brought him in contact with many distinguished visitors to the Twin Cities. Soon his influence was felt in the State House as well as in other parts of Minnesota.

In 1961 he accepted a call to Holy Blossom Temple in Toronto, one of the continent's most prestigious congregations. Here, too, he became the undisputed leader of the Jewish community and, in time, the voice of Canadian Jewry. In 1977, just before he chose to retire from the active rabbinate, he was elected the official head of Canadian Jewry and assumed the presidency of the Canadian Jewish Congress, Canada's central Jewish organization. In addition to his responsibilities at home, my father traveled widely, lectured abroad, and published at an increasing rate.

His decision to leave the congregational rabbinate was motivated above all by his desire to finish his magnum opus, *A Modern Commentary*, on the Torah. The work was published in the fall of 1981 and quickly achieved international acclaim.

Norman Cousins once characterized my father as ''one of the wisest, most compassionate human beings I have ever known.'' He was impressed with my father's ''knowledge of the issues, his historical insights, his comprehension of the workings of public opinion, and, in general, with his leadership capabilities.''

How many great preachers are there in North America today—those who can electrify an audience and cause a hush in the crowd? My father has that charisma and capacity. His presence at a program draws the people to hear his message. His strong views have often found equally strong opposition, but always he has had the respect of those who disagreed with him.

My father is a disciplined human being. Throughout his entire existence, everything has had a time and place. His family came first, although the pressures of his rabbinic career made quality more important than quantity. He is more at ease with a book and a pen than with the frivolity of a social gathering. Seemingly aloof at a first encounter, his warmth and concern for people soon become apparent. Uninterested in the trivia and gossip of the day, my father is, however, a compassionate pastor, a sought-after counselor, and an eminently fair judge. He is a man whom anyone would be honored to call father.

Dr. Robert Gordis wrote, in a message attached to his article, about my father's place in world Jewry:

> Rabbi Plaut is a living demonstration that Judaism in its most creative period and in the careers of its greatest exemplars has always been deeply sensitive to the mysteries and complexities of existence, recognizing that no single approach can do justice to all the manifold strands in the pattern of life. Judaism has, therefore, developed the ability, in the face of two apparently contradictory positions, to take hold of both antinomies and find in the tension between them a stimulus to creativity and a new and higher level of integration in the tradition. Rabbi W. Gunther Plaut is a scion of German Jewry who grew to manhood before the eruption of the monstrous horror of Nazism. Thus, he incorporates all the values of the German-Jewish community, which for a century and a half was the great laboratory for every creative movement

in Jewish history, religious, cultural, and political. Coming to the American continent, he brought these values to creative tension with the pragmatic spirit of North American Jewry, whom he has served with dedication and distinction in the United States and Canada. The age-old dichotomy of tradition versus modernity he has resolved by stressing the values of tradition for modernists, seeking to win their appreciation and loyalty to Kelal Yisrael. The increasing complexity of modern life has driven a wedge between the scholar, who is conceived of as sitting in an ivory tower, and the congregational rabbi, pictured as being mired in the marketplace and seduced by the sirens of popular success. Rabbi Plaut's career demonstrates that the gap can be closed.

Certainly the fitting climax of my father's career is the magnificent commentary on the Torah which occupied him for some seventeen years. In an article in *Commentary*, Robert Alter, a contributing editor to the magazine and professor of Hebrew and comparative literature at Berkeley has written that, "for Jewish readers of the Bible, nothing like it exists in English or, indeed, in any language. The commentary," Alter says, "manages to be intellectually honest and sensitive about the possible contemporary relevance of the text without . . . touches of preacherly exhortation."

My father's interests have reached far and wide, and the essays in this book will, by their variety, testify to his many concerns, which reach from law to art, from biblical studies to human rights. (He has also made sculptures and published chess problems, but no master of the plastic arts or the chess world is represented in these pages.) All contributors have a personal relationship to him. Most of the essays have been written specifically for this book, the others have been adapted from lectures or were previously published in journals. Each one of the authors' particular fields of interest coincides with an aspect of my father's endeavors—for he is in fact a renaissance man, a person of many interests and concerns.

Above all, of course, he is now a man of letters who

spends some time each day working on his new book, magazine article, or regular newspaper columns. A few years ago he ventured into fiction and published a book of short stories, *Hanging Threads*, which appeared in the United States under the title, *The Man in the Blue Vest and Other Stories*. He is now working on an historical novel.

The bibliography of close to a thousand books and articles appended to this volume reflects a lifetime of labors that are by no means finished. Although the bibliography reaches only to the end of 1981, an impressive list of new titles has since reached print.

A number of individuals helped to make the publication of this volume financially possible. I should like to extend my deepest thanks to them: the families of Sidney Barrows, Sylvan Mack, Hess Kline, of St. Paul, Minnesota; Monroe Abbey, Charles Bronfman, Jack Cummings and Reuben Zimmerman, of Montreal; Edgar Bronfman, of New York; Sol Kanee of Winnipeg; Stan Alter, Karl Bald, Donald Carr, Dr. Joshua J. Chesnie, George A. Cohon, Carl Cole, Max Enkin, Dr. Arnold A. Epstein, Earl Farber, Alex Fisher, Joesph Frieberg, Gerry Goldenberg, Maxwell Goldhar, Harold Green, Dr. Gerald Halbert, Dr. Ralph Halbert, W. Bernard Herman, Harold Hertzman, Murray Koffler, Morris Latchman, Morris Levy, Lou Libman, Elliott Marrus, Ben, Bert, and Lou Mendelson, Donald Rafelman, Alvin Rosenberg, Harold Rosenberg, Gurston Rosenfeld, Lou Ronson, David Satok, Lionel Schipper, Milton Shier, Wayne Tanenbaum, Leon Weinstein, Ray Wolfe, Sam Young, of Toronto.

Last but not least, there are twenty-three authors whose voices join as a tribute to my father who has been their co-worker and associate. Their contributions are an expression of friendship which, more than my word of thanks, is its own reward.

I also wish to acknowledge gratefully the help rendered by my secretary, Mrs. Judy Hochberg, in the preparation of the manuscript.

This is a tribute to my father from his friends and associates, and it provides, from a personal standpoint, a special occasion for my grandmother, mother, sister, wife, and children to express their love and admiration.

JONATHAN V. PLAUT

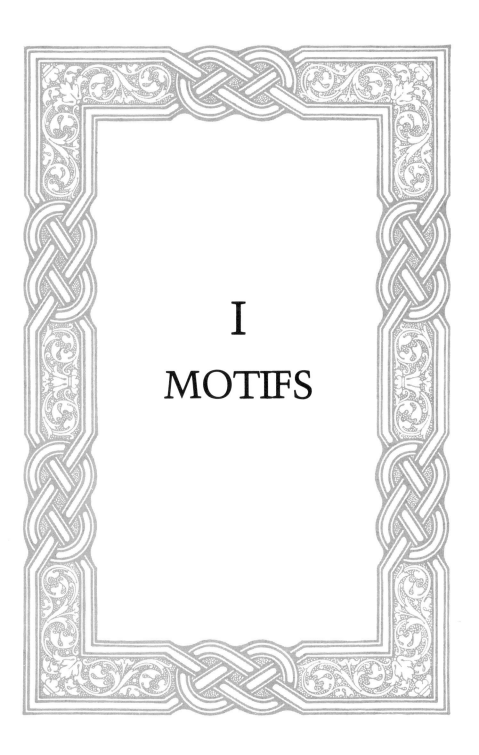

I
MOTIFS

FRIENDSHIP
Elie Wiesel

He is my age though he appears older; he appears as if he carried the weight of centuries on his shoulders.

He wears Chasidic garb and has a beard, its gray hair streaked with white. His bushy eyebrows, his soft yet penetrating gaze—everything in him moves me.

He is my friend, and he frightens me.

We have known each other since the war. We came from the same Orthodox Jewish milieu: I was born in Sighet, he in Ungvar. Both of us went to cheder and yeshivah; then we both found ourselves at camp. There, in the kindgom of night, we met for the first time.

Though we did not know it at the time, we inhabited the same barracks, experienced the same terror, the same hunger, the same solitude.

Only later, much later—when we reconstructed those events—did we discover that we had in fact lived together.

"Do you remember the first selection?"

"And Rosh Hashanah?"

"The first snow?"

"The long night march towards Gleiwitz?"

"The evacuation of Buchenwald?"

Ah yes, we had common memories. Yet, today, we resemble each other so little. He, a famous Talmudist, directs a large yeshivah in Brooklyn. I often visit him, to talk. Few friends understand me as he does.

Withal, why does my heart pound every time I go to visit him?

The sadism of Buna. The corpses of Buchenwald.

"Do you remember?"

"I remember."

The first minyan after the camp's liberation. We both were there. The Kaddish, recited by all—never will I forget it.

Unbelievable but true: we did not forget our prayers. Even stranger: some amongst us never abandoned them. Nothing baffles me more than to think of it today: all the starving, emaciated, humiliated, condemned who, despite danger, mumbled their prayers as they had always done at home, imploring the Creator to have pity on His creation.

I hope these remarks will not be misinterpreted; I am not theologizing, and I am content merely to be a witness.

I knew them, those believing Jews; I rubbed elbows with those pious youngsters, there in the depths of the netherworld. How could they chant the praises of a merciful God just a few steps away from the killers, under a smoke-blackened sky? I don't know. I only know that mornings and evenings, and above all on Shabbat, I heard them, in low and pained voices, submitting themselves to the Father of our ancestors, for they had faith in Him and His mercy.

I don't know how, but someone had managed to smuggle in a pair of tefillin by bribing a Kapo. He must have been paid dozens upon dozens of bread and margarine rations. I don't know who made the bargain or secreted the tefillin. I only know that every morning many of us rose before the call-up to still make the rear of the queue in our block in order to do this *mitzvah*.

Actually, I should note, the Law would not require it under these circumstances. One is not obligated to sacrifice his life for the sake of donning tefillin. And yet: Jews who did not know each other, who perhaps did not even speak the same language, met each morning at dawn, exposed themselves to nameless dangers, for the sake of not interrupting a millennia-old tradition.

I don't understand it. I will never understand whence they derived so much courage and marshaled so much self-denial, even while the world was forsaking them and surrendered them to death.

A childhood friend who lived quite near our home would

never eat non-kosher food at camp. I heard this from his companions. He never touched meat. He had made a decision better to die as a Jew than to live—or even exist—in violation of Torah.

More: he set himself to observe all religious commandments. He worked less on Shabbat, fasted on Tisha b'Av, and hardly touched any bread during the eight days of Passover.

They told me how he managed to light the candles according to the Law during the Chanukah week. He actually approached the camp commandant and very respectfully asked for potatoes. Not to eat, but to make primitive lamps from them: one for the first night, two for the second, eight for the eighth. Now the camp commandant was known for his brutality and cruelty. Normally, the man's logic would impel him to punish my friend for his audacity and kill him on the spot. Except that at that time nothing was normal.

That friend, I am afraid, is no longer my friend. An adherent of the Satmar Movement and the Neturei Karta, he espouses their extremist ideologies. For them, Jews like myself are not Jews. Were one to go by them, the Jewish people today would count only a hundred thousand souls: theirs.

Sometimes I have a mind to provoke a confrontation with my erstwhile friend. I would love to ask him quite simply: "Having lived through what you have, what all of us have, why be so hard, so intransigent, toward your brothers?" Unfortunately I know his answer, for he gave it to me twenty years ago during a chance encounter:

"God," he said, "God alone counts. When God is the issue your very brothers are unimportant."

"And you think that you can please God by speaking in this manner, by acting in this way—in His name?"

"I try to live in accordance with Torah; I hope that by doing this I accomplish His will."

I no longer see this one.

But I do see my first friend, my companion of Buna and Buchenwald. He is no less pious or less erudite than the other one; he is, however, more open, more indulgent—in other words, more human.

We were among the four hundred children whom the government of Charles de Gaulle had brought from Buchenwald to France. Having arrived in Normandy we were put up in a sumptuous castle, and then separated into two groups: one religious, the other secular. My friend and I joined the former. We were hardly settled when we appealed to the management: we wanted strictly kosher food, ritual objects, books for prayer and study.

At once my friend made himself our guide, our spokesman. When there were matters to discuss with the management, he did it. He had enough to keep him busy, certainly at first. That was to be expected, for those responsible for the group were French Jews with an Alsatian or German background, who did not know our habits, the things we stayed away from, our superstitions, our inhibitions. After all, between us there were two worlds, two apprehensions of the universe, which were colliding with each other. Those responsible for us were the first free men and women we had encountered. What they did appeared strange to us; we could not help but suspect them. Of what? Of every beastliness imaginable. Of wanting to convert us, for instance, of trying to corrupt our souls, to poison them with Western culture. So we were determined not to let them do it. Guided by my friend, we put up a ferocious battle so that Shabbat would become a real Shabbat, so that the service would be dignified, and the study room similar to those we had known in our childhood.

Beaten down by distress and sorrow we now spent a year in fervor and exaltation.

Together we made the acquaintance of Rav Shushani. I have elsewhere tried to describe this stupendous, disquieting, mysterious person. No one knew whence he came or how he managed to live; nothing about him was known. Despite his appearance and droll comportment he overwhelmed us with his knowledge. He taught Talmud and commentaries by heart; his courses lasted eight hours or more. He astonished, he amused, he enraged his students. Ancient and modern philosophies, medieval literature and nuclear science, poetry and painting, politics and mysticism—he was at ease in all these disciplines and taught us to follow him toward the dizzy heights of the spirit, where it is dangerous to take a step forward or backward without using a guide like him.

Shushani remained my master teacher for several years. My friend refused to follow us. In fact, he tried to persuade me to do as he had done and break with my teacher.

"He is dangerous," he told me. "I can feel it, I know it. I have no available proof, but my instinct tells me: get away from him."

"But why? You admit he is a great Talmudist?"

"Yes."

"You don't deny that he is intellectually superior to all of us?"

"No, I don't deny it."

"Well then, what else do you need?"

"I don't know. But I can feel it. I feel myself threatened in his presence. And because you are my friend I allow myself to give you advice: leave him as soon as possible. Don't see him again, the welfare of your soul is at stake."

Ah well, I chose to be deaf to his counsel. Education appeared to me more important than everything else, more important even than my salvation. I was burning to know, to understand. Nothing intimidated me. I craved to search and explore, to examine what appeared to be below the surface, the forbidden, hidden, obscure—in short, the other side of reality, of thought, of certainty.

That is why I stayed with Rav Shushani, while my friend and fellow student went to study and learn in the United States.

Some years went by when we had no direct contact with each other. I traveled much at that period; I encountered friends old and new; I rediscovered camp companions; we spoke of the war and the time after the war; sometimes we brought up Shushani and his disciples. And my friend, what had become of him? In the sixties, when I was already living in the United States, I was seized by curiosity. Why not pay him a visit?

He had changed, yet not really, not inwardly. Author of works which had made a mark in talmudic jurisprudence, he directed a yeshivah of four hundred students. His smile was warm and reassuring.

I love to meet him and we see each other often. Still, each time I set out for Brooklyn I go with an unnamed anxiety. Why? Because when I find myself with my friend I realize how little it would have taken to have ended up like him.

HAPPINESS
June Callwood

A number of elderly people, consulted by anthropologists, sociologists, paleontologists, and others interested in the study of relics, have assured their interrogators that there is a second wind in life. In old age, a feeling of youthfulness and beatific happiness pervades the senses.

Ah, happiness.

Balm of toilers and weepers; the carnival's promise; the heart's abiding hope; eternity's reward for the pious.

The Chinese offer a choice of good luck wishes. One is "long life." The other is "happiness." Ashley Montagu, in *Growing Young*, says that these are, in some cases, indivisible.

Happy new year. Happy anniversary. Happy bat mitzvah. Happy birthday to you; blow out the candles and wish: happiness. Here's a toast to the bride and groom: happiness.

It isn't the happiness of a good time that people crave. That's something else, distraction from unhappiness, sea foam teased prettily by the wind but impossible to hold. Nor is it the happiness of an end to anxiety: the warrior's home, the rent is paid. And it isn't the pleasures of possessions which are vulnerable to use, misuse, and mud slides.

> And there is even happiness
> That makes the heart afraid.
>
> Thomas Hood

That's elation born of a fine day; the reveler basks uneasily, anticipating the storm.

This is a person-on-the-street interview, and we're stopping people at random. You, madam, what do you want out of life? You, sir, what do you want for your children? Speak up, grannie, what matters most?

Happiness. All-purpose, all-day, and, especially, all-night, all-weather self-esteem. Being one's own best friend for life. The real thing.

Morton M. Hunt, a writer, flew solitary reconnaissance with the Eighth Air Force during the Second World War. When the war ended, he began to have an emotional breakdown. For weeks his nights were fitful and reamed with terror. By day he was rigid with the effort to continue to seem sane. Then the panic began to loosen. His handwriting looked less like that of a palsied stranger. One afternoon he heard a shard of Mozart on a car radio. He felt a flood of intense joy, as if he had just seen his dearest friend.

"It's me," he thought gratefully. "I'm back."

Philosophers rarely consider the study of happiness a suitable pursuit for a learned person. There is something sappy about examining a state of mind that isn't famous for being productive. Creativity comes from different clay. Approved happiness is the by-product of usefulness. Or, like fingerprints, it is so individualized as to be indescribable as a pure entity.

Still, Thomas Jefferson thought happiness was so desirable that he included its pursuit in the Declaration of Independence, among such American rights as freedom. The United States is the only country on earth with an astonishing guarantee for all citizens to search for happiness by any legal means that come to mind. Efforts by the courts to define what this entitles Americans to do have failed in every test; by common consent, Jefferson's aberration is now a museum artifact.

Of late psychologists have been conducting expensive surveys to ask what makes people happy. There are even Gallup polls on the subject. Norman M. Bradburn, a social scientist at the University of Chicago, spent several years studying happiness. Some two thousand people in four different American communities were asked a range of questions about their lives, the key one being, "Taken altogether, how would you say things are these days—would you say that you are very happy, pretty happy, or not too happy?"

The results appeared in *The Structure of Psychological*

Well-Being. Approximately 35 per cent of Americans told the researchers they were very happy; 54 per cent called themselves pretty happy; only 11 per cent admitted to feeling sub-par. That study was done in the seventies, half-way between the sixties protest and euphoria and the eighties arms race and recession. Still, exactly the same results were noted in a Gallup poll in 1946 and another in 1952.

That's an impressive number of happy people, if the figures are true. Human pride makes the results suspect. When a stranger asks, "How's it going?" even the tormented reply, "Fine."

Bradburn found the highest level of reported unhappiness among unemployed black men in a Chicago ghetto. The most happiness was in a stable, all-white working-class neighborhood in Detroit, with an affluent all-white suburb of Washington, D.C., close behind.

Weather, religion, age, gender, marital status, and education weren't significant factors. Bradburn could single out only one element consistent in the patterns of response: self-described happy people tended to be socially mobile. He concluded that poverty's stagnation, its drabness and restrictions, reduce the likelihood of happiness. The Romans were right to provide bread and circuses to cheer up the masses. For which, substitute television.

This is nonsense. An absence of options is unpleasant, but not particularly relevant to the alchemy of happiness. People who hop on airplanes are not observably ecstatic. Mobility produces variety, stimulation, and delight, as well as digestive upset and anxiety. Mobility isn't the bearer of happiness, or people wouldn't fight on vacations or following promotions.

The relationship between activity and happiness is a subject that engrosses people who like to keep busy. A few years ago Dr. Harry Maas of the School of Social Work at the University of British Columbia reported on a seven-year study of old age. He deduced that the happiest people he found were old women who had a full schedule of outside activities and home-management.

John P. Zubec, University of Manitoba psychologist, in

Human Development, cited a number of research projects that supported the view that happiness in old age is dependent on a full appointment book.

Voltaire agreed: "The further I advance in age, the more I find work necessary. It becomes, in the long run, the greatest of pleasures." Nietzsche said the same thing, but backwards: "I do not want happiness; I want to do my work."

As a tool for acquiring happiness, activity is suspect. People who are deeply unhappy not infrequently immerse themselves in the oblivion of compulsive work or play, or both. Ceaseless distraction is not possible, however, and the subject inevitably must endure the burden of whatever emotional state lies at the bottom of the cave.

Everyone wants happiness: the bluebird, it has been called; the holy grail; free fall; Freud's "oceanic feeling." Robert Louis Stevenson wrote: "The habit of being happy enables one to be freed, or largely freed, from the domination of outward conditions."

That's it, the habit of being happy. Small wonder that its temporary acquisition through booze, drugs, copulation, chocolate sundaes, and a new suit is ultimately depressing. Still, they are better than no happiness at all.

Happy people have no edges. They don't take offense easily. They notice what's going on around them, being largely free of the consuming effort of protecting themselves. They don't snap at others. They don't envy. They don't worry about their hair, hold grudges, or wake up at four in the morning wishing they were dead. Happy people are easy to love, which makes them even happier, which renders them even more lovable. And so on.

Happy people get asked to everything.

Nathaniel Hawthorne once cautioned that happiness is a butterfly. If you chase it, the butterfly will elude you. If you sit still, contemplating clouds, a butterfly may light on your finger.

Aristotle proposed a theory called *audaemonia,* which maintains that happiness springs from activity governed by reason. This is the ruling principle of workaholics and appears to have nothing to say about butterflies. Skip Plato;

listen to Epicurus, who said, "True pleasure consists in serenity of mind and absence of fear."

The Stoics declared that only the virtuous are happy, defining virtue so narrowly as to eliminate everyone but their unhappy selves. Augustine, Kant, and Sophocles did not have a cheerful view of happiness: they maintained that no one could be happy who was not dead.

Aquinas said happiness was an active, moral life.

Horace and Disraeli believed that the basis of happiness is health.

Thoreau, Marcus Aurelius, and George Bernard Shaw subscribed to the active theory. "To be is worn out before you are thrown on the scrap heap."

Cicero, Edmund Burke, Bertrand Russell, Henrik Ibsen, and Buddha believed that happiness was inseparable from tranquility. "Happy indeed," sang the unmoving Buddha, "we live unanxious among the anxious."

Conn Smythe, builder of Maple Leaf Gardens, a patriot, and a tyrant, when he was in his eighties informed a reporter that his secret for happiness was sex twice a week and clearing his bowel once a day.

William Lyon Phelps said the happiest person is the one who thinks the most interesting thoughts.

Lin Yutang: "The man who knows what he wants is a happy man."

Ted Twetie of Vancouver, on the occasion of his one hundredth birthday: "Always have a strong notion for smoking cigarettes, drinking rum, chewing Irish twist, and spitting up against the wind."

The light dawns. They are all, from Aristotle to Twetie, speaking about what makes *them* happy. It is hypothesis by projection, Linus the Philosophy King passing out pieces of his security blanket as his contribution to human wisdom.

It is necessary to look elsewhere. Perhaps the truth lies in the phenomenon that happy people get happier without seeming effort. Butterflies land all over them.

The October 1975 issue of *psychology today* contained a happiness survey that was answered by 52,000 readers. Designed by two psychologists from Columbia University,

[12]

Phillip Shaver and Jonathan Freedman, it was provocatively entitled "What Makes You Happy?"

The responses almost lamed the computer. One respondent was in a hurry. He wanted to be notified at once if his answers indicated he was happy. How else would he know, except by printout?

Seven out of 10 of *psychology today's* admittedly upper-income, higher-educated readers said that they had been happy over the previous six months. Eight out of 10 brooded about happiness all the time. One-third felt "constant worry and anxiety." Forty per cent said they often felt lonely; 13 per cent of men and 32 per cent of women had frequent headaches. Eighteen per cent of men and 30 per cent of women felt so low they sometimes thought they couldn't go on.

Despite this, 70 per cent claimed to have bouts of happiness. Happiness should be made of sterner stuff.

George Bernard Shaw with another observation about happiness: "The man with a toothache thinks everyone happy whose teeth are sound." Thanks.

The happiness mentioned most frequently in recent years, that which adheres in particular to some elderly people, appears to have the element of self-realization. Scholars credit Spinoza, the seventeenth-century misfit, with the first insight into this reality. The essence of his philosophy is contained in this breathtaking sentence: "Happiness consists in this: that man [or woman] can preserve his [or her] own being."

William McDougall, in *An Introduction to Social Psychology*, expressed the Spinozian vision this way: "The richer, the more completely unified or integrated is the personality, the more capable is it of sustained happiness, in spite of intercurrent pains of all sorts."

As Nietzsche advised: "Become what thou art!"

"What a man [or woman] has in himself [or herself] is the chief element in happiness."

Forty years ago, Abraham Maslow, the sage of Brandeis University, examined the mystery of emotional wholeness. He reported that he was awed before the splendor of a well person, a fully-realized, free-standing individual.

Unlike the upbeat surveys, he estimated that only one per cent of adults, three per cent at most, attain full maturity, which is the basis for habitual happiness. These artists in living "make full use and exploitation of talents, capacities, potentialities." They are fulfilled. They have Erich Fromm's "inner productiveness." Active or inactive, they are at peace with themselves.

Fromm, Maslow, and others have faith in human perfectability. They note that happiness is achieved most commonly by those whose childhoods were affectionate, consistent, and stimulating, but that others lamed early in life nonetheless also manage to limp to completeness. Paavo Nurmi, a cripple, became the world's greatest runner; a lonely, anxious child can grow to serenity and bliss.

As explanation for this miracle of the human spirit, Maslow postulates that people have an innate instinct for higher development, something indomitable in their essence. This will not only to grow but also to flower takes the person past the struggle for basic needs: food, safety, love, and esteem. The next level involves certain assertions. The person must have freedom to speak, freedom to investigate and seek information, freedom to defend the self, and also justice, fairness, honesty, and order in the society. The latter is what Jefferson was getting at when he conceived the flawed theory that in a democracy everyone would have the tools to become happy.

The concomitant is skill of a high order to determine consequences and make informed decisions.

"I have done as I pleased all my life," said Katharine Hepburn serenely, ". . . and paid the price."

Maslow listed some people he was "fairly sure" had achieved happiness: Thomas Jefferson and the older Abraham Lincoln; in the "highly probable" category were Einstein, Eleanor Roosevelt, Jane Addams, William James (who once said that people who haven't considered suicide before reaching thirty won't mature), Aldous Huxley, and Spinoza; among the "possibles" were Eugene V. Debs, Pablo Casals, Sholom Aleichem, Robert Browning, Renoir,

Benjamin Franklin, Walt Whitman, Harriet Tubman, and Martin Buber.

"In a word," said Maslow, "they are capable of gratitude. The blessedness of their blessings remains conscious. Miracles remain miracles even though occurring again and again. The awareness of undeserved good luck, of gratuitous grace, guarantees for them that life remains precious and never grows stale."

Lovely. Except that Maslow also stated, in *Motivations and Personality*, that permanent happiness isn't possible. He went on to explain that happy people have the permanent ability to return to happiness, however shaken by desolating events.

"A lifetime of happiness!" groaned Shaw. "No man alive could bear it; it would be hell on earth."

Nothing is more helpful to growth than people. Humans are herd animals and need their tribe. Living with one's self is an epic achievement, but living comfortably with others not only sustains self-worth, but is necessary for its very existence. Nothing is more useful to a person than people.

"And the wider the circle, the greater the gain," comments V. J. McGill, in *The Idea of Happiness*.

Child's play is preparation for the adult ability to be happy. So is skin contact with an infant; stroking a baby induces responsiveness and a sense of safety. The play of children consolidates those beginnings; it is a serious activity. Laughing children are growing themselves.

If people were happier, they would be kinder. If they were kinder, everyone would be happier. As happiness increased, so would kindness. As kindness increased, so would happiness. . . .

Etc.

[15]

HOPE
Norman Cousins

The ultimate adventure on earth is the adventure of ideas. The times favor new ideas. Old dogmas and ideologies are losing their power to inspire or terrify. They are no longer prime sources of intellectual energy and have become instead traditional enduring symbols, objects of generalized attachments and loyalties. Compartmentalized man is giving way to world man. The banner commanding the greatest attention has human unity stamped upon it.

"Something is happening," Teilhard de Chardin wrote, "to the whole structure of human consciousness. A fresh kind of life is starting. In the face of such an upheaval, no one can remain indifferent." The century of Marx and Engels has ended. Marxian doctrine is breaking up, both outside and inside the Soviet Union. The Marxian prophecy about the emergence under capitalism in the United States of a working class with an intense class-consciousness has not materialized. Quite the contrary. The working class in the United States insists on seeing itself much more in middle-class terms than in terms of the class struggle. Edward Bellamy has proved to be a far more accurate prophet than Marx, predicting even more fluidity in the social structure than existed a century ago. Capitalism in the United States has undergone profound modification, not just under the New Deal, but through a consensus that continued to grow after the New Deal and that is now beyond major political debate.

The dethroning of dogma, apparent in politics and ideology, has spared neither philosophy nor religion. New and open currents are at work everywhere. People are breaking through traditions and barriers that obstruct or run counter to ideas of human unity. In philosophy, the familiar notion that a meeting of East and West can best be brought about by a confluence of Eastern spirituality and Western technology now lacks charm and historical force. The splendor or limitations associated with spirituality and technology are no longer assigned to vast geographical blocs.

Old ideas of separatism and group identity don't move men as much as new perceptions of human solidarity. What is happening is that the human race is fighting back. It is responding to the accumulation of dangers and terrors that could put a torch to the human nest. It is facing up to the bizarreness of gamesmanship applied to human destiny, and to the insanity of making the earth a warehouse for holocaust-producing weapons. It dares to think that ethics can be applied to the behavior of nations.

All sorts of magnificent notions are at large in the human mind today, and the most revolutionary notion of all is that the problem of human survival is not beyond human intelligence.

The starting point for a better world is the belief that it is possible. Civilization begins in the imagination. The wild dream is the first step to reality. It is the direction-finder by which men locate higher goals and discern their highest selves.

The case for optimism goes beyond the recognition of a divine itch or the sudden notion that there is an extra minute before midnight. The American experiment has succeeded in a way that Madison and Hamilton never dared dream it would. Its essential idea—that nothing is more important than individual man—has met the test and has been echoed on every continent. The individual man has come into his own. Thinking, feeling, musing, complaining, fending, creating, building, evading, desiring, he has become more important to the operators of his governments than ever before. The question, therefore, is not whether man is capable of prolonging and ennobling his stay on earth. The question is whether he recognizes his prime power—and also his duty—for accomplishing that purpose.

Hope may be fortified by experience, but that is not where it begins. It begins in the certainty that things can be done that have never been done before. This is the ultimate reality, and it defines the uniqueness of the human mind.

[17]

II
ON
SCHOLARSHIP

ON JUDAISM AND
JEWISH LEARNING
Robert Gordis

No student of Judaism can fail to be impressed by the many unique attributes it displays. Not the least is the fact that Judaism is the oldest living religious tradition on the face of the globe, with the possible exception of some cults in the African jungle or the Australian bush. Christianity and Islam, both daughter-religions of Judaism, are obviously younger than their mother. But even the religions of the Far East, the faiths of India, China, and Japan, emerged centuries after Judaism had appeared on the stage of history.

This uniqueness is by no means merely a matter of longevity; it is expressed in many features of its world view, several of which I should like to highlight here.

I am, of course, well aware that every religion, culture, and ethnic group, indeed, every living thing, is individual and unique. Hence, this attribute is to be understood here as descriptive, not as eulogistic.

One of the outstanding qualities of historical Judaism is its capacity for embodying antinomies, its ability to incorporate what might superficially seem to be irreconcilable opposites, and by the resolution of that tension—or even by maintaining both unresolved—to enrich the content of the tradition. Some of these antinomies are biblical, while others are rabbinic, though resting on biblical foundations. In very cursory fashion let me cite a few examples from each period.

Ever since the days of the prophets, Judaism developed an antinomy between particularism and universalism, and persisted in holding on to both! Surely one of the noblest and earliest expressions of universalism is the great prophetic vision of the End-Time, which looks forward to the establishment of world peace, when nations will recognize the sovereignty of the moral law and resolve their conflicts, not through the sword, but through standards of equity. The prophecy occurs in both Isaiah, chapter 2, and Micah, chapter 4.[1] The passage is of course famous, and deservedly so. It is inscribed on the Isaiah Wall at the United Nations, where it stands as a silent condemnation of the international Immoral Majority that now rules those precincts.

But this is only one side of the coin. What is noteworthy is that immediately after proclaiming this universalistic message, each prophet adds a special lesson for his Jewish contemporaries. Isaiah says: "O house of Jacob, come let us walk by the light of the Lord" (2:5). Loyalty to the God of humanity requires that Israel set the example by a stronger attachment to his God. Micah makes the same point by indulging in a Jewish *qal vahomer*: "For as all nations walk each in the name of his god, so we must walk in the name of the Lord our God forever and ever" (4:5).[2] If all nations steadfastly maintain the worship of the national deities, unworthy though they may be, Israel should remain loyal to the God of all the earth.[3] It is precisely the goal of a united humanity that should impel the Jew to deeper devotion to his own tradition.

Even in later periods, when persecution and exile tended to narrow the perspective of an exiled and persecuted people, Judaism retained its commitment to both universalism and particularlism. The *Alenu* prayer from the High Holy Day ritual became part of the daily service, and both paragraphs are recited three times each day. The first paragraph emphasizes the uniqueness of Israel and its destiny, setting it apart from the nations of the earth. The second paragraph looks forward to the day when evil will be uprooted and all creatures of flesh and blood will accept God's sovereignty and live by His law. Rab, the great Babylonian Amora who laid the foundations of the Babylonian Talmud, like the prophets before him, held fast to his concern for both Israel and humanity.[4]

Through the centuries, lesser spirits, both within the

Jewish community and without, have been unable to reconcile these antinomies. Some have opted for a universalism, a love of humanity so pervasive that it left no room for love of their own people. Others, particularly in times of stress like our own, have developed an all-consuming love for the Jewish people and, brushing aside the basic ethical teachings of Judaism, have dismissed any concern for the needs and rights of other ethnic or racial groups. Neither alternative is the Jewish way.

Another instance of basic antinomies held in creative tension is the biblical faith in both the love and the justice of God. The prophets never cease to warn their people that divine justice will bring retribution upon sinful men and nations, including their own. With equal vigor they call upon Israel to return from its evil path and put its trust in the love and forgiveness of a merciful God.

The classical statement on God's attributes is in Exod. 34:6-7: "Lord, Lord, a God merciful and gracious, slow to anger and abounding in steadfast love and faithfulness, keeping steadfast love for thousands, forgiving iniquity and transgression and sin, but who will by no means clear the guilty, visiting the iniquity of the fathers upon the children and the children's children, to the third and fourth generation."[5] It is restated time and again in the Bible and becomes central in the liturgy.

Rabbinic Judaism hypostasized both attributes as *Middat Hadin*, the quality of judgment, and *Middat Harahamim*, the quality of mercy, and spoke of the two thrones upon which the Holy One, blessed be He, sits in heaven.[6] Here again the failure to encompass the antinomy explains the assumption by many modern biblical critics that the pre-exilic prophets brought only a message of doom and destruction to their people. Hence contemporary critics often declare that all passages in the pre-exilic prophets that speak of consolation and rebuilding are later interpolations. We are asked to believe that the prophets from Amos to Jeremiah courted hatred, exile, and even death, merely to proclaim an inevitable catastrophe, and that whenever a

[22]

passage expresses love and pity for their people and a faith in God's mercy and forgiveness, it is to be excised from the text. As Eissfeldt put it, *Für ihn, ist Gott alles, Israel nichts,* "For Amos, God is everything, Israel, nothing."

This may be a position entirely congenial to a German theologian, but not to a Hebrew prophet. This alleged attitude is theologically, as well as psychologically, impossible for a Hebrew prophet. For if Israel, a tiny island in a pagan sea, were to be annihilated, who would be the bearers of God's cause in the world? On the one hand, the prophets never cease to warn their people that divine justice will bring retribution upon sinful men and nations, including their own; on the other, with equal vigor, they call upon Israel to return from its evil path and put its trust in the love and forgiveness of a merciful God. For them and for the religion they helped to create, God's justice and mercy are inseparable.

This antinomy is not merely the result of theological speculation about God; it is an insight reflecting the realities of human nature and the life of society, for justice without mercy is cruelty, while mercy without justice is sentimentality.

In addition, in maintaining these antimonies that are biblical in origin, Rabbinic Judaism articulated several others. Because it created an elaborate system of Halakhah, Rabbinic Judaism confronted the age-old problem of the relationship between liberty and law, and insisted that both were compatible. Citing the scriptural passage that informs us that the Decalogue is *ḥārūt*, engraved on the tablets (Exod. 32:16), Rabbi Joshua ben Levi revocalized the word as *ḥērūt*, liberty, in the great affirmation: "Only he is truly free who occupies himself with the Torah" (*Abot* 6:2).

As old as human thought itself, and not limited to Judaism, is the age-old crux of God's foreknowledge and man's freedom. Rigorously logical theologians and philosophers such as Calvin and Spinoza have insisted unflinchingly on the iron-clad law of predestination or causation, which renders man's moral freedom impossible, or, in Spinoza's view, an illusion. But as Samuel Johnson wisely remarked,

''With regard to free-will, all philosophy is against it and all experience is for it.'' Innumerable attempts have been made to resolve the paradox.[7] Whether or not the contradiction is succesfully resolved, the standpoint of Judaism is clear. What matters is man's moral freedom, and hence his moral responsibility. In Rabbi Akiba's famous utterance, ''Everything is foreseen, but man is given freedom of will'' (Abot 3:15). Judaism holds fast to both elements of the paradox, because it highlights a reality of the human condition.

These are some of the familiar antitheses which have been held in tension in the Jewish tradition. I should like to call attention to one other that has not always been recognized as such, but which has been highly meaningful to me personally. I refer to the two traditional concepts of Torah Lishmah, study for its own sake, and Torat Hayyim, study for the sake of life. On the one hand, Judaism is dedicated to learning for its own sake, the quest for the truth as far as it is given to a fallible human being to achieve. On the other hand, there has been a constant preoccupation with Torat Hayyim, an insistence that the Torah is not to be an esoteric pursuit sundered from life and indifferent to its problems. On the contrary, its real significance and abiding value lie in its contribution to meeting vital problems and the enhancement of human well-being.

To be sure, there have always been dedicated students of Torah, even distinguished scholars, who have been unable to embody both ideals in their careers. They have, therefore, retreated into an ivory tower and immersed themselves in study and research that could never have any relation to reality. They spend their lives in what Thorsten Veblen has called ''uneventful diligence.'' However, the greatest teachers of Judaism throughout the ages have been those who have been able to incorporate both ideals in their lives.

We have only to recall the achievements of Hillel and Johanan ben Zakkai, Akiba and Judah Hanasi, Rab and Samuel, Saadya and Rambam. In modern times the tradition has lived on in such disparate figures as Rabbi Isaac Elhanan and Rabbi A. I. Kook, Solomon Schechter and Abraham Heschel, Leo Baeck and Mordecai Kaplan. These scholars and leaders, as well as many others, have been able to find in this tension between *Torah Lishmah* and *Torat Hayyim* a fountain of stimulation and enrichment.

It is no accident that it is precisely the greatest and most creative scholars who have been able to hold fast both to *Torah Lishmah* and *Torat Hayyim*. On the one hand, *Torat Hayyim*, the concern for learning for the sake of life, has given to *Torah Lishmah*, learning for its own sake, a vitality and a relevance that has enhanced its value and significance immeasurably. On the other hand, the standards of unswerving loyalty to the truth and freedom from ulterior considerations that are demanded by Torah for its own sake have prevented Torah for the sake of life from degenerating into the vulgar popularizations and the bigoted distortions that pass for Jewish learning in many quarters today.

To keep *Torah Lishmah* and *Torat Hayyim* in creative tension and, thus, help make Jewish learning a significant instrument for Jewish living in our time is the great imperative for Jewish scholarship in our age. If Jewish studies are to be meaningful in the world and retain the respect of intelligent and sensitive men and women, and, what is more important, attract the attention and activity of creative men and women in the future, they must have an impact on life. We must strive, on the one hand, to hold fast to these two antinomies of objective and disinterested scholarship—not uninterested or uninteresting—and learning that is responsive to life, on the other.

These reflections on the nature and goals of Torah suggest a few observations on the nature of humanistic scholarship. It is, of course, a truism that all humanistic studies have a difficult lot in our day, while philology and exegesis occupy the lowest rung on the scale of values. In this, the golden age of natural science and technology, we who are engaged in humanistic disciplines often feel a crushing sense of inferiority, vis-à-vis the natural scientists. Nor am I thinking now of the vast difference in the material rewards granted by society to nuclear physicists and to editors of classical texts. We envy our colleagues in the natural sciences the instruments supplied to them by technology that are not available to us. Most important of all, they are often able to verify their theories and check their accuracy by repeating the experiments. Finally, they have the capacity to achieve a high degree of exactness in their researches by quantifying their results, rendered even easier in our computerized age. No wonder that they exude a sense of self-assurance and certitude, or so it seems to us, to which we cannot lay claim.

While humility is a virtue, extreme self-abasement is not. We fall prey to this sense of inferiority because we fail to remember that the material we deal with, namely, the human being, is infinitely more complex, varied, and intractable than the nonhuman world, which is the area of observation and research of the natural scientist. Moreover, much of the apparent certainty that prevails in the natural sciences is itself imaginary: witness the sharp controversies among natural scientists working on the frontier areas, such as subnuclear physics, biogenetics, and space exploration.

If the natural scientists are increasingly sensitive to the tentative nature of their enterprise, the lesson for humanistic scholars should be all the more obvious. Whether as historians of a past that cannot be repeated for verification, or as interpreters of texts and artifacts that are fragmentary remains of a past that can be only partially known, humanistic scholars should always be conscious of the mysterious reality they are seeking to reconstruct and of the tentative character of their undertaking. Since rival hypotheses in these fields cannot be verified or disproved by repeating the experiment, the only valid test is the elegance and simplicity of the various hypotheses advanced and the degree to which they "satisfy the phenomena," to use the older classical phrase.

Fueled by a sense of inferiority, many humanistic scholars are tempted to imitate the methods employed in the natural sciences by putting their faith in computers and statistical tables. To be sure, computers can be of enormous help in reducing the drudgery involved in dealing with statistical data, but they cannot replace original ideas, creative insight, and rigorous thought. Originality, insight, and sound method have always been rare commodities. All too often their paucity is papered over by questionable methodology, by uncritical repetition of the latest fashionable theories, and by ignoring decades and centuries of earlier research.

At this late date, it need not be emphasized that the comparative method is indispensable to modern critical scholarship. But there are pitfalls along its way. We fall prey to what has aptly been called "parallelomania," the search for similarities, apparent or real, genuine or farfetched. A related symptom of this failing is "footnote-itis," the piling up of references to books and papers that may impress the reader, but do not necessarily illumine the subject. In seeking to shed light on an aspect of one culture-sphere by evidence from another, humanistic scholars are sometimes tempted to explain *obscura per obscuriora*, what is unclear by what is even more unclear and uncertain.

In the desire to achieve certainty, we lapse into dogmatism and hostility to rival views. We are tempted to use the verb "demonstrate" and eschew such locutions as "we believe", "we suggest", "it is possible", "perhaps." Moreover, to "guarantee" our results, we are led to carve out ever more minute areas as our field of specialization, so that we are in danger of knowing more and more about less and less.

We often speak of scholarship as a "calling" or a "vocation," but these are simply honorific terms for an occupation. As in every activity, there are levels of dedication and ability that we may designate imperfectly as apprentices, journeymen, artisans, master craftsmen, and creative artists, and there is useful work for all. There come to mind the words spoken by the great Greek scholar Williamowicz–Moellendorf to his students: "When you are digging for diamonds and you find earthworms, do not be disheartened, but do not mistake the earthworms for diamonds."

The disparity among scholars aside, we need a true understanding of the nature of humanistic scholarship. Basically

all humanistic disciplines are exegesis, the effort to interpret one age, society, or culture to another, whether by the
exposition of a text or by the reconstruction of an earlier
and different epoch through the medium of archaeology or
the writing of history.

First and foremost, it needs to be recognized that exegesis
is not a science, but an art, resting upon a complex of scientific disciplines. An illuminating analogy is afforded by the
practice of medicine. Though medicine is often described as
a science, it is actually an art, utilizing many sciences, such
as anatomy, pathology, pharmacology, and psychology, but
requiring such intangible qualities in the practitioner as intuition, experience, and insight into the constitution of the
patient. Similarly, the interpretation of a text requires not
only a background knowledge of phonetics, morphology,
syntax, linguistics, history, comparative religion, literature, and many more, but also insight, creative imagination, and empathy with the material.

Many of the most distinguished practitioners of scientific
research have emphasized the importance that intuition has
played in their discoveries. It is the presence or the absence
of these indefinable qualities that explains why two
scholars of comparable competence will produce exposi-
tions of the same text, varying widely in quality and perti-
nence. The inescapable, indeed, essential basis of subjectiv-
ity in all exegesis is the reason why literature, particularly
the literature of religion, needs to be interpreted anew in
every age in the light of new knowledge and new perspectives and concerns.

The distinguished Palestinian archaeologist, Paul W.
Lapp, after a meticulous analysis of the problems involved
and the techniques available in the writing of history, sets
forth conclusions that are strikingly parallel to our own
observations on the nature of exegesis:

It seems to me that the ultimate source of history is the
will of the historian to assert his particular faith in
humanity and the will of people to accept the assertion.
To be sure, he must have sources, he must employ con-

siderable time and thought in order to understand and evaluate them, he must tax his reason to produce a convincing framework to present his views; in the end, he sets down statements based upon his own convictions about man and his world. In the end, he wills to be human, to present his own conception of humanity. If his conception convinces many, he is honored as a historian.[8]

What is true of history is at least equally true of literature. The interpretation both of events and of words is essentially a work of art, a construct of the creative imagination and the expression of a particular world view. To be sure, the synthesis or the interpretation must conform to the objective data available. But the choice among various competing approaches, all of which may meet the test of external evidence, will depend on the degree to which each interpretation reveals a congruence of structure within the various elements of the work and the extent to which it succeeds in conveying a sense of its significance to the reader. In the deepest sense, the test of exegesis is aesthetic.

It is noteworthy that philosophers of science have long recognized that their enterprise is aesthetic in character. They speak of "an elegant hypothesis," and "a beautiful theory." Ever since William of Occam's dictum, *essentia non sunt multiplicanda praeter necessitatem*, "essences are not to be multiplied beyond necessity," scientists have regarded as "true," or "the truest," the theory that requires the least number of assumptions, because they postulate the doctrine of the economy of nature and the rationality of the world. Let it be noted that these assumptions are an act of faith and not the result of logical demonstration, Q.E.D. Even in Euclidean geometry, axioms and postulates precede theorems, which depend upon them for their validity. Without faith, not only life but science would be impossible.

The author of the book of Jonah ended his work with a characteristically Jewish exercise in logic, employing a *qal vahomer*, an *a fortiori* argument. Following humbly in his footsteps, let us do the same. If natural science is increasingly being recognized as art, the time has come for humanistic scholars to make the same discovery about their own pursuit.

If these observations are valid, they should help minimize antagonism among scholars and increase an openness toward differences of opinion and approach. Whether our field be Bible or Talmud, history or medieval literature, or any other aspect of the Jewish experience and expression, we need to remember that we are practitioners of an art, resting, to be sure, upon a variety of scientific disciplines that check and protect us against illegitimate procedures and unwarranted conclusions. In the light of this understanding, the great dictum of Rabbi Hanina takes on the shape of a rational hope: "Scholars increase peace in the world" (B. Berakhot 64a).

Notes

1. For the various views of scholars as to the original source and date of this prophecy, and the grounds for sharing the view that it is older than Isaiah and Micah, both of whom cited and commented upon it, see my paper, "Micah's Vision of the End Time," in *Great Expressions of Human Rights*, ed. R. M. MacIver (New York, 1950), pp. 1–18, reprinted in my volume, *Poets, Prophets and Sages—Essays in Biblical Interpretation* (Indiana, 1971), pp. 268–80.
2. Slightly different nuances of the first clause will be found in RSV, NEB, NAB, and NJPV; see, also, the commentaries ad loc. Basically, the point is the same: the prophet cites the devotion of the nations toward their religions to urge the loyalty of his own people to its faith.
3. Hence Jeremiah (2:11) excoriated his people: "Has any nation changed its God—though they be no God? Yet my people has exchanged its glory for what is altogether powerless."
4. On Rab as the author of the Musaf service for Rosh Hashanah, see P. *Rosh Hashanah* i, 57a.
5. See also Num. 14:18; Joel 2:13; Jon. 4:2, Nah. 1:3; Pss. 86:15; 103:8; Neh. 9:17.
6. For a conspectus of rabbinic thought on the subject, with references to non-rabbinic attitudes, see Ephraim Urbach, *Hazal* (Jerusalem 5731), pp. 396-407.
7. The present writer has not been guiltless in this regard. See the chapter "The Freedom of Man" in my book, *A Faith for Moderns* (New York, 1960; 1971). An excellent brief treatment of this question by Louis Jacobs, "Divine Foreknowledge and Human Freedom," has recently appeared in *Conservative Judaism* 34 (1980), 4–16. See, also, my "A Note on God's Foreknowledge and Man's Freedom," *Conservative Judaism* 34 (1981), 5–10.
8. See Lapp's *Biblical Archaeology and History* (New York, 1967), pp. 33f.

ON JEWISH SCHOLARSHIP
Alexander M. Schindler

There is a breach in our leadership ranks that needs to be repaired. That breach, that gap of which I speak, is this: that the scholars of our community are separated from it, that they do not hold their rightful place in the councils of those who determine our destiny.

I begin with the assumption that the linkage which I seek, between the academy and the community, between Jewish scholarship and Jewish life, is something more than a desideratum, that it is an essential ingredient of our community's continuity. Without it, power rests solely in the hands of those who are not fully prepared to wield it, and their decisions run the risk of being inauthentic Jewishly.

It is a linkage which obtained and sustained us in the past but which no longer does, and we are the weaker because of it. Franz Rosenzweig spoke of this weakness when, alluding to the tradition of the "academic quarter-hour," that time period during which German university students were compelled to wait for their docent, he spoke of an academic "quarter-century" separating Jewish scholarship and the Jewish community.

This gap is due no doubt to that sheer physical distance that sets us all apart, because of the openness of our society, our increasing mobility, and the fragmentation that ensues. It is due also, and in no small measure, to the obtuseness of a communal leadership that fails to provide a fitting framework for the scholar's function, that does not really call upon his talents by offering him a meaningful leadership role. Why, say, should a Jewish scholar be something more than a passive member of a congregation, when the rabbi of that congregation insists that all substantive issues affecting its inner life are his alone to decide on, that they are the province of the pulpit and never the pew.

But our problem is rooted also in a disjoining of tasks, a sundering of that unity of purpose which once bound Jewish scholarship and the Jewish community—the scholar pursues his quest for truth and the community leader means to help his followers come to terms with their Jewishness. Viewed from such a perspective, that lag of which we speak is in the reverse. Sometimes, and in certain respects, Jewish scholarship trails the Jewish community by that quarter of a century.

Such a twofold lag in fact obtains. The teachers of Jewish studies in our seminaries and on campus have the right to complain that those students whom synagogue and community schools send them are ill-prepared, that they learned too little, that so much of what they learned falls far below the level of understanding that contemporary Jewish scholarship has reached; they were taught a kind of pre-Newtonian Judaism in a post-Einsteinian age. Yet the teachers of these synagogue schools, and especially those who are charged with the responsibility of evolving its curriculum and preparing its supportive materials, have an equally valid counter-plaint: that in their efforts to help the student in his Jewish becoming—which involves, after all, not just the transmission of subject matter, but also the energizing of the will to be Jewish and an enablement to express that will, to translate it from *midrash* to *maaseh* in the modern world—that in these larger efforts the fruitage of contemporary Jewish scholarship is not sufficiently serving.

Both claims have their merit. The first is too manifest to require further elaboration. But as we confess the one, let us acknowledge the other, too. By and large modern Jewish scholarship shuts out the community's claim for help in its efforts to cope with the problems of Jewish identity and Jewish continuity. The professionalization of Jewish scholarship is the first and foremost reason for this denial of the community's claim. Most Jewish scholars simply do not see it as their function to respond to it. They see themselves as professional scholars, citizens of the academic world, fully loyal to its canons of objectivity and value-free research. A deepening of the student's Jewish commitment might be a by-product, but is not a design of their doing.

A colleague of ours, a friend of mine, who teaches biblical literature at an eastern university, put the matter bluntly: "I am not a functionary of the Jewish community," he wrote me. "I approach my teaching as I do my research, with objectivity and dispassion. It is my task neither to defend nor to criticize, but to illuminate. It certainly isn't my job to resolve issues of faith or to coddle students who have problems with their Jewish identity. We have Hillel directors and rabbis for that."

My friend's tongue is sharper than his teeth. He has helped many students with such problems. He is presently engaged in coauthoring a text for our religious schools. He is a committed Jew. So are most Jewish scholars. Their choice of profession gives evidence of at least antecedent convictions. But when they give expression to these convictions by devoting a portion of their work to these concerns, or by becoming personally involved in the synagogue or the religious school, they tend to see these expressions as something apart from their work, totally alien to its higher purposes. And there's the rub.

And thus it is that most higher-level Jewish studies are approached with a strict, almost exclusively academic bent. The *daggesh chazak* is never allowed to suggest the *pintele yid*. Everything is kept as free as possible from the taint of odium theologicum.

It is interesting to remember in this connection that the *Wissenschaft des Judentums*, which began that process of professionalization eventuating in scholarship's turning away from the identity-needs of the community, was itself, paradoxically, a response to such a need of that community which spawned it. Zunz's call for the scientific study of Judaism and its literary heritage was motivated not only by the desire to preserve it, but also by the hope that these scholarly endeavors would lead to a greater appreciation of Judaism and to the more ready acceptance of the Jew. The needs of the community moved Zunz as much as did his concern for its literary heritage. But the spiritual descendants of Zunz see only one purpose for their work: to preserve that heritage of learning and to expand it.

Another factor which slows the flow from the academy to the community and back again is the academy's preoccupation with the past. Modern Jewish scholarship is still, in the main, past-oriented. That's what Jewish learning was all about from its beginnings, I suppose; conviction compelled rabbinic scholars to refer and always to defer to the Torah. *Die Wissenschaft* did not really redirect this orientation; it opted for new, more modern methods. But one of its main goals, as we have seen, was to preserve the gifts of yesteryear, and so the focus remained essentially on the past.

Contemporary Jewish studies are still not given their proper place in the constellation of scholarly creativity. Of course, there are those who labor diligently in this field, but think of the imbalance—they are the few against the many. The preposition "against" is not ill-chosen, for one senses almost an antagonism here by those who constitute the establishment in Jewish academia. It is the classicist's disdain for the social sciences, born of a presumption that the present is vulgar and only the past is worthy of serious concern.

In our synagogue schools the study of the past likewise predominates—and it is not sufficient for the need. Our students want more. They are not content, say, when, in dealing with ideas, we present them developmentally, in their historical unfolding from genesis to present state. When we do, they listen to us politely, perhaps even with interest. But they do not offer their hearts in full involvement until we explore these concepts in their fullness, until we expose them to the winds of challenge which come from contemporary thought, and then proceed to demonstrate their value for today.

Efforts have been made of late to alter the approach to teaching, to make it thematic rather than developmental. But by and large these efforts have been feeble in their effect. How could it be otherwise, since so much of the needed supportive scholarly work is lacking. The religious-school teacher can well be asked to keep abreast of the scholar; he cannot be expected to lead him.

One more matter must be brought to light in this connection. I refer to that historicism which has come to mark so much of modern Jewish scholarship. Historicism leads to relativism, which culminates in nihilism; it is not compatible with any concept of transcendence. Thus, when we apply the methods of historical research to the corpus of Jewish literature and thought, and then see it in all its patterned divergence—ideas appearing from many sources, blending with one another, then disappearing again; and all this without a metabolizing principle independently rooted in nature or beyond, for history sees only Jews as agents of this blending—such a seeing inevitably prompts the question whether there is, after all, *a* Jewish idea, never mind *the* Jewish point of view.

It is precisely on this level that the Jewish community, and especially its teachers, stand most in need of help. Our charges press us on this point of Jewish distinctiveness above all others. They understand full well why they must be just and merciful, and even humble with God. But they do not understand why they must be Jews to be so, not just as a matter of *Pietaetsgefuehl*, of loyalty to a tradition because it is tradition, but in order to preserve for themselves, and to preserve for others, those values that we insist on designating characteristically Jewish. There is an urgent need then to probe carefully those assumptions on which so much of modern Jewish scholarship is based.

Which brings us full square to another node in that network of causes which contributes to that lag problem with which we are concerned: the disinclination of too many Jewish scholars to deal with questions of value. The professional factor undoubtedly fosters this reluctance; there is the ever-present danger of crossing that line which separates the scholar from the apologist. Positivism clearly comes into play, with its insistence that facts and values are absolutely heterogeneous. Whatever the reason, an ethical neutrality obtains, which might be good and proper were it not so stern that not just moral judgments, but moral issues, too, are frequently disdained.

[36]

Few Jewish scholars in their work address themselves to normative ethical issues. What little there is is of the neighborhood variety; it is scarcely present- and never future-oriented. Where, for instance, can we find a critical analysis, from a Jewish perspective, of some of those moral problems which biology's imminent mastery of social engineering presses upon us? Metaethical questions are *shoin obgeret*. Indeed, the philosophical enterprise in its entirety seems shunned among us; too few Jewish scholars make this their field. And yet no other study is of greater potential usefulness to the Jewish community than the history of Judaism's successful response to outer intellectual challenge.

Of course, Jewish scholarship is not value-free. Values, after all, are an intrinsic element of that raw material with which every Jewish scholar works. He may not evaluate these values, but he does not ignore them; he elucidates them, by tracing them to their origins, their causes, and so they are there, implicit in his work. But the need for Jewish education and the Jewish community demands that they be made explicit, and that they be related to the problems of the day.

Education, if it is to be successful, must move from the immediate concerns of the student toward that material which the teacher wishes to transmit. Now, our religious-school students are not interested as much in facts as they are in values; moral issues are at the core of their concern. Begin with facts in the teaching of the Holocaust—the root causes of German antisemitism, its evolution from discrimination to extermination, a listing of the Nuremberg Laws, the names of the concentration camps, and the like—and they will listen, but only with half an ear. To reach them, we are better advised to make some other matters our point of departure, moral matters, issues whose resolution can help them in their quest for faith and for a life reflective of it: how does the Jew confront evil? how does one resist an enemy? does collective guilt obviate individual responsibility? what can we say about the face of God, can we believe in Him in spite of it? These are the questions which stir them, stir within them like a flaming fire. They cannot be ignored; some effort must be made to speak to them. And in his quest for an answer, the teacher should be aided, and not abandoned, by Jewish scholarship.

Without such aid the teacher is lost, and with him his school. Without the support of Jewish scholarship, the Jewish community is lost. This is why I am so determined to repair the breach, to restore the linkage between the academy and the community, to do everything I can—at least insofar as the Union is concerned—to bring Jewish scholars into the forefront of those who point the way of our work.

This task exceeds the scholar's wonted function, I know; it may even compete with it, in that it steals the time and energy required for his customary work. But the professionalization of his calling has not yet obliterated the qualifying adjective "Jewish"—he is a student of Jewish lore, the guardian of Jewish letters—and this Jewishness, too, has a valid claim on him. In a sense, the fulfillment of his narrower task depends in direct measure on his response to the wider claim. For without that response—without the collective response of many Jewish scholars—the community will surely sink into nothingness, and with it will sink from sight all the schools of higher learning and all the seminaries and all the chairs of Judaica on the American-Jewish scene.

As for those who fear that such engrossment in community concern will somehow pervert the nature of Jewish scholarship, let them take heart. Without such an involvement, "modern Jewish scholarship will be neither modern nor Jewish."

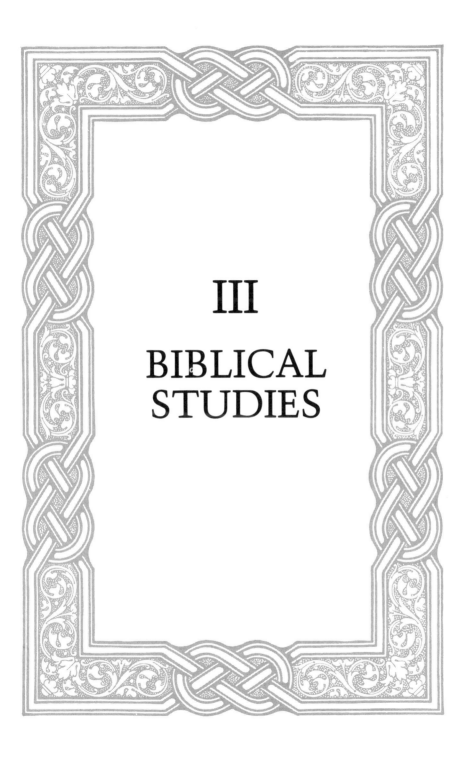

III
BIBLICAL
STUDIES

NEBUKADNEZAR COMES
TO JERUSALEM
William W. Hallo

Recent events in the Near East have left many people breathless with confusion. Wars have broken out between ostensible allies, peace has been concluded between traditional rivals. Nations divided by geography and tradition have surrendered a part of their sovereignty to try to unite with each other, while countries that seemed to have a long history of national cohesion have split apart on religious or ethnic lines. Nationalism, religion, and political ideology have combined in a bewildering variety of mixes that baffles the outside observer.

Is there an explanation to all these paradoxical and shifting patterns of alliances and enmities? Or do we throw up our hands in despair and treat it all as inscrutable? To a historian of the Near East the answer is clear: what is happening today is in some ways merely another chapter in the millennial history of the region, determined now as in all earlier ages by some of the same enduring factors: geography, demography, natural resources, patterns of trade, patterns of state formation, and more. What divides the Near East today, and what has kept it divided throughout most of history, is not religious diversity. What united the area for shorter but more glorious periods in the past was not a sense of common nationhood. The dreams of the Arab awakening during the collapse of the Ottoman Empire envisioned one Arab nation from the Zagros Mountains in the east to the Atlas Mountains in the west; but today that nation is divided into a score of separate states, each jealously guarding its sovereign prerogatives. And in the past, when that unity was briefly a reality, it was precisely the religious factor that supported it: for the victorious march of Islam in the seventh century united diverse nations and cultures in

Africa and Asia, as Christianity had done before it.

Thus, we should not be surprised by today's headlines, and should keep them in mind as we focus our attention on another and perhaps equally momentous period in Near Eastern history, a period in which Israel played as pivotal a part as it does today; again, it is a period that we can assess properly only in the light of a larger, panoramic view of the area's historical patterns and their enduring determinants.

I am referring to the sixth century before the Common Era, or that part of it which, in Jewish history, is generally known as the Exilic Age. This was the period when the Jews of Israel, or, literally, the "better" part of them anyway, were transported bodily (that is, exiled) to Babylonia, there to endure (or, in some cases, to enjoy) the Babylonian captivity until, fifty or sixty years later, Babylon itself capitulated to the all-conquering Persians and the Jews, along with the exiles of other lands, were invited by the magnanimous Persian conqueror to return to their ancient homeland, there to resume their worship and even a measure of their political autonomy. Of this generous offer, some of the exiles availed themselves, becoming the first ôlîm, as the Chronicler designated those who became actual immigrants to Zion, or, literally, "ascendants, those who go up" (Ezra 2:1, 59; Neh. 7:5f., 61). But others, having put down roots in Babylonia, were free to stay there and support the returning ôlîm with money and other encouragements. They thus founded the first enduring diaspora (apart from the doubtful fate of the "10 Lost Tribes"),[1] and set the pattern for the relationship between the land of Israel and the dispersion which prevails to this day. But more than that, the Exilic Age produced some of the most significant portions of the Hebrew Bible—the prophecies of Ezekiel and Deutero-Isaiah, among others—and a general ideological confrontation with the realities of the new age which assured that Judaism as a religion, albeit transformed, would survive the destruction of Judah as a kingdom, much as, centuries later, yet another form of Judaism was to survive the destruction of the Second Commonwealth. Characteristic of the new ideology was an emerging universalism combined with a reassertion of national identity.

But these developments did not take place in a vacuum. Judean exiles were not alone in devising new systems of thought and belief in the face of political turmoil. The entire Near East, indeed the entire *oikumene*, or inhabited, civilized portion of the globe, was in upheaval during the sixth century. The political convulsions of the period elicited an intellectual ferment that swept the *oikumene* from Italy in the West to China in the East. Pythagoras, Heraclitus, Thales, Anaximander, Xenophanes, and the other pre-Socratic philosophers of Greater Greece; Zoraster in Iran; Buddha in India; Confucius and Lao-tse in China— all these great founders of philosophic and religious systems are traditionally associated with the sixth century. It is hard to escape the conclusion that these seminal thinkers, who have had so much impact on all subsequent thought and belief, were somehow responding to the breakdown of traditional structures of authority and their concomitant systems of belief then sweeping the globe. In the case of the Near East, then still in many ways the best-documented part of the world, this conclusion is most readily demonstrated, and the Exilic Age is a case in point: a sure illustration of the interaction of historical events and intellectual response and, more particularly, of the Jewish response to and involvement in the course of general history.[2]

In the view of one notable Jewish interpreter, Yehezkel Kaufmann, the response was equal to the challenge. The greatest threat of the exile was not its harshness—for it was quite mild, contrary to the dire warnings of Leviticus, chapter 26, Deuteronomy, and the pre-exilic prophets—but its attractions. The exiles suddenly found themselves in the midst of a thriving economy, and face to face with the impressive achievements of an ancient culture and its literary and artistic monuments. They were permitted to participate in this economy and could easily have assimilated to the culture, as did some of the other exiled populations (though not, perhaps, all of them: research done since Kaufmann wrote suggests that others, too, retained their identity against a hope of future restoration).[3]

But before the Judean exiles came to Babylonia, Babylonia had to come to Judea: Nebukadnezar came to Jerusalem. How did he happen to do so?

To answer this seemingly simple question, it is best to provide some historical background. Now, when an Assyriologist speaks of a little historical background, he is likely to be thinking in terms of millennia. And, indeed, Babylonians, or Babylonian influence, had been felt in Israel from its beginnings. But here it will suffice if we retrace our steps by a mere century and a half before Nebukadnezar's first documented appearance in front of the walls of Jerusalem in 597 B.C.E. For it is precisely in 747 B.C.E. that there began a new era in the political history of the Near East which, on the one hand, displayed that uncanny resemblance to its current convulsions referred to at the outset and, on the other, climaxed in the watershed events that characterized Nebukadnezar's relations to Judah. Picture the Near East in 747 about as follows: at one end of the Fertile Crescent was Egypt, weak and divided among at least four competing dynasties, including a Nubian one, which was destined to reunite the country under a certain king, Piankhy, whose accession may have taken place in this very year. Palestine, on both sides of the Jordan, was divided into the so-called Divided Monarchy: Judah in the south around Jerusalem, the ancient capital of the Davidic Dynasty, and Israel in the north, around the more recently founded Omrid capital of Samaria. In what is today approximately Lebanon, there ruled the great Phoenician trading cities, their eyes turned westward to their sister-colonies around the Mediterranean. In Syria a number of Aramaic-speaking principalities coalesced then, as now, around the leadership of Damascus. Finally, the present area of Iraq was divided between the resurgent Assyrian Empire in the north and the older but weaker kingdoms of Babylonia, ruled from the ancient capital city of Babylon by a constantly shifting succession of short-lived dynasties, each aspiring and in turn failing to revive the ancient glories of the greatness that was Babylon —or had been, long before.[4]

Thus, the Near Eastern stage was set, then as now, for international diplomacy, intrigue, and shifting alliances, alternating with short, brutal campaigns often mounted across great distances. Then as now, alliances were based on perceptions, or misperceptions, of mutual interest, more often than on sentimental ties of kinship or ideology. Our quick survey will amply demonstrate this. It is based chiefly on three groups of sources: first, the Bible, notably the Second Book of Kings and its parallels in the Second Book of Chronicles; second, the annals and other cuneiform inscriptions of the kings of Assyria, a most abundant source, but one to be used with caution as the royal scribes wrote for the greater glory of the god Ashur and his royal representative on earth, rather than for the primary purpose of enlightening future historians; and third, the so-called Babylonian Chronicle, a record compiled not by the kings, but by the priests of Babylon, and recording not only the religious highlights of each year, as might be expected, but also, and with surprising objectivity, the chief military and political events that had transpired. This record is unusually nonpartisan and correspondingly valuable; it often serves as a useful check both on the bombastic exaggerations of the Assyrian royal inscriptions and on the theologically motivated accounts of the biblical writers, be they those of the pre-exilic prophets, the Deuteronomist, or the Chronicler. There are other sources as well, of course, such as the inscriptions of the Egyptian pharaohs or of the Aramaeans of Syria or of the Babylonian kings; but these sources are far fewer or less informative: in particular, the later Babylonian kings, though they left great numbers of inscriptions, used them almost exclusively to commemorate their temple constructions and other pious works, and are modest to the point of secretiveness about their military achievements. Hence follows the great interest that historians have shown for each new chapter of the Babylonian Chronicle as it has turned up in successive publications of the great cuneiform treasures in the British Museum, where they began to arrive as early as 1876 and to be published by 1882. The process of discovering and publishing the fragments of the series in the British Museum

[44]

has continued intermittently ever since, with the latest instalment only published in 1975. And still the record is not complete.[5]

It begins precisely in 747 B.C.E., a time when the priestly astronomers of Babylonia appear to have refined their calendar, introducing the regular intercalations and luni-solar months that still characterize the Jewish religious calendar —derived at a later date from the Babylonian one; when they began an annual record of astronomical diaries and associated earthly events; and when a new era was thought to have dawned for Babylonia in general.[6] Almost at once, the record indicates, the Assyrian king intervened in Babylonia's affairs—doing so, it would appear, in order to rid Babylon of the twin threat of Chaldeans and Aramaeans inside and outside the country's borders. If so, this provides a curious parallel to events in the west.[7] For there, the same Assyrian king was similarly called upon for help by the king of Judah, Ahaz, hard-pressed by a coalition of Israel and the Aramaeans. In both instances the results were similar. Once on the scene, the Assyrians stayed—in Babylonia the Assyrian king soon took the throne himself, while in Palestine he contented himself with annexing most of the northern kingdom and extracting tribute from Judah. The folly of an Assyrian alliance was seen by prophets such as Isaiah before their royal patrons, but the lesson soon sank in, and henceforth both Judah and Babylonia tended to pursue an anti-Assyrian policy, sometimes in alliance with each other and in opposition to Egypt, whose Nubian rulers were gradually driven up the Nile with Assyrian help, and whose new native (Saite = XXVI) dynasts therefore tended to side with Assyria.

The highlights of the next one hundred years, circa 701–605 B.C.E., may be briefly summarized. Jerusalem was besieged by the Assyrians and saved in almost miraculous fashion; then, for more than fifty years, an uneasy peace was maintained between a chastened Judah and an all-powerful Assyria. But when Babylonia raised the standard of revolt behind its own ambitious Assyrian viceroy, Assyria was put on the defensive. Judah gradually reclaimed the lost territories of the northern kingdom as Assyrian power receded, and even intervened at Megiddo to stop an Egyptian army marching north in a final desperate attempt to shore up the tottering Assyrian Empire. That intervention proved unsuccessful, but a few years later, the intervention of a once-again independent Babylonia proved decisive at Carchemish: Egypt was banished from Asia and Assyria wiped from the face of the earth.[8]

The chief agent of the Babylonian success was Nebukadnezar, at first still in the role of crown prince, but soon to be, in his own right, the greatest member of the tenth and last dynasty of Babylon, sometimes known as the Chaldean Dynasty. This king, destined to reign for fully forty-three years (604–562 B.C.E.), had assumed the name of one of the greatest Babylonian kings of the second millennium, a name pronounced "Nabu-kudurri-uṣur" in Babylonian, where it means: "Oh divine Nabu, protect my offspring." That is more or less the way in which the name, or at least its consonants, appears in most of Jeremiah, in Ezekiel, and in Ezra, in other words, as Nebukadrezar. But in Kings, Chronicles, and Daniel, as well as portions of Jeremiah, we have a variant form, Nebukadnezar, or the like, which has recently been explained as a nickname based, whether intentionally or not, on a kind of scurrilous etymology according to which the name means: "Oh Nabu, protect the mule."[9] Elsewhere in the Bible, such scurrilous etymologies are applied as a polemic against unpopular neighbors, such as Moab and Amon (Gen. 19:36–38), and against the self-serving etymology "Bab-ilim," or gate of God, favored for their own city by the people of Babylon (Gen. 11:9).

Be that as it may, it is clear that the sixth century dawned on a vastly changed political stage, and that Nebukadnezar was prepared to play the leading role in it. He marched many times against the Westland, and appeared before the walls of Jerusalem at least twice, the first time, it has sometimes been argued, perhaps still as crown prince, following his great victory at Carchemish. This is so, at least according to the opening verse of the Book of Daniel. Daniel is said to have gone into exile on the occasion of a siege of

Jerusalem by Nebukadnezar, "king of Babylon," and the capitulation of the city in the third year of Jehoiakim (606–5 B.C.E.). But if Nebukadnezar only became king of Babylon in the fourth year of Jehoiakim, as most scholars would argue, then the date in Daniel may need to be emended. Daniel is, after all, a later source, and even earlier ones have chronological statements that are irreconcilable with cuneiform or even with other biblical evidence, as when Jeremiah dates the battle of Carchemish to Jehoiakim's fourth year (46:1f.). Nebukadnezar was back campaigning in the west almost as soon as he had time to rush home from Carchemish and assume the rule in his own right upon his father's death twenty-three days earlier! The following year he campaigned again in the west, and the year after he somehow secured Jehoiakim's submission and consent to payment of tribute. Two years later he fought an inconclusive battle with the Egyptians, and Jehoiakim was emboldened to withhold the tribute. Retribution was now inevitable. Though it was delayed while the Babylonian king disposed of other threats, including those from some Arab tribes, when it came, it was with the full force of Nebukadnezar's own presence. Jehoiakim died as the Babylonians approached—perhaps, indeed, he was assassinated so as to make way for the more tractable son and successor, Jehoiachin (cf. Jer. 22:18f.).[10]

The Bible records the first coming of the Babylonian king in several passages. Here is how it sounds, in the most explicit and probably the most original one (2 Kings 24:10–17), according to the New Jewish Version:

At that time, the troops of King Nebuchadnezar of Babylon marched against Jerusalem, and the city came under siege. King Nebuchadnezar of Babylon advanced against the city while his troops were besieging it. Thereupon King Jehoiachin of Judah, along with his mother, and his courtiers, commanders, and officers, surrendered to the king of Babylon. The king of Babylon took him captive in the eighth year of his [Nebukadnezar's] reign. He carried off from Jerusalem all the treasures of the

House of the Lord and the treasures of the royal palace; he stripped off all the golden decorations in the Temple of the Lord—which King Solomon of Israel had made—as the Lord had warned. He exiled all of Jerusalem: all the commanders and all the warriors—ten thousand exiles— as well as all the craftsmen and smiths; only the poorest people in the land were left. He deported Jehoiachin to Babylon; and the king's wives and officers and the notables of the land were brought as exiles from Jerusalem to Babylon. All the able men, to the number of seven thousand—all of them warriors, trained for battle—and a thousand craftsmen and smiths were brought to Babylon as exiles by the king of Babylon. And the king of Babylon appointed Mattaniah, Jehoiachin's uncle, king of his place, changing his name to Zedekiah.

Other accounts, like those in Chronicles, Daniel, and Josephus, are largely dependent on this one. As for Nebukadnezar himself, we have already noted his habitual reticence in regard to his military triumphs. Thus it is that, for some two thousand years, biblical scholars have had only the same few sources to mull over. The eight-odd verses in Kings and their reflexes in later biblical and post-biblical sources all provided the Judean report of the event, and left it to imaginative historians to supply the details. But this situation changed dramatically a few years ago, that is, in 1956. Donald J. Wiseman, now professor at the University of London, was then assistant keeper in the Department of Egyptian and Western Asiatic Antiquities at the British Museum. As such, he was privileged to publish for the first time four previously unknown chapters of the Babylonian Chronicle, including one covering the years 605–595, which had lain untouched in the museum for some sixty years. And this is how it reports the same event, this time from the perspective of a Babylonian observer: "In the seventh years of his reign, in the month of Kislev [December 598], the King of Akkad [Nebukadnezar] mobilized his army and marched against the Hittite land [Syria–Palestine] and pitched his camp in front of the city of

Judaea [Jerusalem], and in the month of Addar, on the second day of the month [March 16, 597 B.C.E.], he seized the city, he captured the king, he appointed a king of his own choosing in the midst [of Jerusalem], he accepted heavy tribute from it and brought it to Babylon."

Thus, this precious and unique cuneiform source provides not only verbatim confirmation of the biblical record, but also adds details not preserved in the Bible, including the exact date of Nebukadnezar's first coming to Jerusalem! His second and more fateful coming occurred a dozen years later, after Zedekiah, in his turn, had raised the standard of rebellion, in 586 B.C.E. Would that we had the Babylonian Chronicle's chapter for this year as well—so far we don't, so we must rely on Jewish tradition, which fixes the date for Nebukadnezar's second campaign, the final destruction of Jerusalem, and the burning of the Temple as the ninth of Ab, while Kings gives it as the seventh and Jeremiah as the tenth (cf. also Zech. 7:3, 5; 8:19). There is not even unanimity as to the year of the great event, for some scholars still hold to a date of 587, not 586. Nor do the Lachish letters fill the gap, nor the Arad ostraca.[11]

But I do not mean to enter into these details, but rather to conclude with an appreciation of the larger picture. Why did Jerusalem loom so large in Nebukadnezar's strategy, and why in his turn did this last great Babylonian monarch prove so fateful for Jewish history? The answer, it seems to me, lies contained in the basic nature of the Near Eastern matrix: a strategic crossroads of the world, the center of the *oikumene*, the envy of its neighbors, and the source of many of their inspirations; a place of commercial enterprise, of military innovation, and, above all, of intellectual ferment; too large to be long united, yet so lacking in natural frontiers as to present a perennial temptation to imperial designs; in short, an area of the world living in perpetual tension between centrifugal and centripetal tendencies, where petty nationalisms repeatedly conflict with grand strategies of world conquest. The Davidic kingdom, inspired by faith in the God of Israel, had conquered Philistines and Canaanites, survived Assyrians and Aramaeans, and fought Egyptians to a standstill. Is it any wonder that its last kings dreamed of besting the Babylonians?

Until Nebukadnezar appeared on the stage of world history, Babylonia had been a distant eminence for Judah at best—occasionally an ally, never a foe. The great kings of Judah, like Hezekiah and Josiah, had been adamantly anti-Assyrian, Judean patriots and nationalists who combined a zeal for the God of Israel with a hatred of idolatry and pagan polytheism. In this they were staunchly supported by the true prophets, such as the first Isaiah. When Assyria made common cause with Egypt, the "patriots" opposed Egypt as well: Josiah first at Megiddo, then his luckless son and successor Jehoahaz, and, finally, that short-lived king's full brother Zedekiah. Meanwhile, there was the tendency to befriend Babylonia as the arch-rival of Assyria—from Hezekiah, who dealt with Merodach-baladan, to Zedekiah. What Jeremiah realized soon enough, but Zedekiah too late, was that the Battle of Carchemish had decisively altered the balance of power: Babylon was no longer a counterweight to Assyria, but its successor. When Zedekiah did wake up to the fact, it was too late: too late to rely on effective help from Egypt, which soon enough even made common cause with Babylon, or to stave off Babylonian retribution. It was Zedekiah's personal tragedy and Judah's misfortune to have crossed swords with the one neo-Babylonian ruler who aspired to world dominion and briefly achieved it. Jerusalem had to bow to his grand design, however fleeting a phase it represented in the long continuum of Near Eastern history.

But even in defeat and captivity, the kings of Judah were yet held in honor, for other cuneiform documents confirm that while in exile, the deposed Jehoiachin enjoyed special privileges even before being freed by Amel-Marduk. Indeed, the whole exilic period proved an extraordinarily creative one. "By the waters of Babylon there we sat and there we wept when we remembered Zion," said the Psalmist (137:1). But at the same time the exiles heeded Jeremiah's injunctions to "build houses and dwell [therein], to plant gardens and eat their fruit, to take wives and bear children, . . . and to pray for the peace of the city whither you have been exiled!" (cf. Jer. 29:5-7)—in other words, to pray for it but not to sacrifice for it, for unlike the earlier exiles to Egypt, the Babylonian exiles adhered to the Deuteronomic reform and its centralization of the cult, to the exclusive prerogative of the temple at Jerusalem to accept sacrifices.[12]

The Diaspora, thus begun, built on millennia of prior contact and interchange between Jerusalem and Babylon. Jeremiah himself did not join the Babylonian captivity. Spared by Nebukadnezar (Jer. 39:11–14; 40:1–6) in recognition of his consistent if futile attempts to wean the last kings of Judah from their anti-Babylonian ventures, he chose instead to lead another contingent of exiles to Egypt —where he and they vanished. But another prophet rallied the exiles in Babylonia. Ezekiel sustained the hope of those who had been disappointed by the false promises of an early restoration proclaimed by lesser prophets. So even while the exiles became integrated into the flourishing economy of Babylonia, they retained their national identity. A new generation was born on the foreign soil but, fired by the polemics of the second Isaiah, they rejected the blandishments of idolatry and the ancient polytheistic culture of their new surroundings.

Thus was built a new faith at once nationalistic and universal; a belief that God could be worshipped abroad as well as in Jerusalem; that God could be entreated by fasting and prayer as well as by temples and sacrificial rites; but that the ties between God and his special land should be restored. Both Zionism and a viable diaspora therefore first emerge in the Babylonian exile. The exiles here, unlike those in Egypt and elsewhere, were able to build on prior millennia of fruitful interchange between Babylon and Jerusalem without giving up their own identity.[13] When the captivity ended, those who returned and those who stayed behind both professed a common faith. And when Jerusalem fell for the second time six centuries later, Babylon was ready to become the center of world Jewry for another millennium. The interconnections between the parts of the Near East run deep. We can only hope that today, as in times past, the bonds of mutual interest will once more reassert themselves.

APPENDIX

Limestone bricks stamped with the standard inscription of Nebukadnezar II of Babylon (604–562 B.C.E.) are not exactly a rarity, either in the museums or in the antiquities market. The successive compilations by Langdon, Borger, Berger, and Walker attest to the growing number of published and unpublished examples.[14] The only reason for adding two more to the record is their alleged provenience. Their present owner, Professor Henryk Minc of the Department of Mathematics, University of California at Santa Barbara, with whose kind permission they are presented here, purchased them from different dealers, both located in Jerusalem. In the case of the larger fragment, the information supplied was that it had been found in Jericho.

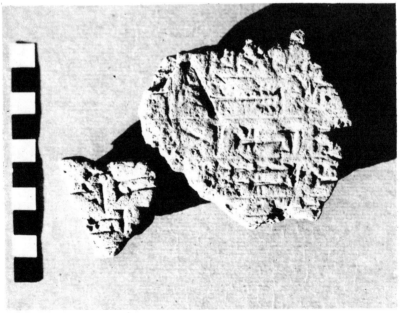

Fig. 1

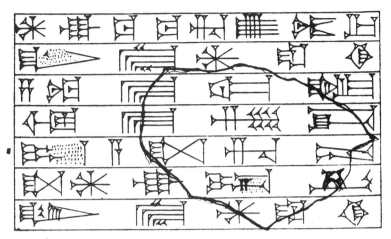

Fig. 2

Fig. 3

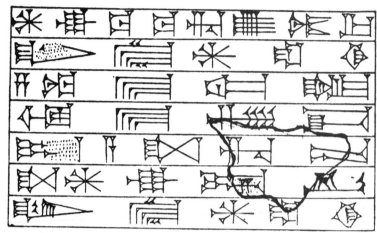

Fig. 4

Fig. 5

There is no need to attach particular significance to this report, and the fragments probably found their way to Israel in modern times, like the comparable ones published by Levy and Artzi.[15] On the remote chance of an alternative explanation, they are offered herewith in photographs supplied by the owner (figs. 1, 3, and 5), and in the form of facsimiles based on Stephens's hand-copy of a more complete exemplar of the seven-line version (figs. 2 and 4).[16] Note that the smaller fragment lacks dividing lines.

"Standard inscriptions" and especially "standard bricks" are by definition valid for royal building-operations throughout the realm,[17] and Nebukadnezar may have availed himself of this medium to exalt his name.[18] However implausible, a connection between the fragments and the Chaldean campaigns against Jerusalem should perhaps not be entirely ruled out. When complete, they presumably read as follows: (1) *Nabu*(^{d}AK)-*ku-dúr-ri-ú-ṣu-ur* (2) *šar Bàb-ili*$_3$ (KÁ.DINGIR.RA.KI) (3) *za-nin É-sag-íl* (4) *ù É-zi-da* (5) *aplu* (IBILA) *a-ša-ri-du* (6) *ša Nabu-apla-uṣur* (URI$_3$) (7) *šar Bàb-ili*$_3$, that is, (1) Nebukadnezar, (2) king of Babylon, (3) provider of (the temples) Esagila (4) and Ezida, (5) first-born heir (6) of Nabopolassar, (7) king of Babylon.

Notes

1. Presumably settled in Assyria after the fall of the northern kingdom in 722 B.C.E. The first exile of Judeans to Assyria took place in 701 B.C.E., at least according to the Assyrian sources; see Stephen Stohlmann, "The eighth century B.C.E. Judean exile," in *Scripture in Context II*, eds. W. W. Hallo et al., in press. The famous Jewish colony at Elephantine in Upper Egypt, though it may date back to the seventh century and the reign of Manasseh, was not to endure beyond the fifth century; see Bezalel Porten, *Archives from Elephantine: the life of an ancient Jewish military colony* (Berkeley and Los Angeles, 1968).
2. Jean M. Davison, "The oikoumene in ferment: a cross-cultural study of the sixth century," in *Scripture in Context: Essays on the Comparative Method*, eds. Carl D. Evans et al., Pittsburgh Theological Monograph Series 34 (Pittsburgh, 1980), pp. 197–219.
3. Yehezkel Kaufmann, *The Babylonian Captivity and Deutero-Isaiah* (New York, 1970), chap. 1; I. Eph'al, "The western minorities in Babylonia in the 6th-5th centuries B.C.: maintenance and cohesion," *Orientalia* 47 (1978), 74–90.
4. H. W. F. Saggs, *The Greatness that was Babylon: a sketch of the ancient civilization of the Tigris-Euphrates valley* (New York, 1962); see, especially, ibid., chap. 4.
5. For the latest edition, see A. K. Grayson, *Assyrian and Babylonian Chronicles* (Texts from Cuneiform Sources 5, 1975), chap. 2 and part II, Chronicles 1–13a.
6. On the "Nabonassar Era" see Grayson, *Assyrian and Babylonian Chronicles*, pp. 13f., and idem, "Assyria and Babylonia," *Orientalia* 49 (1980), 174; 178; 193.
7. The notion that Tiglat-Pileser was invited to do so by Nabonassar was first suggested by Abraham S. Anspacher, *Tiglath Pileser III*, Contributions to Oriental History and Philogy 5 (1912), p. 19, and has since been widely accepted; see, for example, J. A. Brinkman, *A Political History of Post-Kassite Babylonia*, Analecta Orientalia 43 (1968), p. 229, note 1443; and W. W. Hallo and W. K. Simpson, *The Ancient Near East: A History* (New York, 1971), pp. 144f. But it rests on the assumed parallel with Judah rather than on independent evidence.
8. Anthony Spalinger, "Esarhaddon and Egypt: an analysis of the first invasion of Egypt," *Orientalia* 43 (1974), 295–326; idem, "Assurbanipal and Egypt: a source of study," *Journal of the American Oriental Society* 94 (1974), 316–28; idem, "Egypt and Babylonia a survey (620 B.C.–550 B.C.)," *Studien zur Altägyptischen Kultur* 5 (1977), 221–44.
9. A. van Selms, "The name Nebuchadnezzar," in *Travels in the World of the Old Testament: Studies presented to . . . M. A. Beek*, eds. M. S. H. G. Heerma van Voss et al., Studia Semitica Neerlandica 16 (1974), 223–29.

10. Alberto R. Green, "The fate of Jehoiakim," *Journal of Near Eastern Studies*, in press; cf., also, Elias J. Bickerman, "Nebuchadnezzar and Jerusalem," *Proceedings of the American Academy for Jewish Research* 46–47 (Jubilee Volume, 1979–1980), 71–85.

11. For convenient surveys of the evidence and various scholarly interpretations, see Abraham Malamat, "The last kings of Judah and the fall of Jerusalem," *Israel Exploration Journal* 18 (1968), 137–56; idem, "Josiah's bid for Armageddon," *Journal of the Ancient Near Eastern Society of Columbia University* 5 (The Gaster Festschrift, 1973), 267–79; idem, "Megiddo, 609 B.C.: the conflict reexamined," in *Wirtschaft und Gesellschaft im Alten Vorderasien*, eds. J. Harmatta and G. Komoroczy, Acta Antiqua Academiae Scientarium Hungaricae 22, 1974 (Budapest, 1976), 445–49; idem, "The twilight of Judah: in the Egyptian-Babylonian maelstrom," *Supplements to Vetus Testamentum* 28 (1975), 123–45; idem, "The last years of the kingdom of Judah," in *World History of the Jewish People*, ed. Abraham Malamat, 4/1 (New Brunswick, N.J., 1979), pp. 205–21; 349–53.

12. Porten, *Archives from Elephantine*, pp. 115f. For recent studies of the Babylonian diaspora see M. D. Coogan, "Life in the diaspora: Jews at Nippur in the fifth century B.C.," *The Biblical Archaeologist* 37 (1974), 6–12, and Ran Zadok, *The Jews in Babylonia during the Chaldean and Achaemenian Periods according to the Babylonian Sources*, Studies in the History of the Jewish People and the Land of Israel Monograph Series 3 (1979).

13. The stories of Daniel and Mordechai (and perhaps Joseph) may be regarded as fictional prescriptions to this end; see, especially, W. Lee Humphreys, "A life-style for diaspora: a study of the tales of Esther and Daniel," *Journal of Biblical Literature* 92 (1973), 211–23, and A. Meinhold, "Die Gattung der Josephgeschichte und des Estherbuches: Diasporanovelle," *Zeitschrift für die Alttestamentliche Wissenschaft* 87 (1975), 306–24; *Zeitschrift* 88 (1976), 72–93.

14. Stephen Langdon, *Die neubabylonischen Königsinschriften*, Vorderasiatische Bibliothek 4 (1911), 43, nos. 39–41; Rykle Borger, *Handbuch der Keilschriftliteratur* (Berlin, de Gruyter) 1 (1967), 283; ibid., 2 (1975), 173f. ad loc; P. R. Berger, *Die neubabylonischen Königsinschriften*, Alter Orient und Altes Testament 4/1 (1973), 179–82; 185–200; C. B. F. Walker, *Cuneiform Brick Inscriptions in the British Museum* (London, 1981), pp. 80–86, nos. 100–4.

15. S. Levy and P. Artzi, *Sumerian and Akkadian Documents from Public and Private Collections in Israel* (Atiqot 4, 1965), nos. 95–97.

16. Ferris J. Stephens, *Votive and Historical Texts from Babylonia and Assyria*, Yale Oriental Series: Babylonian Texts 9 (1937), no. 86.

17. W. W. Hallo, "The royal inscriptions of Ur: a typology," *Hebrew Union College Annual* 33 (1962), 20f.

18. For which see Brinkman, *A Political History*, p. 104, note 565; and above, note 9.

BIBLICAL VIEWS OF
KINGSHIP AND SOVEREIGNTY—
WORLDLY AND DIVINE
David Polish

The issue of the place of kingship in Judaism is debated in
Scripture, and the debate is carried on in rabbinic literature.
Commentators discuss whether selecting a king is a commandment or whether it is optional, and the issue is even
joined politically when, in 63 B.C.E., certain representatives
of the people appealed to Rome to dismantle the Jewish
state as violative of Jewish faith.[1] Thus, an institution
which has been perceived as a given in Jewish tradition was
highly controversial. This essay will deal with the idea of
kingship as presented in biblical literature and as trans-
figured by prophecy.

The first fact that must be noted is that the monarch
entered comparatively late upon biblical history, although
Israel's encounters with foreign kings were extensive. As
Gen. 36:31ff. tells us, "These are the kings who reigned in
the land of Edom before any king reigned over the Israelites." Jewish monarchy is mentioned in the Torah in Deut.
17:14–15; 28:36; and 33:5. The dominant theme of Scripture is the kingship of God.

In light of the development of the people Israel, monarchy
was an innovation. There is even some biblical indication
that it was artificially grafted to the people's corporate existence, and then only after initial rejection. The social
organization of early Israel was regulated by law, not by
kings. The law was from God, Who had established His sovereignty over Israel at Sinai. When heroes would arise to
rescue the people from oppression, they could fulfill their
tasks only because they were instruments of God. "The

spirit of God descended upon Jephthah," who won a notable victory. Without God's spirit, the leader was powerless.

It is important to note that these heroes have little in common with rulers among neighboring tribes and nations. Their rule is not hereditary. They do not come from any special class. Their tenure is not fixed. Most remarkable of all, absolute power is not given to the hero, and in one instance, it is even declined. Kingship is offered not only to Gideon but to his descendants, but he rejects it. "I will not rule over you, nor will my son rule over you. God will rule over you" (Judg. 8:23). It is clear that true sovereignty is God's alone, that the leader governs not by divine right, but by divine consent.

Monarchy is even held up to scorn. A scathing fable in the book of Judges, chapter nine, contrasts the richly endowed and productive men who spurn leadership with the sterile and mean aspirant to power and tyranny. The fable judges an historical situation in which Abimelech kills off seventy potential rivals and contrives to have himself made king. The parable tells how fruitful trees such as the olive, the fig, and the vine are invited to rule over the trees of the land, but decline, while the prickly and unproductive bramble hastens to accept authority. This has been called "the most forthright anti-monarchial poem in world literature." The bramble's call to the trees of the forest to take refuge under its shade "is a piece of ludicrous arrogance."

When monarchy finally did come to Israel, it arrived as a departure from the people's traditions and institutions. The looseness of national ties was conducive neither to central authority, nor to the absolute power of a strong man. Judges came and went, and asserted their leadership, as the exigencies of the time demanded. But always "God raised up" a redeemer, who was clearly nothing but a divine instrument, fulfilling himself and the people's destiny only in accordance with a cosmic plan. From the beginning, the people neither knew the kind of kingly rule to which their neighbors were subject, nor was the need for it expressed until much later. In its earliest development, Israel's sole king was God. The covenant established a clear relationship between the divine ruler and the ruled.

Certainly no society can be devoid of political and social structure, nor of government and authority. But in Israel, through the very terms of the covenant, these were restricted at their very source to the transcendent and lasting control of God. More specifically and correctly, the tangible and readily accessible basis of authority was the Torah, first in its fragmentary and orally transmitted sense, finally in its canonized sense. The legal and social system of the Torah was regarded as supernaturally ordained. What is more, the line of human "command" in the tradition moved through the Patriarchs and Moses. And Moses had trouble enough asserting authority, albeit as God's delegate, over the people. The real authority, however, was not Moses but divine law. This chain of command is never challenged, but eventually it is joined to monarchy from David on. As we shall see, the Davidic line never superseded the other. It derived its validity from its dependence upon divine law. Ultimately, in order to be able to claim something of its royal aura, it had to transform itself into a messianic cast, with temporal rule subordinate to the kingdom of God.

In his *Old Testament Theology*, Gerhard von Rad tells us: "The institution of the monarchy was a new-comer in Israel, indeed almost something born out of season. Consequently, it was inevitable that its relationship with the central traditions of the faith was strained from the outset and, right down to its end, the monarchy never succeeded in extricating itself from the strain."[2] The contrast between this conception of sovereignty and that of other groups is revealing. Perhaps the contrast can best be illustrated by the recurrence of the biblical preface to the laws of Israel—"God said"—or their summation—"I am the Lord."

While this view of the ruler-subject relationship obtained in Israel, other contemporaneous societies were already under the domination of kings. It is highly significant that while there is a remarkable similarity between many ancient laws and those of the Torah, the sources of authority are altogether different. The kings of Egypt were considered sons of God and each was called "gracious God." Their subjects prayed to them. Pharaoh Amnufis III and Raamses II offered sacrifices in their own honor. The same was true in Assyria and Babylonia, whose king was regarded as God's representative. The statue of Tiglath Pileser is found among the idols of the gods, and before another king's statue there is an altar.

Although there are some similarities in ancient Israel, they stop far short of deifying the king. While Ps. 82:6 describes the princes of Israel as Elohim, it proceeds to assert that if they are unjust, they will die like men and fall like princes. Ps. 45:7 refers to the king as Elohim, but it quickly refers to God as the king's Elohim (45:8). Parker writes: "The tradition of monotheism, the strength of which . . . has probably been underestimated by many expositors dominated by nineteenth-century presuppositions of gradual and inevitable progress, was sufficient to clip and restrain the old tendency to political apotheosis."[3] The theme of the priority of monotheism in the very origins of Israel echoes that of the Jewish authority, Yehezkel Kaufmann. Numerous references in Scripture indicate that the king rules in behalf of God. But in Israel, the king is not declared to be God, and to have set up his image as part of a theophany world would have been utterly unthinkable, even in the most corrupt of times. "Of no king of Israel could it be said as of a Pharaoh of Egypt," Parker writes, "that he was the cause of natural phenomena."[4]

Professor Henri Frankfort, in his *Kingship and the Gods: A Study of Ancient Near Eastern Religion as the Integration of Society and Nature*, says:

The Hebrews, though in the Near East, were only partly of it. Much is made nowadays of Canaanite and other Near Eastern elements in Hebrew culture, and a phenomenon like Solomon's kingship conforms indeed to [a] type of glorified native chieftainship. . . . But it should be plain that the borrowed features in Hebrew culture, and those which have foreign analogies, are least significant. In the case of kingship they are externalities, the less important since they did not affect the basic oddness of the

Hebrew institution. If kingship counted in Egypt as a
function of the gods, and in Mesopotamia as a divinely
ordained political order, the Hebrews knew that they had
introduced it on their own initiative, in imitation of
others and under the strain of an emergency. The Hebrew
king normally functioned in the profane sphere, not in
the sacred sphere. He was the arbiter in disputes and the
leader in war. He was emphatically not the leader in the
cult. The king created the conditions which made a given
form of worship possible. . . . But the king played little
part in the cult. He did not, as a rule, sacrifice; that was
the task of the priests. He did not interpret the divine
will; that again was the task of the priests, who cast lots
for an oracle. Moreover, the divine intentions were sometimes made known in a more dramatic way when
prophets—men possessed—cried, "Thus saith the Lord."
These prophets were often in open conflict with the king
precisely because the secular character of the king entitled them to censor him.[5]

The presentation in Frankfort's epilogue is significant.
He regards the Israelite king as a "third type of King" in the
ancient Near East, distinct both from the Egyptian and Mes-
opotamian forms: "The relation between the Hebrew monarch and his people was as nearly secular as is possible in a
society wherein religion is a living force." This aura of royalty was a derivative from God, not indigenous to it. God
was the only true king, and He was the only true source of
justice and redemption. Whatever wisdom or justice ema-
nates from the king in Israel, it is granted to him by God.
The king dispenses justice (without the king, justice fails),
but he is God's deputy, not his alter ego.

In the early period of monarchy the king performs certain
priestly functions, but this practice is short-lived and comes
to be frowned upon. Saul and David offer sacrifices (2 Sam.
6:13–17). Solomon blesses the people (1 Kings 8:14). The
king could even appoint and dismiss priests (2 Sam. 8:17)
and control worship, as the reforms of Hezekiah and Josiah
indicate. Yet this is a far cry from the king as deity. He is

God's appointee, at first serving both a sacred and a secular function. But this encompassing power is to become circumscribed by the increase in priestly authority and by the persistence of the prophetic denunciation of royal excesses. Even those kings who sinned against the faith itself nevertheless "served as the foundation of the survival of the state. . . . Even a sinful king was the anointed of God. Even the scholars of the Talmud found that only three kings who had sinned most heinously and caused the people to sin—Jeroboam, Rehoboam, and Manasseh—did not have a share in the world to come."[6]

Chaim Tchernowitz comments on a statement by Rabbi Judah concerning the punishment of those who demanded that Samuel give them a king. "Why should they have been punished? Does not Scripture say, 'You shall place over yourself a king?' It was because they were premature in their request." Tchernowitz remarks: "This is a wonderful insight into the events of those times, because the demand for a king was before its time. The time for the unification of the tribes by one king had not yet come, . . . and this is why the reign of Saul did not endure. Monarchy in Israel was not accepted for a number of generations. Even the unity of the tribes hung by the strength of the first three kings and lasted only three generations."[7]

Fragments of the laws of Eshnunna (about 2000 B.C.E.) are frequently reminiscent of the laws in Exodus, but there is no mistaking the meaning of a passage ending, "jurisdiction of the king." Biblical law, to the contrary, identifies God as the source of jurisdiction. Some three centuries later, while Israel as we know it in the Bible is still to emerge, a great code is promulgated by King Hammurabi of the Old Babylonian Dynasty. Both the monarch and a royal class are already highly developed. Clear distinctions are made between the aristocracy and the common people. A feudal hierarchy, at the apex of which is the king, informs the spirit and the body of the code. More striking by far than the similarities between laws here and elsewhere and biblical law is the Torah's rejection of royal power as an ultimate or even a delegated source of authority.

[63]

The transition to monarchy in Israel was accompanied by a severe, moral struggle. The depth of the struggle is described in the story of Samuel's vain effort to dissuade the people from seeking a king. The distance between Israel and its neighbors is reflected in the people's demand to Samuel: "Make us a king to judge us like all the nations." Thus, until that moment, Israel stands as a solitary community, devoid of absolute rule, in the midst of a world where monarchy was long and deeply entrenched. At first, this demand is seen as a repudiation of divine sovereignty: "They have rejected Me, that I should not be king over them." The transition is also accompanied by earnest warnings against the beguiling foreign institution. "He will take your sons. . . . He will take your daughters. . . . He will take your friends. . . . You shall cry out on that day because of your king whom you shall have chosen."

Nevertheless, monarchy did eventually come. Yehezkel Kaufmann writes that the activity of the prophets "lessened, but could not obviate, the need for a monarchy."[8] When the new institution asserted itself, however, it was bound to have a revolutionary effect upon the people and their development. The initial forebodings, that monarchy represented a rejection of an entrenched religious system, possessed great validity. Until that moment in Israel's history, the life and loyalties of the people were encompassed in a loose but free structure in which there was no sovereign but God. This system was now challenged by a new order, which represented an unaccustomed realm of authority. There is no doubt that it became deeply imbedded both in the life of the people and in its psychic development. For good or evil, it became a historical necessity, prompted by the shifting political fortunes of the people. It was not ever to be eradicated as long as they enjoyed even a measure of freedom. And when the people lost their freedom, they never stopped yearning for restoration.

The new institution thus became a dual source of intense loyalty and fierce resentment. We get a clue of the difficulty monarchy had in becoming entrenched in the fact that David's rule over all Israel was held up for seven and a half years. "The time that David was king in Hebron over the house of Judah was seven years and six months" (2 Sam. 2:11). Much of David's authority was imposed upon the people by his military might, and rebellious activities persisted throughout his reign. It created a new factor in which the rival claims of God and king, divine and temporal rule, were often joined in conflict. The denunciation by prophets of royal and aristocratic abuses upheld the moral law of God against tyrannical kings.

It must be noted, however, that in the face of all the denunciations, there was no outright rejection of kingship, certainly not of the "house of David." Some prophets came dangerously close to repudiating the entire cultic system, and there are scholars who argue that Amos and Jeremiah did in fact reject the cult outright, but the claim of the Judean monarchy to survival was not challenged. Individual kings were doomed by outraged prophets. "I give you a king in My anger, and take him away in My wrath" (Hos. 13:11). But the throne, symbol of the endless continuity of the monarchy, was not to be utterly annihilated. "In Judah, defiance was directed against the man, not against the line."[9]

Yet three factors appear to modify these generalizations. The first is that dynastic lines are challenged by prophets. Saul is rejected by God and by Samuel for disobedience to a divine command. The prophet Nathan foretells to David, elevated to royalty "forever," that his dynasty would be destroyed because of his sin with Bathsheba. For the sin of idolatry, the end of Solomon's kingdom is predicted (1 Kings 11:11).

Second, in the northern kingdom, transiency is the rule rather than the exception. Here, the hold of monarchy is much more attenuated. There was no hereditary monarchy, as in Judah. Ten different dynasties ruled in Israel, while one alone persisted in Judah. "A man of God" foretells the doom for Jeroboam and his land, as does Jehu for Baasha, Elijah for Ahab, and Amos for Jeroboam II. Elisha encourages Jehu to destory the Omrides. Kaufmann writes: "The prophetic conception of the monarchy was given fuller expression here than in the south, for the defiance of northern prophecy knew no legitimate check to the freedom of Yahveh's word."[10]

Third, the very idea of monarchy is held to be repugnant by some. Hosea proclaims: "O Israel, you have sinned from the days of Gibeah" (10:9), that is, since the time of the kingship of Saul, whose home was in Gibeah.

These instances are enough to indicate that while normative Judaism adhered to monarchy once it was instituted, the countervailing forces which challenged it persisted. Prophecy made way for royalty, but it never abdicated to it. In fact, prophecy frequently asserted itself in the teeth of royalty and, as in the northern kingdom, defied not only kings but dynasties.

Hosea goes further than other prophets when he indicates the failure of monarchy: "All their kings have fallen, not one of them calls upon Me" (7:7). Yet even Hosea does not call for the repudiation of the monarchy, but he infers, rather, that the monarchy must be directed by God through His spokesmen, the prophets. "They made kings, without asking Me; officers without My knowledge" (8:4). A monarchy removed from the word of God was another manifestation of Israel's trust in the no-gods that Hosea denounced.

Fortunately for the survival of Israel, the conflict between the two sovereignties, divine and temporal, did not become an outright cleavage. Had this occurred, both the viability of the people (wedded to the king but divorced from its covenant with God) and the tenacity of the God-idea (abstracted from a living existence among an historical people) would have been critically impaired. An outright separation could not be sustained. A synthesis of both principles enabled them to interact creatively rather than to destroy one another.

The synthesis achieved partial fulfillment during the period preceding the Babylonian exile. It reached a higher fulfillment during and after the exile, when the idea of the monarchy underwent refinement.

Even during monarchy's most dynamic period, the king was regarded and often treated as a limited sovereign, whose authority came from God and whose powers were circumscribed. The philosophy of history that runs through the accounts of the kings is that the success or failure of their reigns was related to the extent of their obedience to God. This was a gross rationalization, but it reveals the attitude of biblical literature to monarchy.

It is noteworthy that in an absolutist world, Judaism should have developed a restrictive code limiting the sovereignty of the king. Jeremiah, addressing himself to Shallum, King of Judah, says: "Woe to him that builds his house by unrighteousness. . . . Shall you reign, because you strive to excel in cedar? . . . Your eyes and your heart are only for shedding innocent blood. . . . Therefore, . . . he shall be buried with the burial of an ass" (Jer. 22:13–19). Most illuminating are the legal restrictions placed upon the king. The very passage requiring, as most rabbinic authorities assert, the establishment of kingship (Deut. 17:14–15), places restrictions upon it so that he is denied, in theory, absolutist power, and is defined as a limited monarch. His limitation is imposed by the very scroll of the law which must abide with him constantly (Deut. 17:16–20).

The law of kingship is often abused, but its very existence is more remarkable than its violation. It is remarkable that Samuel, as God's spokesman, can depose Saul. It is even more remarkable that the excesses of kings can be openly assailed and on occasion punished or checked. Even though the absolute theocracy of the prophets was shared by monarchy, the prophets never abdicated their prerogative of rebuking and opposing the king.

The rule of David and his dynasty most clearly reflects the self-subordination of the king to preexistent authority. The first authority is God. In order to establish an enduring reign, the king had to fit himself into the unassailable religious system of absolute divine sovereignty. He is commissioned to govern by God, but this is not a mere fiction or a pretext for the seizure of power. Power can be snatched from the king's dynasty, and he is well aware of this dire possibility. Solomon is told, "I will rend it [the kingdom] out of the hand of your son" (1 Kings 11:12).

The second authority to which the king is subject is the divinely ordained Torah. Not only the regulations concerning royalty, but the rules of cultic and ethical existence, stand above him and hold him under their mandate. King Josiah tears his royal robes in guilt and remorse when confronted by the scroll of the neglected law.

The third authority is prophecy, to which kings sometimes submit, and which they rarely reject. Prophecy is first in Israel. It is indigenous. Kaufmann writes:

> What is the latest date that can be assigned to the religious revolution in which Israelite prophecy was born? Not after Israel's entry into Canaan, for in the life of the settled tribes the apostolic idea appears as a vital force from the very start. It pervades the period of the judges; the very institution of judges and its underlying concept of the "kingdom of God" rests on the faith in a succession of messengers of God. The early kingdom of God is founded on the expectation that what happened once—God's sending a savior to Israel—will be repeated when the need arises (cf., e.g., Judg. 6:13). The source of this expectation must lie in the period before the judges, that is, in the period before the settlement.
>
> Apostolic prophecy is an intrinsic part of the historical religion of YHWH. Apostolic prophecy, the faith in YHWH, the battle with idolatry, and the covenant-confederation of Israelite tribes are inseparable elements in Israel's consciousness. Only the assumption that they have one and the same historic root can explain the continuous combination of these phenomena throughout the ages. It was an apostolic prophet, the first in history, who proclaimed the faith of YHWH to the tribes of Israel, made them enter into a covenant concerning this faith, and implanted in them the expectation that other messengers would come after him. Moreover, his appearance must be placed before the entry into Canaan.[11]

Nothing will enable us to understand the Jewish attitude toward sovereignty as much as this central, indisputable fact. Prophecy is inherent in Israel. Monarchy is imposed.

The people are conditioned to recognize the prophet as an agent of God. Even if they detest him, they are compelled to acknowledge him. Kaufmann writes that "the people believed in the appearance of God's messengers, anticipated their appearance, yearned for them after prophecy ceased. . . . In ancient days it believed that God would send it messengers in every generation. . . . The appearance of the first prophet-messenger—in Israel and in the world—is the beginning of the history of the faith of Israel."[12]

How can we account for the deference and fear which royalty manifested to prophecy except that the latter is really "the first-born" in Israel, and also more truly speaks for God than does the king. In the light of Jewish history, the king, however glittering his role has become, is still a parvenu when he stands in the presence of prophecy. The tradition of Israel speaks of Abraham, a prophet, confronting the kings of other lands. Moses is the God-appointed prophet who faces the Egyptian power. If the king comes to be regarded in a symbolic sense as God's adopted son, the prophet has been for generations God's living, burning word to Israel, to mankind, to the king himself.

The failure of royal power, the collapse of royal purpose, occurs when the prophet stands before the king. Then the truth is revealed, and the king knows where authority really dwells. David trembles before Nathan, who condemns the murderous-adulterous king: "You are the man." David trembles because implicit in this confrontation is the clear understanding that the king can be swept away, but "the word of the Lord endures forever." The mighty King Ahab quakes when Elijah tracks him down to the scene of his crime, and he can only babble, "Have you found me, my enemy?"

Nothing is more illustrative of the king's limitation than his moral surrender to the prophet. No absolute ruler, in the ancient world or in ours, could tolerate open defiance. But in Israel this was not defiance. It was divine rebuke, and this gave the prophet immunity. All this stems in large measure from the fact that monarchy was superimposed on Israel. Thus, the prophet dared to speak while the voice of prophecy was stifled in other places. Thus, the king had to listen while in other places kings would have put detractors to death. The king rules. The prophet overrules.

When Elijah the prophet and Ahab the king meet, all the issues of sovereignty and ultimate authority are joined. A man has been killed. False charges of blasphemy and treason have been trumped up against him so that the king might seize this victim's estate. But it is exactly here where we see the rigid limitations of royal authority in Israel. The king wants to pay for a plot of land but the owner, Naboth, refuses to sell, and there is nothing further that the king can do. Expropriation, even by the king, is forbidden in Israel, and there is no way to process the estate other than through stealth. What is more, the treachery involved in hiring lying witnesses and in fabricating a monstrous case against Naboth is contrived not by the king of Israel, but by his foreign wife, Jezebel, whose own conception of royal power is far less scrupulous. It is Jezebel, not the king, who has been harassing the prophets of Israel and driving them into hiding. When Elijah faces the king, he does so not merely as a courageous man, but with the authority of a divine mandate. Ahab listens with fear and trembling to a sentence of doom, and he dare not retaliate.

This is not a solitary example of the collision of power and prophecy. David listens remorsefully to his own sentence at the hands of Nathan. Amos stands up to the high priest, agent of the king, and he sends him back with a message of irrevocable doom. Amos is accused of conspiracy. He is commanded to leave the king's sanctuary, but he holds his ground and pronounces his sentence. Jeremiah is charged with treason; he is accused of preaching surrender to the enemy. But the king, hard-pressed as he is to execute the traitor, not only desists, but in his terror and danger, brings him out of the dungeon to consult with him. The king virtually asks his prisoner, "What do I do now?"

The monarch is not endowed with absolute power. When he does assume it, it is only because he has usurped it. King Uzziah dares to perform a priestly office in the Temple, and the priests stand in his way, accusing him of "trespass against God" (2 Chron. 26:18ff.).

The monarch can be openly deflected from a wayward course. In a bloody civil conflict, Israel inflicts a heavy defeat upon Judah and takes ''two hundred thousand'' captives. A prophet, Odeh, meets the victorious forces on their way home and prevails on them to return the captives (2 Chron. 28:9–15).

If absoluteness resides anywhere, it is in prophecy and not in monarchy. We see Micaiah ben Imlah standing alone before the kings of Israel and of Judah, surrounded by four hundred professional court prophets who goad their rulers on to war. The kings want Micaiah to foretell the successful outcome of the war, as have the other prophets. They want him to make it unanimous, to bless their enterprise. But, solitary amidst the armies and the war-mongering prophets, he says, ''I see all Israel scattered upon the mountains, as sheep that have no shepherd.''

The kings are appalled, but Micaiah is beyond the punitive hand, even of kings. The full measure of both this heroic stand and the moral subordination of the throne can be taken when we compare this moment with another, twenty centuries later, in the England of Henry II. The king calls upon Sir Thomas à Becket, archbishop of Canterbury, to sanction ecclesiastical control by the king. Becket refuses, and because he does not bend to Henry's will, he is put to death. At issue is not any open condemnation of the king's moral conduct. At issue is only Becket's refusal to approve a royal intrusion into the realm of the Church. Micaiah denounces an unjust war—and survives. Nathan says, ''You are the man,'' to an adulterous King David—and David acknowledges his guilt. Becket will not ratify Henry's trespass—and he dies for protecting the precincts of the Church.

Yet we know that power did emerge in Israel and did present a growing threat to the rule of Israel's God. The state did assume a life of its own, and temporal sovereignty clashed with divine sovereignty. The conflict increased with the growth of statehood and all of its attendant and inherent defects.

The clash between the powers of God and the state on which prophecy was to make the most fearless and the most telling judgment illuminated the ultimate national disaster. More clearly than other observers of the national condition, prophets such as Amos, Hosea, Isaiah, and Jeremiah saw calamity not only as a consequence, but as inherent in moral decay and public corruption. National overthrow was set in motion by national evil, which was often ignored either because of national success or national crisis. (The time never seems to be right to put the nation's moral house in order.)

The judgments of the prophets on their society were validated by catastrophe. As a consequence, two extreme conceptions of the fall of Israel and the fall of the house of David have asserted themselves. One is that prophecy not only envisioned but embraced overthrow. Out of disaster, a new Israel could be born, free of the restraints of temporal power and the corrosive forces of statehood. The destruction was to be final. From one view, Christian, the wreckage of the state was to become the rich soil out of which Christianity was to emerge. From another view, Jewish, the state was to be superseded by a higher Judaism, freed of the bondage of territory, free to pursue a purified, universal existence.

A third conception of the fall of the Jewish state is that history's balance could not be redressed until the state was reconstituted. The collapse of the kingdom was a tragedy, hardly a triumph. The restoration of the house of David became a cardinal tenet of faith. From the time of Jewish subservience to Persian and Greek rule during the Second Temple, the Davidic dynasty became idealized and romanticized in the people's memory. They never abandoned hope for the restoration of the ''house of David.''

In the wake of national disaster, the remonstrative and condemning voice of prophecy became muted. Conciliatory, consoling prophecy became dominant. One aspect of the collective fantasy was full restoration and resumption of the nation's fortunes. An extreme and secular version of this fantasy was that prophets such as Jeremiah had actually betrayed the people by counseling submission to the enemy, and that King Zedekiah, in his vain resistance to Babylonia, was a national hero.

Neither of these extreme views regarding the national disaster as beneficial is valid. It is almost a savage assumption that prophecy sought destruction as a prerequisite for salvation. If prophets proclaimed doom, it was not out of hope but out of despair. They persisted to the end to appeal for a turning away from the fateful path. They pleaded for a last minute withdrawal from the brink, though they could not deceive themselves into believing that they would be heeded. They saw the inevitability of destruction, but not of annihilation. Israel would not be swept off the face of history, either to be obliterated or to be replaced by another Israel. It would be this Israel, this people, restored to this land. "I will bring your seed from the East, and gather you from the West; I will say to the North, 'Give up,' and to the South, 'Keep not back' " (Isa. 43:5-6).

Equally untenable is the assumption that restoration meant the full resumption of an interrupted career, the investiture of the banished king, the awakening of the sleeping beauty to her wonted activities. The destruction and the exile to Babylonia had been too traumatic to permit such a simple solution. There could be no going home again in the accustomed manner. A wrench had occurred in the body and the soul of the people. The power of the nation had asserted itself over the sovereignty of God, and the collective fall ensued. Out of the fateful encounter, Judaism saw neither a victor nor a loser; neither the total assertion of God over an obliterated nation, nor the escape of the nation from its God. Instead, exile and despair saw the makings of reconciliation. Jeremiah's recriminations are modulated by a love as intense as his chastisement: "I have loved you with an everlasting love. . . . Withhold your voice from weeping . . . for your work shall be rewarded" (Jer. 31:16).

Just as some prophets saw national disaster as an accomplished fact, so they saw the reconciling act and the redemption. Out of the expectation that the covenant between God and Israel would be renewed, a deepened conception of the place of the nation in God's plan developed.

[73]

This conception did not require the nullifying of the nation but its purifying. As a result of prophetic stress upon renewal, the people was called to resume its former condition of subordination to the sovereignty of God. But the commonwealth and the Davidic dynasty had become so organic to the people's life and spirit that commonwealth and dynasty could not be excluded from this relationship with God. Prophecy foresaw destruction, not abolition. To annihilate the national hope would have been to annihilate both Israel and its God. Out of the dual necessity of restoring the sovereignty of God and also the integrity of the commonwealth and its king came the conversion, in prophetic outlook, of the nation into a sacred instrument of God, and the king as a messianic figure. Kaufmann tells us: "Monarchy is rooted in prophecy. . . . The king is only the bearer of God's love through His messenger [the prophet]. He is only a symbol of the reign of God's will upon earth."[13]

Even before the destruction of the first commonwealth, prophecy was already engaged in transforming both the character of the nation and the task of the king. The transformation was rooted in a recognition that the kings had been failures, and it resulted in the expectation that ultimately an ideal king, "a shoot from the stock of Jesse," would emerge. But this messianic king would be endowed with prophetic influence. Out of the fusion of monarchy and prophecy a messianic monarchy would result.

An ideal of what the true king must be was set forth. He ceased to be a ruler in the accepted sense, and he became a wonderful counselor, a prince of peace, a righteous judge, a champion of the afflicted. In a real sense, he was to become the instrument for fulfilling the pristine virtues of justice and righteousness. He was not to be God's son in the primitive, mythical sense, but the agent of God's will, endowed with God's spirit. What the monarchy had superseded, it was, in prophetic vision, to fulfill. The king was "to restore the order of society which the monarchy itself had dissolved."[14]

The king was to become the embodiment of prophetic ideals. Ultimately, he was to loom larger and larger in the people's expectations as the *Melech Ha-Mashiach*, the King–Messiah. While the king enters Jewish history as a superimposed borrowing from the ancient world, prophecy so alters his character and his function that only his title bears resemblance to other rulers. The very assumptions of his office against which Samuel inveighed are now repudiated. His authority is not to rest upon power but upon God's spirit.

"Shall you reign because you strive to excel in cedar? Did your father . . . do justice and righteousness? Then it was well with him" (Jer. 22:15). The unalterable requirement for the king is the renunciation of unbridled power and the resumption of obedience to the moral law. "Execute justice and righteousness, deliver the spoiled out of the hand of the oppressor; do no wrong, do no violence, to the stranger, the fatherless, the widow, neither shed innocent blood" (Jer. 22:3). In a true sense, the king must cease being a king. He must reduce himself to the place of all Israel which is commanded to do righteously. He is not permitted to exclude himself from the requirements of the law. This was the prophetic conception of the ruler, before disaster overwhelmed the people. It became even more definitive when the commonwealth fell. The anointed king is to be not only the champion of the lowly, but will himself be lowly and humble. The king is not to be exalted but to be meek, just, and righteous, unlike the previous kings of Judah. The total repudiation of every other form of monarchy attains its final form. Like the people, the king is to be totally submissive to the sovereignty of God, and thus the people is to be restored full circle to its pristine state. A prophet of the exile, Ezekiel, was to define this new, yet old, condition: "That which comes in to your mind shall not be, in that you say: we will be as the nations. . . . As I live . . . I will be king over you" (20:33–34).[15]

In Ezekiel, kingship is transposed from tyranny before the destruction of the first kingdom to beneficence under the anticipated restoration. Denouncing pre-captivity kings, he describes them as "a great beast. . . . He devoured men" (19:4). He attacks the "dishonored wicked prince of Israel whose day has come" (21:30). He generalizes: "Every one of the princes of Israel in your midst used his strength for the shedding of blood" (22:6). But in the time of restoration, kingship will attain new and moral heights when "he comes to whom it rightfully belongs" (21:30). "My servant David . . . shall be a shepherd to them" (34:23). "My princes shall no more defraud My people" (45:8). "The prince shall not take property away from any of the people and rob them of their holdings" (46:18).

The nation, like the king, is to be transformed in the prophetic outlook. One thing is clear—the main burden of prophecy is not annihilation, but ultimate restoration. However mutilated the people might be, it would be redeemed and resettled upon its land. Seeing beyond national collapse, prophecy saw renewal. "Bid Jerusalem take heart. . . . Her guilt is paid off" (Isa. 40:2). The people is to survive. Survival itself is the very stuff of transformation because, as it applies to Israel, it runs counter to all history and experience. Prophets before and during the exile were well aware that the survival of the people was itself a miraculous event, a merciful act of God. It is noteworthy that an extreme exponent of the final end of Israel has to acknowledge that in the last analysis, it did not come to an end. In one place, von Rad writes of "the twofold message of Israel's end and of Jahweh's making all things new." Yet elsewhere, he attests: "Israel was still to be regarded as a community bound together by nature and history, . . . really a people in the proper sense of the word." It should be added that it was to be a people established upon its own soil.

But if the people as such was to endure, the inner content of its life was to be altered. There is an ambivalence in prophecy about this. There is the stress upon total change and there is also reference to a great reversion to the classical wilderness period. It is the difference between the prospect of the yet unattained future, and the hope of the discovery of the lost golden age. In one instance, it is the "end of days." In the other, Israel is to be purified by a repetition of the wilderness experience. In either event, Israel, healed of its decimation and replanted in its land, and thus a proper continuum of the Israel that had fallen, would undergo a radical change, or restoration.

Micah saw the change as taking the form of reununciation. Israel would no longer depend upon the instruments of war for survival. At the same time it would irrevocably reject every form of paganism and idolatry (Mic. 5:9ff.). The period of its morally endangered involvement with false political and religious values would be dissolved. The new era, like the pristine, golden one, would restore complete reliance upon God, the people's protector; upon God, the Only One. The ancient and neglected covenant between God and Israel would be reestablished. The Torah would enter more profoundly into the life of the people; it would cease to be an external, superficial influence. When Jeremiah envisioned the "renewed covenant," he coupled this with the expectation that as a consequence, "they shall be My people." Ezekiel actually saw the renewal of the covenant in the form of a recapitulation of the Egyptian bondage and the entrance into the wilderness. It will be Sinai all over again. "As I pleaded with your fathers in the wilderness of the land of Egypt, so will I plead with you, . . . and I will bring you into the bond of the covenant" (Ezek. 20:36–37).

An added and indispensable part of the covenant is the prospect of God's future love for Israel and His people. In addition to the allusion to the Exodus, we find reference to the Flood, and Isaiah of the Exile ventures to predict that as God swore never to flood the earth again, so He swears never to be angry again with His people (Isa. 54:9). Prophecy is so redolent with the assurance of the restoration of the national fortunes that one wonders whether exponents of an opposing view were reading a mutilated text. How can one overlook the unmistakable meaning of: "You shall no more be designated forsaken, nor shall your land be called desolate, but you shall be designated My-Delight-in-her, and your land, Espoused" (Isa. 62:4). This passage, like a profusion of others, does not speak of the future bliss of a disembodied and attenuated group, but of a regenerated people on its own soil, a people not only of time, but of space. Prophecy speaks not of the withering of the state, but of its purification. "I will take away all of your alloy; I will restore your judges as at the first, and your counsellors as at the beginning" (Isa. 1:25-26). Israel will be peace-abiding, and will be free of the fear of its neighbors. Its king will not be a warrior, but a protector of the weak. "Prosperity and security will prevail in the land" (Ezek. 34:25ff.).

A fundamental condition for the people's renewal is the establishment once more of the covenant by which Israel proclaims its primary allegiance to God. A corollary condition is that the Torah will fasten itself more firmly upon the consciousness of the people. The inference is that neither covenant nor Torah had really broken through to the inner existence of the nation. The covenant is central. It differentiates Israel from its neighbors. It denies Israel's claim to be "like all the nations." It establishes the chain of obedience as running from the people to Torah. Yet, within these relationships, the temporal texture of the people's existence is both assumed and assured. The land has been integrated into the sacred relationship as evidence of the covenant's promise and truth. The people is the historic witness of the truth. The people's national existence, reaching its highest point in the dynasty of David, has been fused to the prior claims of the covenant. It is not something separate and sovereign. It is an instrument of a higher purpose, and it is not permitted to break away as a deviant entity. The king becomes messianic. The people becomes utopian. Its inner life will be peaceful. Its children will be learned of the Torah. Justice will be firmly established within the nation, and God will be acknowledged as creator and redeemer. Out of its renewal, the people will become the instrument for diffusing the word of God to all mankind. Out of its affliction and redemption, it is called to fulfill a universal task, to proclaim universal truth. Israel, always interlocked in encounter with the world, is summoned to turn to the world in a redemptive way. Israel "shall make the right to go forth . . . [and] set the right in the earth." It has been created to be a "light to the nations, to open blind eyes, to free the prisoner from the dungeon." Suffering and the redemption which is born of it become the catalyst out of which Israel is made conscious of a universal task.

As Jeremiah is consecrated even before conception to be a "prophet to the nations," so is Israel called upon to turn outward toward the world. This is an evocation of the old biblical formula which demands that the people be mindful of the stranger. But this nowhere requires that the people go into exile in order to execute the task. Exile is evil. Exile is punishment. Only through restoration is the task made possible. "Out of Zion shall go forth the Torah." The people requires the land for healing. It requires the land for teaching. The renewal both of life and spirit is contingent upon it. But at the same time, prophecy makes it clear that renewed national life is only the gift with which a spiritual awakening must take place. When the nation faces the threat of a devastating invasion, Isaiah offers the partial consolation: "Out of Jerusalem shall go forth a remnant, and out of Mount Zion they that shall escape" (2 Kings 19:31). But looking far beyond that point, the prophet paraphrases the assurance and transposes it into an altogether different key: "Out of Zion shall go forth the Torah, and the word of God from Jerusalem."

A remarkable dichotomy confronts us. The same prophecy which does not see the state in ultimate terms looks to national restoration as a supreme fulfillment. It would appear that these two conceptions are irreconcilable, and that each must pursue its own divergent path, one toward nationalism, the other toward a universalism which allows no room for national expression. But instead, the prophetic influence fused these two apparently disparate views into a single category. It achieved the synthesis by making national redemption part of the redemption of the world. One was a pre-condition for the other. The restoration of Israel was not to be isolated from humanity, nor was it to be an end in itself. On the one hand, the people could not be redeemed without first being restored. On the other hand, restoration was to be the beginning of universal redemption.

Notes

1. Josephus, *Antiquities*, XIV, 3, 2.
2. Gerhard von Rad, *Old Testament Theology* (New York, 1962), vol. I, pp. 66–68.
3. Parker, *Christianity and the State in the Light of History* (London, 1955), p. 7.
4. Ibid.
5. Henri Frankfort, *Kingship and the Gods* (Chicago, 1948), pp. 337ff.
6. Chaim Tchernowitz, *Toledot Ha-Halakhah* (New York, 1945), vol. I, part II, p. 51.
7. Ibid.
8. Yehezkel Kaufmann, *The Religion of Israel*, translated and abridged by Moshe Greenberg (Chicago, 1966), p. 262.
9. Ibid., p. 272.
10. Ibid., p. 273.
11. Ibid., p. 216.
12. Translated from the unabridged Hebrew edition, *Toledot Ha-Emunah Ha-Yisre'elit* (Tel Aviv, 1952), vol. II, p. 181.
13. Ibid.
14. Johs. Pedersen, *Israel* (Oxford, 1926), vol. III, p. 91.
15. Note Deut. 17:14.

REVELATION,
A PROLEGOMENON
Herman E. Schaalman

The cornerstone of authentic Judaism is the assertion that there is one God. This is the root statement out of which grows the luxuriant tree of the Jewish way of life. Its acceptance is the *conditio sine qua non* which places one into the *kelal*, the embracing totality of the Jewish community. Its denial is the cardinal sin which entails the radical jeopardy of being an outsider. It puts one on the precipitous slope at the foot of which yawns the abyss of inauthenticity or worse.

The declaration of the *ichud hashem*, the uniqueness, the oneness of the divine, was, when first disclosed, the radical opposite of paganism, and so it remains today. It opposed paganism's inevitable fragmentation of reality with a bold statement of an ultimate underlying unity. It challenged its moral diffuseness with the unequivocal moral clarity: "Thus saith the Lord." It enabled the soul to find that center round which could coalesce the vision and, at times, the achievement of wholeness, *shalom*.

Nor has the flow of time from Abraham and Sinai to today lessened the truth or urgency of this assertion. Paganism remains a major option in our world and in our own lives. Its appeal is as enticing as in antiquity. It contains sufficient operative validity to provide an adequate framework for broad reaches of public and private lives and decisions. Its insinuating attractiveness captivates still as it did in ancient times. Its staying power is underrated only at grave risk. Its "why not" and "try it, you might like it" allure remains potent. Its devotees easily outnumber those whose values and attitudes are shaped by the uncompromising consequences of the faith-assertion *adonai echad* of Jewish mono-

[81]

theism. And since the theological and moral consequences of this statement are neither self-evident nor comfortable, tradition has wisely ordained that we recite *Shema* three times daily. Those who instituted this rule surely had in mind more than God's need or joy in receiving this adoring gift from the worshipping individual or community. They understood the proclivity also in the Jew's heart toward denial or evasion which the thrice daily declaration, *shema*, was designed to counteract. It is not easy at all, both privately and publicly, to assert *adonai echad*, and thus to fly in the face of most of the world. It requires faith, courage, and thoughtful discipline. And yet to be thus the witness to this unity, its *ed*, its *martyros*, has been the vocation of the Jewish people. We have carried it out faithfully until now. It has been the source of the driving energy of our history. It has molded our past and present. It remains our destiny, the purpose of our existence.

Tradition unequivocally declares that the discovery of this divine unity was made possible by God. It was initiated by God. *Shema*, hear, was addressed to the entire community and understood and accepted as the culminating summation of human understanding of God. Torah taught it and Jewish tradition placed it at the summit liturgically, theologically, and pedagogically. It was not an achievement of human wisdom, not the ingenious result of careful or brilliant penetration into the mystery of the divine. It came to the Jew not as the proud accomplishment of the searching mind, but as the sudden, radical, perhaps unmerited, and surely overwhelming gift of God.

Or, to put it differently, it was the result of revelation. At the heart of Judaism and its age-old tradition lies the assertion that God reveals, that God is capable of essential and commanding disclosure to human beings, and is willing to do so. The entire structure of Jewish belief and practice rests on this possibility, and on its actual occurrence in the lives of the community and a number of individuals. Without revelation Judaism may at best be a thoughtful philosophical system, subject inevitably and totally to intellectual analysis, evaluation, criticism, and perhaps rejection, or, at worst, a human fabrication incapable of withstanding the ever more powerful cultural and intellectual currents of advancing civilization. Judaism is built squarely on revelation. Revelation is the seal of its authenticity. It has been a major source of its astounding survival and staying power.

Needless to say, the traditionalists in the Jewish community have asserted this root value of revelation right along. *Torah min hashamayim,* "Torah comes from God," has been one of their chief articles of faith and, if necessary, their battle cry. There is an unbroken and massive flow of statements declaring this to be a truth beyond all challenge. From Torah itself to the most recent theological or polemical treatise emanating from the traditionalist camp, revelation is considered an unconditional truth without which there would be no Judaism, or at least none as we know it.

Nontraditionalists, however, and those who are called or call themselves modernists on the contemporary Jewish scene, have by and large experienced grave difficulties with this position. There is probably no other belief in the structure of Jewish religious life which has troubled the modern mind more and drawn more severe challenges. Surely it is no exaggeration to say that the idea of revelation has been the great "scandal" over which not a few have felt compelled to turn their back on the religious traditions and beliefs of their forebears. The inability to accept revelation as possible and real has driven many, and not the least thoughtful, to secularism, scientism, and a whole variety of psychological and sociological substitutes and reductions. It is claimed that there is a basic, fundamental incompatability between the concept of revelation and the modern mind. Revelation, thus, often became the test-stone separating traditionalists from modernists.

Need this be so irrevocably? Is this challenge inescapable and the resulting conflict unavoidable? I believe not. I believe that it is possible to understand the event of revelation in such a way as to avoid the difficulties which modernists inevitably find in the traditional view. There is a way to construct a model of the revelatory moment and act so built and described that it becomes compatible with the modern mind and meets the objections raised against it. In fact, a series of problems inherent in the usual traditional picture of the revelatory process can thus be solved, not by denying revelation, but by understanding it in a manner different from the usual traditional description.

Sinai, the giving and receiving of Torah, is surely the most signal and cardinal moment of revelation in Jewish tradition. The *ma'amad har sinai*, the assembly at the foot of the mountain, and *matan torah*, the giving of Torah by God, are the core of the Jewish people's covenant life. Thus, any attempt to deal with revelation, to structure and interpret it, needs to start with Sinai.

The most commonly used traditional statement of the event of revelation at Mount Sinai goes to the effect that the people of Israel, seven weeks after their exodus from Egypt, are led by Moses to the foot of Sinai. The mountain is wrapped in ominous clouds; flashing fire and terrifying noise so frighten the people, who have been given to understand that God has descended upon the mountain, that they are unable to withstand the overwhelming impact of these phenomena. They shrink back, send Moses into the thick darkness to become their protective interlocutor, and it is Moses who then relates the divinely spoken Ten Commandments. Later, during a forty-day sojourn on top of Mount Sinai, Moses receives Torah, which he then brings and teaches to his people. In all this, Moses is depicted and understood to be the agent of God in the transmission of the divine message.

Revelation thus seen is the act of God whereby Moses is presented with the text of the Torah. God speaks and Moses writes. God gives Moses the Five Books that will bear his name and he receives them. God chose Moses because there had already been unprecedented intimacy between them, as is convincingly corroborated by the statement of *lo kam kemoshe od*, that Moses's place with God was unique, never again to be equalled, let alone surpassed. He was *the* servant of God. And yet there is no overlooking the fact that Moses's role was passive, subservient, instrumental in the original sense of that word. He is understood to be, and

[84]

called, *navi*, the forthteller, who, like Bala'am, could only tell what God had put in his mouth.

Not that Moses is invaryingly pictured in such a passive stance. When compelled, he is shown to be capable of boldly arguing with God, even daring to reverse God's decision. And while he is *anav*, the very model of the humble, he can also boil over in wrath and shatter the very tablets "written by the finger of God." But when it comes to the generally accepted traditional image of his place in the revelatory process at Sinai, Moses is portrayed as God's secretary, faithfully taking down the divine words. Is it not strange that he, whom tradition extols as the supreme Jew of all time, as God's closest and most favored intimate, should have been depicted, and is still seen, as performing a task and playing a part in revelation so subordinate and passive that it might well have been performed by a lesser person? Unless, that is, this picture of the revelatory moment and Moses's part in it is fundamentally wrong, to the point of missing crucial truths and hiding a radically different understanding of the event and its texts.

In its place it is proposed that revelation not be understood as a one-sided event, with an active, speaking God and a passive, note-taking Moses, but as a two-sided event in which the human is as inescapably necessary and active as is the divine, an event moreover that could only occur with the total involvement of the human partner. Revelation is not only a giving. It is also, and equally, a receiving. In fact, there could be no revelation without the human participant. God's would be a voice crying in the wilderness unless there was a human being responding by listening and hearing and understanding. Revelation is a two-way street on which traffic can flow only when both the divine and the human partner are present and on the way toward each other. The human presence and readiness is the inescapable condition for the divine Revealer to be able to function as such.

Our midrashic literature is full of the profoundest insights into this condition. When God is ready to give Torah, to reveal Torah, no willing partners are to be found. Nation

[85]

after nation, though offered the priceless gift, refuses to participate. Finally, Israel does: *na'aseh venishma*, "we will do, we will hear." Not until Israel, in a supreme moment of willingness whose consequences were to last forever, accedes to God's urgent plea and becomes the human participant can God proceed to give Torah. God alone is powerless to reveal. Revelation remains unheard until the human ear and mind are ready and open. And even more telling, and more astounding for its daring and profundity, is the Midrash, which makes God threaten an Israel unwilling to share in revelation with catastrophic death beneath the uprooted mountain which would then become its grave. And only when the terrified people agree, revelation, Torah, occurs. Could the rabbis have been any clearer, any bolder in proclaiming their understanding and conviction that revelation requires two partners, that Torah is the result of interaction between the divine and the human, that to depict Moses as taking dictation from God is so distorted an image as to misread the nature of revelation and Torah?

Moses was totally involved in the revelatory process. If all Israel—the women, the children, the well and the sick, the learned and simple—was indispensable for Torah to come into being, how much the more indispensable was the quintessential Jew, Moses. It is *torat moshe*, Moses's Torah, as much as *torat adonai*, God's Torah. Torah is inevitably both!

The very statement of the rabbis that a servant-maid at Sinai understood Torah better than later learned sages, not only underscores their deference to the compelling nature of the event itself and their awareness of the possible defects in understanding due to the passage of time, but dramatically asserts the individual's share in revelation. This assertion is elaborated upon later by the suggestion that each person present at Sinai heard Torah in his or her own way, that Torah has 600,000 "faces," a veritable infinity of meaning, an inexhaustible depth of interpretation and understanding.

If, then, God did not dictate Torah to Moses, if it is not God's one-sided gift, what do we mean by Torah? If revelation is not the passive act of *kabbalah*, a receiving as though

[86]

poured into the waiting human vessel, what is it? How does it happen?

To answer these questions, we must first deal with the word "speak." It is surely a key concept in all of Torah, in fact, in all of Judaism, which is much more oriented toward sound than sight, toward speaking and hearing, than toward seeing. This emphasis is, also, one of several major distinctions between Judaism and Hellenism.

Speaking is the most distinguishing feature of the human being. It is a unique ability which is both the base and crown of human achievement. *Davar*, the word, is the apex of humanness. Little wonder then that Torah, when attempting to describe how revelation proceeds and how Torah is born, uses "speaking" as the only possible metaphor. Nothing more fitting, nothing "higher" or more appropriate, was available. It is the supreme human experience. When, therefore, faced with a desire and necessity of talking about God's self-disclosure to human beings, of God's encounter with Moses, Israel, Abraham, etc., Torah searches for the most applicable descriptive term; it says: "God speaks." When creating, it is "speaks." When commanding, it is "speaks." When in anger or compassion, it is "speaks." In this context we can understand that later extreme utterance: "God was Word [*Logos*]." And yet, in a most remarkable statement, the wordlessness of God, the soundlessness of God, is suggested equally when it is said that the only sound God made at Sinai and, therefore, the only sound which the people "heard" was the silent aleph of *anochi*.

Search if you will, but what other word would have been more apt, how else might Torah have put it, how else might Moses have said it? But surely "God speaks" was never meant to be equated with "I speak" or "you speak." It is not to be taken literally. It is metaphor. It is the perhaps desperate attempt of the human partner in the revelatory event to put into communicable and universally understandable language what occurred at the moment of revelation. "Speech" came closest to what inherently is ineffable.

There was the Presence, undeniable, inescapable. God

[87]

"came", "descended", "appeared." If God could not do so, then there would be neither relevance nor revelation, then the human and the divine would miss each other, pass each other by, live in unrelated realms, and hence be irrelevant to each other. Religious faith, Jewish faith, asserts as one of its most significant points that such meeting between God and human beings can and does occur, that there was a person or persons who "saw", "heard", "understood." So compelling is the Divine Presence and so unequivocal that the human beings who are graced by being present are inescapably caught up in the experience. Their whole existence is enveloped, altered, even in grave jeopardy. One does not seek out this Presence lightly. Perhaps the four who entered the *pardes*—all of whom, except for Akiba, came to grief—are a classic warning against such adventurism. Not for nothing did the Kabbalists warn any under forty years of age to desist from seeking to penetrate into the Mystery.

The undimmed brilliance of the divine is fatal to humans. The unshielded full brunt of God's presence is unbearable and consuming. As Emil Fackenheim puts it, God in revealing must conceal.

As Judaism sees it, the encounter between the divine and the human is not intended to destroy the individual, to absorb the human person into the divine fullness. On the contrary, the human partner needs to be kept intact to become the messenger, the interpreter of God. The human partner is compelled to speak, to tell, to report, to say what the ineffable Presence meant. It is not enough to be there, to be caught up in the marvelous experience. One must speak. One must become God's articulator, God's forthteller, *navi*, God's "mouth." And therefore, and inevitably: *dibrah torah kilshon bene adam*, "Torah speaks human language," and human language only, for language is quintessentially human. It is always what Moses heard and understood and then spoke or wrote that we find in Torah.

God is there, inescapably, essentially. There would be no Torah without God. But God does not speak and say. Moses, or, for that matter, perhaps others, does the speaking and saying, but only of that which the Divine Presence compellingly imprinted on his being, his mind and soul. Torah is Moses's response to God's presence. This understanding serves also to eliminate difficulties arising from different and even contradictory statements, all claiming to have originated in revelation. They are the inevitable result of different persons, souls, minds, responding to God's presence. Even a Moses at 80 would differ from a Moses at 120. He might hear differently under the variant conditions of joy and sorrow, exaltation or depression of spirit.

Revelation is the interaction between, the joint action of the compelling presence of God and the articulating human partner. Torah is the "expression," coming forth from within the depth of the human partner, of what God in encountering him had "intended" to convey.

The quotation marks around "speaks", "says," etc., are no evasion or equivocation. They are the worshipful tribute which the human being, understanding his limitations of experience and hence expression, pays to the Divine. We use our highest accomplishment, our quintessence, to come close, to hint at, to allude to the Divine. *Dibrah torah kilshon bene adam*, "Torah speaks human language," in our case Hebrew.

Thus, it does not become an overwhelming problem when passages contradict each other or when some are obscure and others difficult. We need not be upset to the point of calling the entire text into radical question, prepared perhaps even to discard it, nor need we expend ourselves in seeking ingeniously to harmonize its contradictions. It is the human factor in the revelatory process that furnishes the explanation. It is human error inevitably rooted in our limitation and fallibility that accounts for mistakes, contradictions, etc.

God's part in the revelatory process is not affected thereby. God knows who the partner is, who the creature is which "is born against its will and dies against its will." God does expect perfection neither from humankind nor even from those specially gifted who, though chosen to be revelatory partners, are nonetheless prone to error. Even Moses sins.

[89]

In fact, precisely because it is God who is the fountain of Torah, the "Giver" and "Ground" of Torah, it is impossible for the human partner to comprehend all, to express all, to be flawless. God is too much. The Presence always exceeds human capacity to grasp and understand. Torah has to be fragmentary, incomplete, a condensed abstract of the divine fullness. Just because God is its origin, Torah cannot possibly tell all, to comprise all either in the *chumash* or *tanach* or in the *torah shebe'al peh*, the oral tradition of the past and of the future. It is precisely the infinity of God that, coming to the human participant in the revelatory moment, must be pared down, channeled, worded. And once a given word has been chosen to be spoken or written, all others are left out, eliminated. Only one word at a time, a given vocabulary, becomes the self-limiting vessel for the meaning that streams forth from the Divine Presence as grasped and expressed by the human partner. The miracle is how much infinity remains, how inexhaustible Torah has proven to be, how millions upon millions of its students and lovers have poured over its lines for centuries, and still there is no end. There never will be an end.

Revelation is the joint enterprise between the Divine and certain human beings, for not everyone has the capacity to be open to the Presence, to make himself or herself present to God in the required total participating fashion. Human beings can perhaps prepare themselves, practice, for example, "radical amazement," but God retains the initiative. Revelation occurs at God's bidding provided there is a person who can share it.

Thus, God is in Torah, in all of Torah, by way of Moses or perhaps others, though this latter point loses much of its force in this model of revelation, and becomes nearly negligible. The important point, the key, is God's presence in Torah.

It is this Divine Presence in Torah which is also needed for an understanding of *mitzvah*, commandment. There is the *metzaveh*, the commander whom Moses "understood" to demand of the covenant-people certain behavior, certain acts and abstentions. By accepting Torah, by entering the covenant, Israel bent its neck under the yoke of *mitzvah* and became *metzuveh*, the one addressed by the command. But that command, those *mitzvot*, are as surely the human expression of what God's commanding presence compelled the human partner to understand and articulate as are all the other sentences and words in Torah. The *mitzvah* is the collaborative result of the Divine-human encounter as surely as the whole Torah text. It is as full of the Divine and as full of the human as all other passages. This, therefore, both impels us to take them with utmost seriousness and at the same time opens the door to the equally serious necessity of further analysis, study, interpretation, revision, even occasional abolition, as rabbinic tradition has demonstrated abundantly and conclusively.

This process of study and sifting, of seeking to hear God's ''voice'' in each *mitzvah*, of taking its original human formulation as the incentive and commission to revise and add, to abolish and intensify, needs to go on unabated. Each stream within Judaism is engaged in it in its own way, each by its own standards and methods. Each derives its authenticity and authority from the seriousness and sensitivity, from the knowledge and devotion of its *posekim*.

The alternative model of revelation here proposed, with its radical emphasis on the human factor as the indispensable part of the revelatory process, serves to break through the presumption that there is an infallible Torah text; that there is the unmediated direct word of God which would discourage God-seeking and God-aware probing for additional understanding or formulations; that there is one and only one licit, authentic path of understanding and interpretation held in the monopolistic custody of self-perpetuating interpreters, who start with a severely limiting perception of the process of revelation. It opens the door to all Jews who seek the Lord and want to live by Torah and *mitzvot*. This view upholds that Torah is *min hashamayim*, from Heaven, but only by way of human beings. Thus, the covenant is reaffirmed for the people of Israel, and the human partner is seen to be God's indispensable ally and friend.

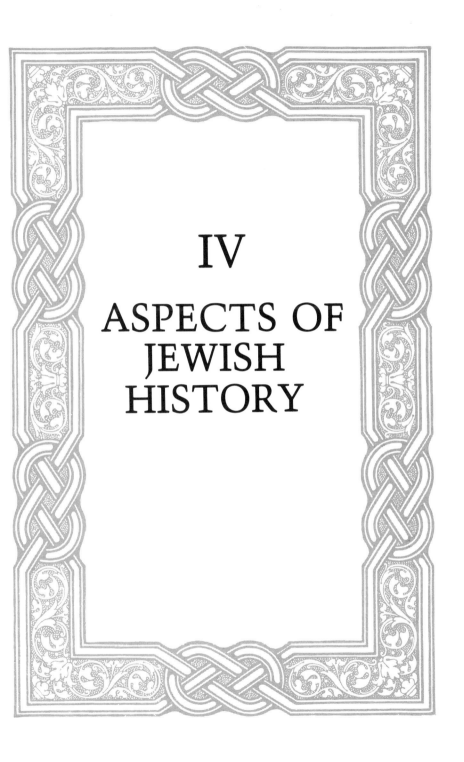

IV
ASPECTS OF JEWISH HISTORY

PERSPECTIVES ON
ANTISEMITISM
Harry S. Crowe

The perspectives on antisemitism which I shall offer are historical and, in part, those of my generation of Canadians and, in part, personal.

I am not an authority on the subject, but it is one in which I have always been most interested.

The expression "anti-Semitism" was first used by Wilhelm Marr, an anti-Jewish agitator and publisher in Hamburg, in the year 1879. At point-of-origin it meant opposition to Jewish economic influence and to Jewish cultural ideas and influences, and support of German economic influence and German cultural ideas and influences.

The year 1879 is very late in the history of the Jews and in the history of activities against Jews. Many scholars have remarked that it is odd that something should go on for centuries without a simple, all-embracing term emerging to describe it. The expression "anti-Semitism" spread very quickly throughout Germany and elsewhere in Europe. Sometimes it is said that the appearance of the expression signified the ascendancy of the opposition to Jews on economic and cultural grounds over the opposition to them on religious grounds, which had become secondary by the nineteenth century.

The use of the terms "Semite" and "Semitism" was racial: it was a total rejection of the people.

Originally, anti-Semite and anti-Semitism were spelled with a capital "S," and always with a hyphen. In the early twentieth century, the capital "S" frequently gave way to a small "s" in England and the United States. I believe that it should be spelled without a hyphen, because the essence of what it conveys is not really opposition to something, but the condition of the person to whom it is properly attached —a diseased or unbalanced condition—to which the original object, the Jew, is essentially irrelevant.

The term "antisemitism" emerged in Europe to describe an attitude toward Jews. Once in the dictionary it is as appropriate to describe an anti-Jewish event in Iraq as to describe one in Germany. It has nothing to do with "semites in general." But it is confusing. "Anti-Jewish" is a less distracting expression when describing events in Arab lands, but not more accurate.

A more recent problem of terminology has arisen since the creation of the State of Israel, or, more precisely, since the Six-Day War in 1967. I sometimes hear someone say he wishes to make it clear that he is anti-Zionist and not anti-semitic. We may look into this later. I have a feeling that those who say this don't distinguish very clearly between the terms. I am sure we will soon hear people say, "Some of my best friends are Zionists."

The *Encyclopaedia Judaica* is an encyclopedia of Jewish history, and to a very considerable extent, it is also an encyclopedia of the history of antisemitism. When I began to prepare this talk, I took down from the shelf a volume of the encyclopedia and opened it at random. I opened it at "Xanten," the name of a town in West Germany—appropriate, as that was where my brigade assaulted the Rhine River in February 1945. This is what I read:

The first documentary evidence for the presence of Jews in Xanten dates from the period of the First Crusade when Jews from Cologne sought refuge there. On June 27, 1096, the crusaders reached Xanten as well, and some 60 Jews were either killed or committed suicide. Among the martyrs was Moses ha-Kohen, Rabbi of Xanten. . . .

In 1197 the Rhenish communities paid the bishop for permission to bury six Martyrs of Neuss in the Xanten cemetery.

Though Jewish moneylenders were found in Xanten in the 13th century, the market day was held on the Sabbath so as to exclude Jews from trade.

[95]

The community suffered badly during the Black Death persecutions of 1349. . . . From 1690 Xanten was the meeting place of the Rhenish Jewish Diet. . . . In 1860 the community had its own elementary school. . . .

A butcher, Adolf Wolff Buschoff of Xanten, was victim of a blood libel in 1892. Accused by a Catholic of murdering a Christian boy, a charge taken up by the antisemitic press. Buschoff was arrested but then discharged for lack of evidence.

A debate in the Prussian Diet, which gave the antisemite A. Stoecker an opportunity to fulminate against the Jews, resulted in the arrest of Buschoff for a second time, but a jury at Cleves found him innocent. (Because of this agitation the community declined. . . . In 1916 [it was] still nearly 10% of the population.)

The synagogue was destroyed on *Kristallnacht*, 1938.

The account stops before the Holocaust.

In the encyclopedia there are not hundreds, but thousands of similar accounts: slaughter by crusaders; suicides; special exactions; trade restrictions, living restrictions; Black Death persecutions; intervening periods of tranquility; assorted accusations, not just "blood libel"; and, where Hitler ruled, the destruction of the synogogue in 1938 and, subsequently, of the people themselves. That is Christendom. But if you look up "Baghdad" or "Tunis" or "Alexandria," the story is not very different. The waves of persecution come at different times, and the final act is not *Kristallnacht* and the Holocaust, but the riots, the restrictions, and the exodus from Arab lands after 1948 and in 1967.

Restrictions and persecution were the intermittent affliction upon Jews throughout the history of the Diaspora. Sociologists and psychologists have many theories about it, and I am not an expert on the subject.

I have wondered, and I have examined documents about it, trying without success to find some reasonable explanation why a man like General Ulysses S. Grant would issue a directive that no Jew could engage in business in any of the southern territories occupied by Union forces under his command. Lincoln reversed the directive, but Grant went on to become president, and the directive against Jews was referred to, not by his opponents, but by his supporters.

This year is the fortieth anniversary of the Evian Conference. I was only fifteen at the time, in July 1938, but I remember the event very well: it intruded upon my consciousness on a farm in western Manitoba, as my father attempted to persuade our local member of Parliament (later a member of Mackenzie King's cabinet) that if Canada would admit several thousand Jews and the United States a proportionate number, then the British government would have to admit some into Palestine; and that other nations would fall into line and the Jews of Germany could be saved. Although the newspapers were still full of horrors being inflicted upon Jews in Vienna, the MP's response was that anyone who would want more Jews in Canada must be out of his mind.

As well as being the fortieth anniversary of the now-forgotten Evian Conference, it is also the thirtieth anniversary of the founding of the State of Israel. There are connections between these two events. On the most elementary level the creation of Israel was the declaration that Jews would no longer have to look for places to hide. But there is a much more substantial relationship than this between Evian and Israel.

If the nations of the world had taken a stand in July 1938 in support of the Jews of Germany, there is a high probability that *Kristallnacht* would not have taken place in November, in defiance of world outrage and world action; and that as Hitler's legions marched across Europe, the policy of *judenrein* would have found expression in great concentration camps, Jewish pales, and ghettoes, and some expulsions to neutral countries, but not in the mass murder of extermination camps. The war would have ended with five or six million Jews hideously oppressed, but alive, an infinitely more potent force than six million dead men, women, and children in the claim upon the conscience of mankind for a national home of their own, and the human resource to build from 1945 (not 1948) a state of such strength that its right to existence would not have become the object of a thirty-year challenge.

An examination of the events at Evian is painfully instructive. We know now that it was the brainchild of American Under-Secretary of State Sumner Welles, sold to Roosevelt through Cordell Hull. It was designed to fail in its announced purpose of helping to rescue German Jews. With the *Anschluss* and the ruthless implementation of the Nuremberg Laws, Jews were subjected to public brutality, confiscation of property, and arrests. There was extensive protest in the American press and a demand that immigration of the Nazis' chosen victims be facilitated.

According to a memorandum in the United States' National Archives, "The Secretary [and] Mr. Welles . . . decided that it would be inadvisable for the Department to attempt merely to resist the pressure and that it would be far preferable to get out in front and attempt to guide the pressure, primarily with a view toward forestalling attempts to have immigration laws liberalized. The idea of the Evian intergovernmental meeting was suggested by Mr. Welles and approved by the President on March 22.''

Roosevelt had invited the nations of western Europe, the Western hemisphere, Australia, and New Zealand. Thirty-one attended, with Italy the main one declining. Germany was not invited, but German observers attended and were accepted in that role. They took copious notes and rose to cheer an extreme antisemitic address by the Swiss delegate. Just before the conference got underway suicides of Jews in Vienna were reported to have reached two hundred a day. Goebbels said: "We cannot protect every Viennese Jew with a special policeman to prevent him from committing suicide.'' On the eve of the conference thousands of Jews in Germany were arrested and put into concentration camps.

The world knew what was happening. The president of the United States had convoked this extraordinary meeting. Much was expected. The address of the American delegate, Myron Taylor, former head of the United States' Steel Corporation, was awaited with great anticipation. Delegates and reporters alike could not believe what he proceeded to say. All the United States was prepared to do was to see that the full quota of about twenty-eight thousand Germans and Austrians—Jews and non-Jews—would be admitted each year.

That, in effect, finished the conference. But other nations made their presentations. The Australians said they did not wish to import a "racial problem." The French said they had reached the "saturation point." The British would accept a few into the British Isles, but no mention of Palestine. In London, Beaverbrook's *Sunday Express* complained that Jewish refugees were already "overrunning the country."

The Canadian position was very much like Mackenzie King's: something should be done if it is clear there is a problem; preferably it should be done by the European nations; in any case, Canada could be expected to accept only a limited number of experienced agricultural workers who qualified in existing categories of Canada's immigration laws. The Dutch, almost alone, were prepared to take more refugees, but hoped that they would be in transit to other countries.

The nations of the world were heard from. The World Jewish Congress was allotted five minutes. Dr. Chaim Weizmann, the spokesman of world Zionism, was not permitted to speak. The assembled nations proceeded to pass an odious motion declaring their unwillingness to finance the migration of Jews out of Germany. A Jew could take only $4.75 out of Germany.

The Evian Conference had gathered to discuss the persecution and plight of the Jews of Germany. It adjourned to a form of adulation from the Nazi press: "The conference serves to justify Germany's policy against Jewry"; the conference had shown "no nation wants Jews"; it had shown "the danger which World Jewry constitutes." Goebbels said that Germany had been trying to get rid of its Jews, but nobody would take them. The French foreign minister told Joachim von Ribbentrop that the Jews were now solely Germany's problem, and that other nations could not object to whatever measures the Germans might employ to solve their problem.

It must be clear that the policy of the Third Reich was to get rid of Jews. They could still go—without their property —but they could go. The problem was that there was no place to go. The Nazis tried one more means of becoming "free of Jews" by having them leave the country. It is another "forgotten event" in history. It was the Nazis' weird response, inhuman and grotesque, to the Evian Conference. Ten thousand Jews were rounded up, many from the streets, many children in schools, taken to the Polish border, and simply dumped into Poland. The Poles did not accept them. They were caught between the forces and the barbed wire of two nations, with little means of sustenance. It was a gesture to the world: "If you want the 'Jewish problem,' here it is."

It was the barbarity of that event, as described in a letter from his father about the family's suffering, which led a seventeen-year-old boy named Herschel, who had managed earlier to get to France, to shoot a German diplomat. This was the excuse for the murder and mayhem and the burning of hundreds of synagogues and Jewish-owned stores on *Kristallnacht*, November 10, 1938. While that was the excuse, Evian was the signal. The world would not interfere. *Kristallnacht* was the testing act for the Holocaust.

While this was the most virulent anti-Jewish outburst to that date in modern times, it aids one's perspective about the creation of Israel to note that in the five-year period before and after *Kristallnacht*, there were about thirty major and minor anti-Jewish outbursts from Morocco to Iraq, in the Arab lands which were to produce some 600,000 Jewish refugees to Israel.

But in 1938 it was the Jews of Germany and Austria who desperately sought a sanctuary. Five hundred thousand was less than the number of Cubans the United States would later absorb after the victory of Castro. That number divided among so many nations, and including so many educated people, would have been absorbed even in the thirties, and their skills would have been of great value to the accepting nations, not to mention their immediate value to the impending war effort.

But it was not to be. Silence gave consent. Freeing Germany and then occupied Europe of Jews was to take the route of the gas chamber and the crematorium. One-third of an ancient people would be destroyed. Arthur D. Morse, in *While Six Million Died*, presents the most convincing case that the six million would not have died if the world had opened its doors to the first half a million refugees.

But they were left to the Germans. Herschel, the boy assassin in Paris, said: "Being a Jew is not a crime. I am not a dog. I have a right to live, and the Jewish people have a right to exist on this earth. Wherever I have been, I have been chased like an animal."

In 1938 there was no place to hide. In 1948 there was Israel. Ten years is such a brief moment in history.

I want to go back, briefly, in history—to nineteenth-century Canada. I want to introduce you to a "righteous Gentile"—an unknown Canadian whom all Canadians, Jews and non-Jews, should know—Henry Wentworth Monk. A very readable biography of Monk was published in 1947 by Richard Lambert, entitled *For the Time is at Hand*, and subtitled *An account of the prophesies of Henry Wentworth Monk, of Ottawa, Friend of the Jews, and Pioneer of World Peace*. Monk lived from 1827 to 1897, most of it in Ottawa, but some of it in London, England, and in the Holy Land. His papers have recently been put into the Public Archives of Canada—extensive correspondence with heads of state and other public figures, and a full set of his pamphlets.

Two things to be noted at once: the first is that Monk had an extensive correspondence with Arthur Balfour in the 1890s—ten years before Herzl first approached Balfour through Joseph Chamberlain, and long before Weizmann first met Balfour—and in this correspondence Monk was pressing the proposal that the British should buy Palestine

[101]

from the Turks in order to establish within it "a Jewish National Home." That is the expression of the Balfour Declaration.

The second point to be noted is that this national home would not only be a haven for Jews suffering persecution in Russia, but its very existence would alleviate the condition of Jews everywhere in the world.

Monk wrote in a similar vein to Lord Salisbury and Lord Roseberry. And he had others write. He wrote to three tsars of Russia, protesting the persecution of Jews—and he got some replies. He visited Abraham Lincoln and discussed with him the condition of Jews in Europe, although not, at that point, the idea of a Jewish national home.

I shall conclude by focusing upon the idea of Monk that antisemitism would wither away with the establishment of a Jewish national home.

In Arab countries, after 1948, anti-Jewish activities, public and private, increased. The pattern varied, and persecution came in waves. Albert Memmi has written extensively on this subject. In the Soviet Union, official anti-Jewish activity, always called anti-Zionism, has increased, again in waves. The *Pravda* cartoon of Dayan and Hitler as twins depicted Dayan, not as he looks, but as the traditional antisemitic stereotype of Germany or tsarist Russia, with an eye-patch. How can you say that is anti-Zionism?

The Jewish community in Argentina is in mortal danger. Elsewhere in Latin America there are growing difficulties. In Communist countries, Arab states, and in the underdeveloped world, Jewish nationalism, alone of all nationalisms, is called "a form of racism," and the General Assembly of the United Nations passed such a resolution.

But what about western Europe and North America? Is Israel a factor in the attitude of the non-Jew? Human rights' laws and commissions have an educating effect. Among non-Jews the Holocaust is a nightmare to the older generations, but not to the younger (although younger people have few hang-ups about racial, religious, and other differences).

But what about the relevance of Israel? In the short run, in the present phase, in which many people have developed an attachment to the cause of Palestinian Arabs—(but, oddly, not to the cause of the Lebanese Arabs)—I am not sure what the effect of the existence of Israel is upon the attitude of non-Jews to Jews.

From 1948 to 1967 there was great sympathy for the creators of the new nation. In 1967 there was euphoria. Then the attitude of many people almost became: "Too bad you won; now we'll feel sorry for somebody else." The switching of roles from scapegoat to underdog to scapegoat leaves one perplexed.

The creation and support of the national home has become entwined with the supply of a vital resource for the industrialized West and Japan—oil from Arab countries. When a congressman weighs conflicting pressures upon him from pro-Israel constituents on the one hand and from oil companies on the other, and measures the competing national objectives of sustaining Israel and sustaining the oil supply (and keeping in check the billions of dollars it produces), at what point does he stop thinking in terms of competing political pressures and national interests, and begin to harbor thoughts of Jews as a problem to him—a new dimension of antisemitism? Henry Wentworth Monk and others did not of course forsee the thirty-year struggle following the creation of the national home and, still less, an "Arab oil" phase to be added to the thousands of years of Jewish history.

But this is only one aspect of what is essentially a problem of non-Jews—of how they relate to Jews. The economic, cultural, and religious aspects continue. I grew up assuming that a society of people of many different origins, as in Canada and the United States, rather than one composed only of French or Poles or Germans, would be one in which the attitude of non-Jew to Jew would be less troubled, more manageable. But I understand studies now show that antisemitism in the United States is most pronounced where there are ethnic mixtures, and it doesn't make much difference whether the mixtures are old or new, and it doesn't depend on how many Jews there are in the locality.

[103]

So I end where I began, by declaring that I am not an authority. Uncivilized conduct of non-Jews toward Jews has come in waves throughout history, and has receded. With the Holocaust occurring in the 1940s, it is especially difficult for an historian to suggest that there has been progress or improvement. There is a golden age now for Jews in North America. But there have been golden ages in the past. My concluding word is to resort, as a caution, to my contribution to Jewish philosophy: "Every silver lining has a cloud."

FORCED TO RECOGNIZE: THE TRUMAN ADMINISTRATION AND THE RECOGNITION OF ISRAEL
Harvey J. Fields

On November 29, 1947, the Truman administration voted for the partition of Palestine at the United Nations. By March 1948, however, the president was having doubts about the wisdom of the United Nations' solution to the "Palestine problem," and was encountering stiff opposition to the creation of a Jewish state from the British, and from James Forrestal, Loy W. Henderson, William D. Leahy, George Marshall, and Robert M. Lovett, among others. They were all strongly advising the administration to abandon its commitment to partition.

Fighting between Arabs and Jews had raged since the United Nations' vote. By March 1948 it was still unclear just who would emerge victorious on the battlefield. Some of Truman's advisors feared that the Russians would use the strife between Jews and Arabs to establish their own base of operation in the Middle East, while others estimated that American troops might be required to preserve peace in the area, and thereby guarantee continuing Western access to its oil.

The British clearly had their own agenda. They hoped that the fighting between Jews and Arabs, and the prospects of continuing instability in the Middle East, would persuade the Americans either to abandon partition or postpone it. The hope was that a United Nations' vote could be manipulated that would put off partition and resolve the conflict by inviting the British to remain as the chief brokers of peace in the Middle East.

Ostensibly, United States' policy was committed to the rescue of Hitler's victims and the creation of a Jewish state. President Truman's understanding of the meaning of that commitment, however, remained rather vague. Commenting, later, on his thinking about the creation of a Jewish state in March 1948, he observed: ''I was not committed to any particular formula of statehood in Palestine or to any particular time schedule for its accomplishment. The American policy was designed to bring about, by peaceful means, the establishment of the promised Jewish homeland and easy access to it for the displaced Jews of Europe.''[1]

With his administration divided between those who favored vigorous support for the United Nations' partition plan and those who wished to disentangle America from its promise of support for it, the president sought compromise. So, apparently, did Secretary of State Marshall. Both men, anxious to avoid the complications of war, agreed, during the first week in March, that a different timetable might be necessary if they were to achieve a peaceful solution.

On March 8 Marshall showed Truman a State Department draft of a speech to be given by Warren Austin at the United Nations. It summarized consultations by the UN Palestine Commission, and suggested that if the Security Council were to find that partition could not be implemented, a temporary trusteeship should be recommended. Truman approved the thrust of the draft statement, though not its actual language.[2] He believed that if the Jews and Arabs, through consultations sponsored by the Security Council, could not resolve their differences, then a ''trusteeship under the UN was not a bad idea.[3] The president later explained: ''This was not a rejection of partition, but rather an effort to postpone its effective date until proper conditions for the establishment of self-government in the two parts might be established. My policy with regard to Palestine was not a commitment to any set of dates or circumstances; it was dedication to the twin deal of international obligations and the relieving of human misery.

In this sense, the State Department's trusteeship proposal was not contrary to my policy."[4]

The notion of trusteeship, however, was anathema to the Jews. Abba Eban later captured the intense feelings: "The vastest anticlimax of Jewish history was being prepared. Having been on the threshold of statehood the Jews were going to be urged back into the vacuum of tutelage."[5] Under the circumstances, Zionist leaders endeavored to make contact with the president. Eddie Jacobson, Truman's old Kansas City friend and business partner, was persuaded to see if he could arrange a meeting between the president and Chaim Weizmann. It was hoped that the ailing chief of the Zionist movement would be able to stiffen Truman's resolve to stand firm behind partition.

Jacobson saw Truman on March 13, and while he had promised not to speak a word about Palestine, he did! Tearfully, he pleaded with Truman to meet Weizmann. The president responded: "Eddie, you son of a bitch, I ought to have you thrown right out of here for breaking your promise; you knew damn good and well I couldn't stand seeing you cry."[6] Truman met with Weizmann on March 18. He expressed sympathy with the Jewish cause, and "a firm resolve to press forward with partition."[7]

By that time, however, General Marshall had set in motion new problems for the president. Without telling Truman, the secretary of state had ordered Austin to convey the State Department's proposals as soon as possible to the Security Council. Whether Marshall intended malice, or whether it was a matter of poor communication, is still in the realm of conjecture. He and Lovett had assumed that the president's approval of the draft statement on March 8 was sufficient. For that reason, according to a later investigation by Clark Clifford, they had not given instructions that the speech or its timing be cleared with the White House.[8]

The day after Truman's conference with Weizmann, Austin announced before the Security Council that the United States favored "a temporary trusteeship for

Palestine'' so as to afford Arabs and Jews ''further opportunity to reach an agreement regarding the future government of that country.''[9] Truman was stunned and angered. On his calendar for March 19, 1948, he wrote:

> The State Department pulled the rug from under me today. I didn't expect that would happen. In Key West or en route there from St. Croix, I approved the speech and statement of policy by Senator Austin to UN meeting. This morning I find that the State Department has reversed my Palestine policy. The first I know about it is what I see in the papers! Isn't that hell? I am now in the position of a liar and a doublecrosser. I've never felt so low in my life. There are people on the third and fourth levels of the State Department who have always wanted to cut my throat. They've succeeded in doing it. Marshall's in California and Lovett's in Florida.[10]

If the timing and tone of Austin's speech surprised the president, they were no less shocking to the country. Emanuel Celler denounced the proposal as a ''shameful decision.'' Leon Henderson, chairman of the Americans for Democratic Action, called the ''abandonment'' of partition a betrayal of ''peoples everywhere.'' Robert Taft, who was already running hard for the Republican presidential nomination, condemned the reversal of policy. Eleanor Roosevelt, enraged by what she considered an undermining of the United Nations, submitted her resignation from the American delegation. It was, to quote Margaret Truman, ''one of the worst messes of my father's career.''[11]

Both Truman and Marshall tried, publicly, to patch over the widening divide between the State Department and the White House. On March 20, the secretary of state issued a statement explaining that the suggestion of a ''temporary trusteeship'' was not meant to prejudice the ultimate solution, but, rather, ''to open up the way to an agreed settlement.''[12] Five days later, the president was a bit more specific: ''Trusteeship is not proposed as a substitute for the partition plan but as an effort to fill the vacuum soon to be created by the termination of the mandate on May 15.''[13]

[108]

While the public statements were being formulated and pronounced, the president was seeking to discover what had happened. Clark Clifford was assigned to investigate. First, he called Lovett in Florida, who said that the whole thing was a complete surprise. He then contacted the State Department's section for Near Eastern Affairs. It was explained that just before Marshall had left for San Francisco, he had authorized a memo which stated that if partition failed in the Security Council, the United States would then recommend trusteeship.[14] A few days later, according to Dean Rusk, who subsequently recalled the events for Marshall, "informal consultations among the non-permanent members of the Security Council indicated clearly that partition could never get votes in the Security Council."[15]

At that point, those at the State Department, who had wanted all along to sabotage Truman's Palestine policy, had their opportunity and took advantage of it. Clark Clifford later recalled that "the incident in March profoundly affected Mr. Truman. He realized that State was going to try to have its policy despite the White House."[16] In a letter dated March 21, Truman revealed his anger to his sister. He confided that the "striped-pants conspirators" on the "third and fourth levels" of the State Department "have completely balled up the Palestine situation. It was not necessary either. But it may work out anyway in spite of them."[17]

Truman's indignation, while well founded, may have been overly self-righteous. After all, he had agreed to the suggestion of a "temporary trusteeship," and was convinced that a war between Arabs and Jews would endanger American interests and, possibly, the security of the world. He agreed with the Joint Chiefs of Staff that it would be extremely difficult to muster the number of troops required to maintain order in Palestine. Above all, he did not wish to provide a wedge through which the Russians might squeeze their way into the Middle East. A trusteeship would postpone the problem and allow for consultation—and, he hoped, for a peaceful settlement.

The "striped-pants" fellows at the State Department also

wanted trusteeship, but for different reasons. Forrestal, Henderson, Merriam, Rusk, and Leahy were determined to dump partition. Trusteeship was a step in that direction calculated to give them time either to place Palestine back in the secure hands of the British or under the wing of the United Nations for a prolonged period of time.[18] Truman's lack of a timetable and program left him vulnerable to those who opposed him.

While the Truman administration floundered between trusteeship and partition, and was condemned for its indecisiveness, determination of the Jews of Palestine to create a state intensified. After Austin's March 19 declaration of American policy, a tough and blunt Ben Gurion defiantly told his people: "The American announcement does more harm to the United Nations, its standing and authority—than it does to us. The change in the American position indicates that the United States has surrendered to Arab terror. But this does not change the situation here or impede the establishment of a Jewish State."[19] As head of the Jewish Agency, Ben Gurion commanded the Haganah to mobilize all available forces, and ordered his officers to secure weapons.

By then it was clear to Ben Gurion, and most Jewish leaders, that war between Jews and Arabs was inevitable upon the evacuation of the British. Seven thousand Arab Liberation Army troops, led by Fawzi al-Qawukji, had entered the country and were poised to attack in the north. Five thousand troops under the command of Abdal-Qadral Husseini, a nephew of the Jerusalem Mufti, had already sealed off the Jews of Jerusalem from the rest of the country. In the south, Moslem Brotherhood volunteers from Egypt harrassed Jewish settlements, and the Egyptian armies were prepared to carry out Farouk's promise of a massive assault as soon as the British were gone.[20]

As Ben Gurion surveyed the situation, there was no alternative between self-defense and surrender. "All we must consider," he told the Zionist General Council, "is how to fight in order to win, and thus ensure our people's freedom, a national future, and international status."[21] A realist, Ben

Gurion understood that unless Jews, on May 15, were in possession of the partitional area granted to them by the United Nations, their national aspirations would be smothered. He reasoned that no power, save Arab military might, would attempt to dismember a Jewish state if it stood strong with borders and administration intact as the British withdrew. Seasoned on a Zionist philosophy of auto-emancipation, Ben Gurion and his associates were determined to present the world with a fait accompli. No other option seemed available or tolerable.

In Washington, Zionists pressed the Truman Administration to lift the State Department's ban on shipping arms to the Middle East. Fearing a protracted battle, they argued that weapons were necessary to assure Jewish security. White House supporters sought to persuade the president and State Department officials.

On March 24 the president met with his advisors on the Palestine issue. At the gathering in the Cabinet Room were Marshall, Henderson, Rusk, and Chip Bohlen, from the State Department; Howard McGrath, Oscar Ewing, Matt Connelly, Charles Ross, David Niles, and Clark Clifford, from the White House Staff. The White House side of the argument made a strong case for lifting the arms embargo to the Middle East. The State Department representatives demurred. Marshall protested that they were now working on plans for a truce and hoped that it would soon be discernible, and indicated that matters would be clear by April 7. Clifford's notes from the meeting indicate that there was a "general understanding" that if a truce was impossible, "steps would be taken to release the embargo."[22]

The "truce" State Department people were pursuing included a plan for the British to continue and extend their stay in Palestine as the designated trustee of the United Nations. It was reasoned that such a trusteeship would enable them to restore order, and the status quo ante.[23] Should the British refuse doing the job themselves, then State Department officials proposed a combined British, American, and French force to supervise the trusteeship.

On March 29 Robert Lovett requested the Joint Chiefs of

Staff to prepare an estimation of how many troops would be required, and spoke with Forrestal about the plan.[24] Forrestal responded favorably and called Truman. The president listened to Forrestal's argument and agreed that "if we had to respond, that we would participate in the implementation of the trusteeship mandate by the associated allied nations (U.K., U.S., France) up to the limit of our ability."[25]

The next day Warren Austin submitted resolutions to the Security Council calling for a truce between Arabs and Jews, and a special session of the General Assembly. In presenting the request for a General Assembly session, Austin explained:

> It will be noted that this resolution does not mention trusteeship. The United States adheres to the view I stated in the Security Council on March 19, and which was reaffirmed by the Secretary of State on March 20 and again by the President of the United States on March 25, that a temporary trusteeship should be established to maintain the peace. This trusteeship would be without prejudice to the character of the final political settlement in Palestine. We believe that a trusteeship is essential to establish order, without which a peaceful solution of this problem cannot be found or put into effect.[26]

The thrust of the United States' proposal was quite clear. If a truce could be concluded and a temporary trusteeship arranged, the bedevilling problem of partition could be postponed. Denunciations of the proposal were immediate. Gromyko accused the United States of plotting to destroy partition.[27] In the Senate, Senator Wayne Morse thundered that Austin's new tactic was meant to undermine the United Nations.[28] Secretary General Trygve Lie, so frustrated by the American position, and what he believed were attempts to cripple the United Nations, decided to resign. It was only when both Austin and Gromyko cautioned against such a dramatic step that he changed his mind.[29]

Austin's resolutions were passed by the Security Council and a special session of the General Assembly was set for April 16. By that time, however, events were to outstrip the slow-grinding gears of both the American government and the United Nations.

On April 4, a few days after the Security Council had voted to hold a special session of the General Assembly, 50,000 American veterans marched down Fifth Avenue in New York City in a record protest against the Truman administration's policy. While the president and his advisors could not remain impervious to the swelling antagonism, there is little evidence to indicate that Truman guided his handling of the Palestine issue on the basis of political pressures. Senator Carl Hatch, after a meeting with Truman, informed reporters on March 23 that the president "intends to do what he thinks is right without regard to the political consequences."[30] The popular thing for Truman to have done, especially facing an election in the fall, would have been to support partition. Politically, it would have yielded a warm response from the widest spectrum of voters.[31] Despite the unpopularity of his position, the president was persuaded to pursue another course during late March and April.

Truman's central concerns were strategic, not political. Of overriding importance was stalemating what he believed was a Soviet advance into the Middle East. It was feared that if the United States did not support a temporary trusteeship under United Nations' authority, the Russians would intervene either by a takeover of Palestine orchestrated through especially trained immigrants, or by capitalizing on the inevitable conflagration between Arabs and Jews. Postponing partition was a small price to pay, if it would result in a peaceful solution and spoil Russian designs on the area. A truce and temporary trusteeship enforced by a United Nations' constabulary composed of American, British, and French participants would not, so the president reasoned, foreclose partition; it would simply slow down the process. Truman was not opposed to a Jewish state. He was opposed to the creation of such a state if it meant risking Russian infiltration or intervention on behalf of Jews or Arabs, and a subsequent loss of the region for U.S. strategic and economic interests. In this sense, the president, Joint Chiefs of Staff, and State Department were of one mind.

The State Department reasoned that the United States should take an active role in achieving a truce, and in pressing for a United Nations' trusteeship guaranteed by American, British, and French forces. If American action was not decisive, it was feared that the Soviets would take advantage of the troublesome situation in order to gain control of Palestine, or a foothold for themselves in the area. Furthermore, it was argued that another "Jewish slaughter" would provoke the necessity for an American response, one far in excess of the troops required if the United States was to participate in sustaining a trusteeship. Not incidentally, Dean Rusk, who presented the State Department's views at a special April 4 meeting on Palestine, attended by Secretary Forrestal and the Joint Chiefs of Staff, pointed out that from a strategic point of view, a trusteeship would provide an advantageous opportunity for the United States to construct bomber fields in the Middle East.[32]

Rusk's final argument on behalf of trusteeship was clearly meant to appeal to the Joint Chiefs of Staff. State Department officials were anxious to replace partition with trusteeship, and by suggesting that such an arrangement would provide an excuse for the construction of bomber fields, they obviously hoped to persuade the Joint Chiefs of Staff. Actually, the latter needed no convincing; they were already in agreement with the State Department in preferring a truce or trusteeship to the outbreak of hostilities. Assuming that a "completely effective truce was impossible in Palestine," they suggested that a force of 104,000 would be required to maintain order. Should the situation explode, the Joint Chiefs of Staff warned that as many as 300,000 troops might be needed. As a preventive measure, American participation in a United Nations' force was considered desirable.[33]

During the first weeks of April, Warren Austin held informal discussions with members of the Security Council in order to test the acceptability of the Truman administration's trusteeship proposal.[34] His hope was to convince the

Security Council not only to accept the American plan, but to present it as its own to the General Assembly. Members of the Security Council easily found the soft spots in the proposal. They contended that it avoided the crucial questions of implementation. Who, they inquired, would be responsible for maintaining the trusteeship?[35] The question was deliberately rhetorical. Everyone at the United Nations knew that while Austin was making his proposals at Lake Success, American officials were seeking cooperation in London and Paris for the joint imposition of trusteeship.[36] On April 20, in a speech supporting an immediate truce and trusteeship, Austin revealed what everyone already knew: that the United States had been discussing, "with certain governments, the question of joint responsibility for the security of a trusteeship. The discussions," Austin continued, "have thus far produced no tangible results." He then announced:

The United States is willing to undertake its share of . . . trusteeship, along with other members who may be selected by the General Assembly and who are willing to carry out such a task in accordance with the will of the Assembly and with the provisions of the Charter.

While the United States is prepared to carry its fair share of the United Nations' burden involved in such a temporary trusteeship, it is not prepared to act alone in this matter. Our participation will be conditioned upon a readiness of other governments to provide similar assistance.[37]

Two days later, at his news conference, the president was asked if United States' troops were to be sent to Palestine. He responded: "We offered to furnish our share of a UN police force. That is the only way we will send troops anywhere under the UN. As a part of a UN police force for the enforcement of the orders of the UN, we will furnish our share, just as Mr. Austin said we would."[38]

The measure of agreement between Austin and Truman on April 22 indicates just how fully the president shared the commitment to a truce and a temporary trusteeship over

[115]

what he perceived were the hazards of partition. In the third week of April the State Department, Joint Chiefs of Staff, and White House were, albeit for different reasons, still in agreement and in pursuit of the same Palestine policy. What shattered the unified approach during the next critical weeks were the surprising battle reports from the hills of the Holy Land. At the beginning of April a shipment of Czechoslovakian arms, undoubtedly sent with Soviet permission, gave Jews the weapons with which to mount their offensive. Two weeks later, outmanned three to one, Haganah forces dealt a major blow to the Arabs by taking the Galilee capital city of Tiberias. On April 18, at Mishmar Ha'emek, Jews with just over 300 men destroyed three Arab brigades, totalling 3,200 men, led by al-Qawukji. That blow was followed three days later by the capture of the Mediterranean port city of Haifa. By early May, as the last British soldiers were making preparations to leave, a tattered Jewish army composed of 16,400 combat troops and 13,500 armed settlers had gone on the offensive. Jews were not only successfully holding the borders of the patchwork partition plan, but were administering local needs effectively as well. The Zionist policy of assertion was working. All attempts to stall or thwart Jewish independence from that point on were to fail.

On April 26 Moshe Sharett (then Shertok) of the Jewish Agency was shown a new State Department proposal for a truce between Arabs and Jews. It called for a suspension of efforts to carry out partition pending decisions to be made at the September sessions of the General Assembly. Meanwhile, Arabs and Jews would agree to administer the areas then under their control, and Jewish immigration would be limited to four thousand per month.[39] Sharett rejected the draft and, three days later, in a letter to Marshall, wrote: ''The proposed truce entails the deferment of statehood and renders its attainment in the future uncertain, thereby gravely prejudicing our rights and position.''[40]

The administration's next gambit was no more successful. On May 3 Dean Rusk contacted Sharett with a proposal that Arab and Jewish leaders, together with representatives from the United States, Belgium, and France, be flown in the president's "Sacred Cow" to Jerusalem, in order to arrange a truce. The conditions set out included an immediate ceasefire, and an extension of the mandate for ten days.[41] Again Sharett rejected the American suggestion. In a telegram to Rusk he explained that Jewish authorities in Palestine "are ready forthwith to agree to a 'ceasefire' order provided the Arabs do likewise." Sharett called attention to the fact that the American suggestion seemed to bypass "action already taken by the Security Council on the appointment of a Truce Commission," and that, in any case, the Jews could not possibly accept "the suggestion that the British mandate should be prolonged, whether de jure or de facto, beyond the appointed date."[42] On May 7 Sharett reiterated his position in a letter to Secretary of State Marshall: "As things stand, I see no prospect of agreement which would preclude the setting up of a Provisional Government for the Jewish State or entail the prolongation of British rule."[43] Despite last minute State Department attempts to block their efforts, Jews were not to be stalled or to waver from proclaiming a Jewish state the moment the mandate ended.

Marshall, however, was not at all satisfied with Sharett's response. At a meeting in Washington the next day, as Sharett was scheduled to depart for Palestine, General Marshall and Robert Lovett tried their powers of persuasion on the Jewish Agency's man. They were no more successful than Rusk had been. Sharett at one point sharpened the exchange by asking Marshall whether the United States wanted or did not want a Jewish state. Neither Marshall nor Lovett had an answer for that. Lovett warned that if the Arabs invaded Palestine after the proclamation of a state, the Jews should not count on American help. According to Sharett, "both spoke with great earnestness about the truce. They showed complete sincerity when they depicted the situation as disastrous and capable of developing into a danger to world peace."

While the American leaders did not threaten, it was evident that they were deeply concerned about the impact of a Jewish state and a war between Arabs and Jews. That Marshall was running out of arguments which might convince Jews to postpone their intention to create a state is seen in the lame advice he offered Sharett at the conclusion of their meeting. "It is not for me to advise you what to do, but I want to tell you as a military man, don't rely on your military advisors. . . . However, if it turns out that you're right and you will establish the Jewish State, I'll be happy. But you are undertaking a very grave responsibility."[44] The advice was gratuitous. In international terms, the colossus power was being dragged, kicking and complaining, to the birth of a new, though already highly independent, national entity.

While the State Department and United States' delegation at Lake Success were bending every effort to line up opposition against partition and the creation of a Jewish state, the White House was rethinking its position. A handwritten Clark Clifford memorandum, dated May 4, lists five reasons for extending immediate U.S. recognition:

1. Recognition is consistent with U.S. policy from beginning;
2. A separate Jewish State is inevitable, it will be set up shortly;
3. As far as Russia is concerned we would do better to indicate recognition;
4. We must recognize inevitably. Why not now?
5. State Department resolution doesn't stop partition.[45]

Clifford's notes are an index to the arguments that flowed across President Truman's desk during the first two weeks of May. Jewish victories in Palestine had completely altered the strategic situation. It could no longer be contended that 100,000 to 300,000 troops would be required to keep peace, or to save the Jews from another slaughter. Indeed, quite the opposite was argued. Without help, save a small shipment of Czechoslovakian arms, Jews had taken control of the area alloted by the partition plan. Arab strength had been overestimated. Truman's advisors were now declaring that the Jews were "the strongest military force in the Middle

East," and that a Jewish state would emerge as "the only true bastion against the Bolshevists." Furthermore, it was pointed out that British companies were already making large financial investments in Jewish Palestine, apparently with approval from the British Foreign Office, and by contrast the Arab countries were in a state bordering on chaos.[46] The new realities suddenly cast doubt on all the assumptions that had justified a policy of putting off partition.

By the beginning of May the president's advisors were mounting a strong case for an immediate recognition of the Jewish state. Delay would allow the Soviets to preempt the United States and deal an embarrassing diplomatic blow. It would prolong Arab opposition and strengthen the bonds of Arab leaders who might rely upon American ambivalence as a sign that the United States would eventually come to their rescue with sanctions, embargoes, or even troops. Critical of the State Department proposals, which were labeled "grandiose as well as futile," White House counselors suggested that prompt recognition could accomplish much in retrieving the lost prestige of the American government and the United Nations.

The advice dispensed to Truman did not overlook the domestic political fallout of recognition, yet by no means was it the paramount factor. Later, as Clark Clifford recalled the arguments for recognition, he noted that "while we were interested in the Jewish vote, it wasn't a major issue. Our major thrust was to labor, farmers and blacks."[47] What White House staffers realized was that once May 15 arrived, pressures for recognition would mount from Republicans and Democrats alike. An early announcement would effectively "end the issue."[48]

It seems clear that by the first week in May, President Truman was convinced that the United States should grant recognition just as soon as the Jewish state was declared. The major question was how to convince his secretary of state. Truman had no desire to assume a position that would put him at odds with the man whose judgment he respected and trusted so completely. In the hope of winning Marshall's concurrence, the president convened a special meeting on May 12 to discuss Palestine. In preparation, he ordered his counsel, Clark Clifford, to organize a presentation favoring immediate recognition. "Prepare the case," Truman told Clifford, "as if you were arguing before the Supreme Court!"[49]

On the morning of May 12, General Marshall, Robert Lovett, Robert McClintock, David Niles, and Clark Clifford joined Truman in the Oval Office. The president opened the meeting by stating that he wanted a "thorough airing" of the Palestine issue. He then turned to Marshall and asked the secretary of state to define his position. Marshall indicated that he and his department were "unalterably opposed" to extending recognition. He explained that the borders were still unsettled, that the battle was still being fought, and that the United States ought to leave the problem to the United Nations rather than interfere.[50]

Clifford, who had diligently prepared a counter-argument, made the case for immediate recognition. He pointed out that the Jewish state was an actual fact and that all the State Department maneuvers had not prevented it from coming into existence. The president was on record as favoring a Jewish State, and would be severely weakened if he failed to recognize it.

Clifford's presentation was followed by a heated and angry exchange of views. Seeing that he could not counter Clifford's arguments, Marshall focused his frustration upon motivations and personalities. Turning to Truman, he declared: "This is not a matter to be determined on the basis of politics. Unless political questions were involved," he continued, with face flushed, "Mr. Clifford would not even be at this conference." Clifford was shocked by Marshall's vehemence, and recalls, with some note of bitterness, that "the General did not speak to me for six months after that meeting." Realizing that he dare not push the matter any further, Truman closed the discussion by indicating that he would certainly not wish to take a position which his secretary of state opposed so strongly.[51]

After Marshall, Lovett, and McClintock had left the Oval Office, Truman remarked to Clifford, "Quite a meeting, huh Clark?" Clifford, who felt as though he had lost his case, answered, "I think they left thinking they have carried the day." To which Truman responded, "Give him a little time." Apparently, the president believed that despite Marshall's "bludgeon," the secretary of state would eventually come around. In any case, until he did, Truman was not about to take action which might severely damage their relationship.[52]

The next day, when the President was asked by a newsman if the United States would recognize the new Jewish state when it was proclaimed, he curtly replied: "I will cross that bridge when I get to it."[53] With one day to go until the British mandate expired, there was still no unanimity on United States–Palestine policy.

Meanwhile, doubts about the wisdom of withholding recognition were beginning to bother the "striped-pants conspirators" at the State Department. Fear of being upstaged by Russian recognition of a Jewish state began to worry several ranking officials. The hope of preventing or postponing a declaration of a Jewish state through the United Nations was fast fading. Haganah victories made it certain that Jews would declare their state the moment after the British mandate ended. The urgent question was what to do with a fait accompli.

Just after Lovett returned from the May 12, Oval Office meeting, officials on the Near East desk shared their concerns with him. Already disturbed by what he perceived was a major disagreement developing between Marshall and Truman, he decided to call a meeting of State Department people in order to discuss the entire question. He also put through a call to Clark Clifford at the White House. After being informed that there was some rethinking going on at the State Department, Clifford told Lovett that Truman was convinced about recognition, but did not want to break with George Marshall. He urged Lovett "to persuade Marshall not to buck the President." At the end of their conversation they decided to meet for lunch in two days.[54]

While eating together at the 1925 F Street Club, on May 14, Lovett informed Clifford that he and Marshall had concluded that the United States should recognize the Jewish state.[55] Having reached agreement on recognition, the only obstacle remaining was timing. Clifford favored an announcement immediately following upon the declaration in Palestine. Lovett hesitated. He would need time to inform the French and British, and secure a formal request from the Jews. At Clifford's suggestion, they split up the tasks, hoping to meet the deadline of 5:00 P.M.

At three in the afternoon, Clifford met with President Truman to tell him that Lovett and Marshall had changed their position. The president then agreed with Clifford that the United States should be the first to recognize the Jewish state, and authorized him to direct Lovett to inform the British and French, but not to wait for their replies.

Clifford then telephoned Eliahu Epstein at the Jewish Agency, in Washington, and asked him to dispatch a formal request for recognition as quickly as possible. Forty-five minutes later copies arrived at the White House and State Department.[56] At 6:11 P.M., eleven minutes after the British mandate expired, Charlie Ross, Truman's press secretary, released a terse, two-sentence statement: "This Government has been informed that a Jewish State has been proclaimed in Palestine and recognition has been requested by the provisional government thereof. The United States recognizes the provisional government as the de facto authority of the new State of Israel."[57]

What emerges out of this Palestine–United States' odyssey is that, in the final analysis, United States recognition was not determined in Washington, but in the ancient hills and plains of Judea. It is true that the Truman administration favored a Jewish home in Palestine as a solution to the desperate plight of Europe's homeless survivors. Yet, the president had no plan or schedule for the creation of a Jewish state. He had reluctantly agreed to partition because it was a United Nations' proposal. By the middle of March, fearing that American troops might be required to save Jews from a slaughter should partition be effected, and that hostilities might invite Russian intervention, Truman endorsed the State Department's plan for a temporary trusteeship. From March 20 until the second week in May, no effort was spared in seeking a truce and postponing partition. United States' policy, as articulated by Dean Rusk, was "directed towards a truce, armed and political in the sense of excluding the proclamation of States."[58]

While one American initiative after another faltered or failed at the United Nations, Jews in Palestine were forging a new political and national reality. The invading Arab forces were thrown back and into disarray. As Arab armies collapsed, the Haganah offensive took over crucial British fortresses and strategically important villages and cities. By the second week in May, British military commanders in Palestine and Egypt were reporting that Jews were in complete control of their partitioned area.[59] Even some Arab leaders were in agreement. A United Press dispatch quoted a member of the Syrian Parliament as saying, "The battle is over. The Jewish State has arisen."[60] As May 15 approached, the White House and State Department were faced with a whole new set of circumstances. Jewish victory and power had to be reckoned with, and so did the impending declaration of the first Jewish state in two thousand years.

To withhold recognition would have meant risking diplomatic disadvantage, if not disgrace. Not only would it have let the Russians champion another triumph of the people over imperialism, but it would have encouraged enraged Arabs to hold out and, possibly, even to widen the hostilities. The Truman administration reasoned that if it recognized the Jewish state, the Arabs would recognize their own, and peace might be achieved.[61] Standing aloof would have been costly in international terms, and domestically as well. In refusing recognition of a declared Jewish state, one which fulfilled the declared platform of both the Democratic and Republican parties and countless resolutions of Congress, the Truman adminstration would have become a target of political ridicule and reproach. While, as we have seen, politics played a minor role in the definition of Truman's Palestine policy, the consequences of non-recognition would have severely crippled any future political plans for the president. Had State Department officials and Lovett not had second thoughts, however, Truman might very well have accepted those consequences. It is unlikely that he would have taken a step so strongly opposed by a secretary of state he revered.

The most critical factor in the recognition of Israel was the success of the Jews themselves. Had they failed to secure their borders, or caved in to the pressures put on them to postpone declaring their state, then American officials might have succeeded in blocking the creation of the State of Israel. Later, when President Truman recalled his reasons for recognizing Israel, he wrote the following: ''Partition was not taking place in exactly the peaceful manner I had hoped, to be sure, but the fact was that Jews were controlling the area in which their people lived and that they were ready to administer and to defend it.''[62]

Presented, as it was, with a fait accompli, the Truman administration moved to accept the inevitable, and fit it into the shaky status quo it had been seeking to build throughout the Middle East.

Notes

1. Harry S. Truman, *Memoirs—Years of Trial and Hope, II* (Garden City, N.Y., 1956), p. 157. See, also, Kenneth M. Birkhead, Oral History Interview, July 7, 1966, pp. 17–18, Truman Library.
2. A handwritten and undated memorandum by Clark Clifford reveals the set of circumstances around the March 19, 1948, speech by Warren Austin. Memorandum by Clark Clifford, undated, Clifford Papers, Box 14, Truman Library.
3. Harry Truman, *Memoirs*, p. 163.
4. Ibid.
5. As quoted in Robert St. John, *Eban* (New York, 1972), p. 189.
6. Merle Miller, *Plain Speaking* (New York, 1973), p. 207.
7. Chaim Weizmann, *Trial and Error* (New York, 1949), p. 472.
8. Memorandum by Clark Clifford, undated, Clifford Papers, Box 14, Truman Library.
9. *Department of State Bulletin (SBD)* (Washington, D.C., 1940–1953), March 28, 1948.
10. Margaret Truman, *Harry S. Truman* (New York, 1974), pp. 424–25.
11. Ibid., p. 425.
12. *New York Times*, March 20, 1948.
13. *Public Papers of the Presidents of the United States (PPP)* (Washington, D.C., 1948), March 28, 1948, no. 55. A draft of the president's statement in Clifford's handwriting contains the following: "I have always believed in the establishment of a Jewish National Home. I strongly favored the plan of the partition and hoped that it might be carried out at this time." The sentiment did not survive in the final draft of the president's statement. Palestine Statement, March 25, 1948, Clark Clifford Papers, Box 14, Truman Library.
14. The reconstruction of these events is based upon Daniels, pp. 318–19, and research notes used in connection with *The Man of Independence*, part 1. Notes on interviews; interview with Clark Clifford, Jonathan Daniels Papers, Truman Library.
15. Rusk to Marshall, March 22, 1948, Clark Clifford Papers, Box 14, Truman Library.
16. Interview with Clark Clifford, August 7, 1974.
17. Margaret Truman, *Harry S. Truman*, pp. 425–26.
18. Max Lowenthal, who advised Clifford on Palestine, sent him a memorandum on March 26, 1948, which referred to State Department activities in London. Basing himself on a news item which appeared in the *New York Times* on March 26, Lowenthal wrote: "You remember that we were told one of the big grounds for distrust is the charge, sound or incorrect, that what goes on in Washington or at Lake Success in this matter is quite unimportant and that the real job is being done in London—the charge that American representatives are talking with the British in London to get them to continue in Palestine with their troops, as the trustee. The statement is made that if such an intrigue succeeds, the situation will in fact be where it was for some years past, with the British in control, but this time, for the first time, at the express request of the U.S. Government, and

with its moral support. . . . The claim is made the alleged intrigue will merely pay lip service to partition and to the UN decision, but will in fact restore the status quo ante." Lowenthal to Clifford, March 26, 1948, Clifford Papers, Box 13, Truman Library.

19. David Ben Gurion, *Israel: A Personal History* (New York, 1971), p. 72.
20. George E. Kirk, *The Middle East, 1945-1950* (London, 1954), pp. 251-70; Howard M. Sachar, *Europe Leaves the Middle East, 1936-1954* (New York, 1972), pp. 505-29; Jacob C. Hurewitz, *The Struggle for Palestine* (New York, 1950), chap. 23.
21. Ben Gurion, *Israel*, p. 67.
22. Memorandum of Conference on Palestine, March 24, 1948, Clifford Papers, Box 14, Truman Library.
23. Lowenthal to Clifford, March 26, 1948, Clifford Papers, Box 13, Truman Library.
24. *Forrestal Diaries*, ed. Walter Millis (New York, 1951), March 29, 1948.
25. Ibid.
26. *SBD*, April 18, 1948; UN Security Council, *Official Record*, 3rd Year, 275th meeting, Docs. S/705 and S/705, pp. 247-48.
27. Ibid.
28. U.S. *Congressional Record*, 80th Congress, 2nd Session, March 31, 1948, XCIV, Part 3, p. 3806.
29. Trygve Lie, *In the Cause of Peace* (New York, 1954), pp. 170-71.
30. *New York Times*, March 24, 1948. In Clifford's memorandum of March 8, he wrote to the president: "I know only too well that you would not hesitate to follow a course of action that makes certain the defeat of the Democratic Party if you thought such action were best for America." Memorandum to the President, March 8, 1948, Clifford Papers, Box 14, Truman Library.
31. An analysis of editorial opinion for the week ending March 27 revealed that 62 per cent of comment opposed the new U.S. position, 20 per cent supported it, and 18 per cent were mixed or neutral. U.S. Christian Palestine Committee, *American Public on the United States and the UN*, New York, 1948.
32. *Forrestal Diaries*, April 4, 1948.
33. Ibid.
34. Ibid.; see, also, *New York Times*, April 14, 1948. See Jessup's remarks, United Nations General Assembly, *Official Records*, 2nd sess. 1st Committee, 140th meeting, May 13, 1948, p. 243.
35. *New York Times*, April 16, 17, 1948.
36. *New York Times*, April 14, 1948; see, also, *supra*, n. 54.
37. *SBD*, May 2, 1948.
38. *PPP* (1948), April 22, 1948, no. 84.
39. Joseph B. Schechtman, *The United States and the Jewish State Movement* (New York, 1966), p. 288.
40. Shertok to Marshall, April 29, 1948, Clifford Papers, Box 13, Truman Library.
41. Schechtman, *The United States*, p. 161.
42. Shertok to Rusk, May 4, 1948, Clifford Papers, Box 13, Truman Library.

43. Shertok to Marshall, May 7, 1948, Clifford Papers, Box 13, Truman Library.
44. Sharett, pp. 226–28.
45. Palestine Memorandum, May 4, 1948, Clifford Papers, Box 13, Truman Library.
46. Lowenthal to Clifford, "Supplemental Memo," May 9, 1948, Clifford Papers, Box 13, Truman Library.
47. Interview with Clark Clifford, August 7, 1974.
48. An anonymous memorandum, perhaps by David Niles, in the Clifford Papers, dated May 9, 1948, details the arguments for recognition. "Statement," May 9, 1948, no. 20, Clifford Papers, Box 13, Truman Library.
49. It should be noted that the account of events described here is contrary to that found in Daniels, *The Man of Independence*, pp. 318–19, also in Daniel's notes used in connection with writing *The Man of Independence*, Part 1, interview notes pp. 46–47, Daniels papers, Truman Library. In a discussion with Clifford the author called attention to the discrepancies. Clifford maintained that the May 12 meeting had taken place in the Oval Office ("I can remember where we were all sitting") and that Marshall, not Lovett (as Daniels maintains) did all the talking for the State Department. In Clifford's words, "Marshall took the lead, Lovett came along as second man and didn't say very much." Clifford recalls that "Marshall's presentation was not very well prepared—he had a lot on his mind." Interview with Clark Clifford, August 7, 1974.
50. Ibid.
51. Ibid.
52. Ibid.
53. *PPP* (1948), May 13, 1948, no. 97.
54. Interview with Clark Clifford, August 7, 1974.
55. Ibid. Forrestal indicates that on May 14, when Lovett called him to tell him that the U.S. had recognized Israel, he said that the decision had been made by the White House and communicated to Marshall and himself. It is likely that Lovett may have misrepresented the details knowing full well Forrestal's hostility toward partition and the creation of a Jewish State; see *Forrestal Diaries*, p. 440.
56. Epstein to Sharett, 5/14/48, Weizmann Archives, Rehobot, Israel; see, also, Memorandum by Clifford, undated, Clifford Papers, Box 13, Truman Library. The memorandum contains notes in Clifford's handwriting of a talk with Epstein.
57. *PPP* (1948), May 14, 1948, no. 100.
58. Memorandum of Telephone Conversation with Dean Rusk, May 8, 1948, Box 13, Clifford Papers, Truman Library.
59. *New York Times*, May 8, 1948.
60. Ibid.
61. Truman to Neely (Personal and Confidential), May 18, 1948, *PPP*, 1821, Box 534, Truman Library.
62. Harry Truman, *Memoirs*, p. 164 (emphasis added).

HUMAN RIGHTS AND THE NEW ANTI-JEWISHNESS
Irwin Cotler

The Jewish condition, as we enter the 1980s, is not only that of *am levadad yishkon*, a people that dwells alone, but of a people that today alone stands indicted at the bar of mankind; a people whom it is sought once again to portray as pariah; a people whose group defamation is increasingly receiving the sanction of public international law, in which arena de-legitimization has become the idiom of defamation. This new anti-Jewishness says more about the state of the world the Jews inhabit than it does about the state of Jews in the world today. While grounded in classical anti-semitism, it is distinguishable from it; while formally originating in the "Zionism is racism" resolution, it goes beyond it. The anti-Jewishness can best be defined as the denial of, or discrimination against, national particularity whenever that national particularity happens to be Jewish—be it the State of Israel as the political sovereign expression of the Jewish people, or be it Jewish collectivity in the Diaspora wherever Jews are found.

Israel is the enemy of labor, health, culture, women, peace, love, human rights—indeed, the enemy of mankind. Why? Because Zionism is racism. This indictment of Israel and Zionism as racism is neither fortuitous nor accidental; its authors know that the worst label one can affix in the world today is that of a racist. The very label supplies the indictment; no further proof is required. If further proof is necessary, associate Israel with the consummate evil of our time—apartheid—and speak of the Tel Aviv–Pretoria axis, the South African connection. Israel is therefore to be seen not only as the enemy of all that is good, but as the personi-fication of all that is evil. This de-legitimization unfolds in a general atmosphere of moral corruption: the politics of indifference, the culture of appeasement, the indulgence of terrorism—physical, intellectual, moral, and economic—and the banality of evil. In this general assault on human rights, the Jewish condition stands uniquely exposed.

In the terror of the Gulag in the Soviet Union, it is Soviet Jews who emerge as the most threatened minority in Russia today, where, to quote André Sakharov, "antisemitism has been raised to a level of a state religion in a godless society." In the disappeared of Latin America, a disproportionate number of those who disappear happen to be Jewish, and a differentially severe punishment is being meted out to those prisoners who are Jewish. In the universality of torture and terror in the world today, only the Jew in Syria, in Iran, in Latin America, in the Soviet Union, and elsewhere emerges as the universal victim across national boundaries. In the famine of Black Africa, it is Black Jews, Falashas, who stand uniquely exposed. In the virus of racism and terrorism in western Europe, Jews—by the communiqués of the attackers themselves—are the most intended victims. In the proliferation of arms in the world today, the largest arms sale in the history of American foreign policy, $8.5 billion of the most sophisticated arms in the world today, is made to Saudi Arabia, a state that in the same year called publicly for a *jihad*, a holy war, against Israel.

The new anti-Jewishness must be approached with caution. It is clear that not all Jews are necessarily Zionists, nor are all expressions of criticism against Israel, or even anti-Zionism, antisemitic. If we tar the brush too indiscriminately and accuse everybody of being antisemitic, then in a sense nobody will be antisemitic. But when antisemitism is proclaimed in denial of Israeli statehood, when "Zionism is racism" is asserted in denial of Jewish peoplehood, when Farouk Kaddumi can say from the Security Council of the United Nations that "this ghetto Israel must be destroyed," then that anti-Zionism must be labeled for what it is: the new anti-Jewishness, a contemporary group-libel of the Jews in our time.

Less overt, but no less sinister, is a callous indifference to

Jewish rights or Jewish sensibilities which finds expression today in the singular, obsessive, unidimensional indictment of anything and everything that Israel and the Jewish people do, with a corresponding waiver of immunity to anything and everything that is done against Israel. This is not to say that Israel is somehow to be above the law, or that Israel is not to be held accountable for any breaches of law. The problem, however, is not that Israel is above the law, but that Israel is being systematically denied equality before the law; not that Israel must respect human rights, but that Israel is regarded as not having any rights; not that standards of human rights apply to Israel, but that the same standards are not being applied to anyone else.

Witness the following: how does one account for the fact that whereas all nations in the world are universally regarded as having the right to self-determination, only the Jewish people continuously have their right to self-determination called into question? How does one account for the fact that whereas all nations in the world are regarded as being entitled to the right of self-defense in international law, only the Jewish exercise of self-defense is labeled an act of aggression? How does one account for the fact that of some forty-five million refugees since the Second World War, only Palestinian Arab refugees—whose pain and suffering I do not discount—are regarded as having rights of return and compensation, whereas Jewish refugees from Arab lands are not regarded as having any standing in the debate at all? How does one account for the fact that Jewish trade with South Africa is singled out for condemnation, whereas trade by France and England and even Black African states in greater percentages with South Africa bears no mention at all? How does one account for the fact that in the recent battle over the sale of AWACS, Saudi Arabian blackmail threats were somehow regarded as being permissible, indeed encouraged, whereas Israeli concern regarding threats to its vital interests was labeled as a surreptitious attempt to dictate American foreign policy? How does one account for the fact that when we press for the prosecution of Nazi war criminals in Canada, we are told that only Jews want it, as if those who belong to the class of the victims have no standing to petition on behalf of those victims? We are told not to protest because we might invite anti-Jewishness, as if we should repress and censor our speech in the name of those who can no longer speak.

A consequence of this anti-Jewishness, which in turn generates further expression of it, is the innuendo of double-loyalty which surfaced during the AWACS' debate in the United States' Senate. Jews were warned against acting ''in a manner inimical to the American national interest.'' Lobbyists for AWACS were seen as good Americans, while opponents of the sale were regarded as un-American or as followers of the dictates of a foreign power. The implication was that it was illegal in America for American citizens—indeed, even U.S. senators—to petition government for redress of grievances, that it was immoral for American citizens to exercise the democratic process if that democratic process was somehow associated with the cause of Israel, that Jewish rights were not human rights.

We must make it clear, as Jews and as Canadians, that such politics of intimidation, the beginnings of which can be seen in Canada as well, are threatening not just to Jews, but to Canadians as a whole and to the integrity of the democratic process. If any group in Canada is ever told that they cannot protest on the grounds that their stand will invite some backlash against them, be they Greek, Italian, Portuguese, or members of any other national group, there will result a chilling effect on free speech everywhere. An example of this effect was seen in the admission of Senator Cohen of Maine, in explaining his change of vote from opposition to the AWACS' sale to support for it, that he did so due to concern for the future of American Jewry and Israel if the sale was defeated. He could not vote as an American loyal to the principles of American integrity. Senator Cohen spoke for many whose views were not given public expression.

Let us not delude ourselves by saying that resolutions in the international arena can be confined to the abstractions of history, or that the United Nations and its specialized agencies have no bearing on reality. These resolutions, the ongoing de-legitimization, the attempt to portray Jews as the pariah—all have concrete effects everywhere.

Jewish students in England were refused the right to speak in university forums on the grounds that they were Zionists, Zionists are racists, and racists have no right to speak. In 1980, at Harvard Law School, a symposium was organized under the theme: ''The So-called State of Israel and its Policy of Genocide and Terrorism in the Occupied Territories.'' At the symposium, organized by alleged progressive and black-nationalist Harvard law students, an award of Harvard Law School was conferred on a representative of the government of Libya, the consummate terrorist agency of our time. When Jewish students at Harvard Law School wished to intervene and protest, they were shouted down with epithets of ''Zionism is racist.'' Hugh Trevor Roper, the distinguished Regis professor of history at Oxford University, who has written movingly of the Holocaust in the past, writes, in the book-review section of the *New York Times*: ''There are common characteristics between Nazism and Zionism.'' This is regarded by the *New York Times* book-review section as part of ''all the news that is fit to print.''

The leader of the Quebec teachers' union, one of the largest trade unions in Quebec, goes to Libya and attends a conference on Zionism is racism. This he has a perfect right to do. But upon his return to Quebec, in his capacity as head of the union, he calls upon all teachers in that province to teach the Zionism is racism theme. The Polish trade union, Solidarity, finds itself accused of being Zionist. Here we witness a new phenomenom in our time, that of antisemitism without Jews, reminiscent of Jean Paul Sartre's comment: ''If the Jew did not exist, the antisemite would create him.''

In Iran, Syria, the Soviet Union, and elsewhere, formal legal indictments are brought against Jews, not for what they do, but for who they are. The most compelling image of the systematic denial of the rights of Jews occurred in Copenhagen in July and August 1980, at the United Nations' mid-decade conference on women. In one of the sessions, during a brutal vilification of Israel, Zionism, and the Jewish people, the representative of the State of Israel sought the right to speak on a point of privilege and was denied permission. Not one political leader from other Western countries represented at that conference stood up to defend, not what the Israeli representative would say, but simply his right to speak in the debate. It is no longer a question of the merits of a case, but rather a denial of our right to make the case to begin with. The message cannot be heard because the message is being impugned.

What, then, can we do? Have we learned nothing from Jewish history? Is the Holocaust to continue to be defamed in the obscenities of the present? Is the loyalty of American or Canadian Jews to be questioned and the cause of Israel and Jewish rights to be defamed in the process? Are we simply being benumbed, overwhelmed by it all? What is our responsibility as Jews, as Canadians, in the face of the ongoing de-legitimization of Israel, Zionism, and the Jewish people, which is as much a threat to the integrity of the democratic process and civil rights anywhere as it is to Jews?

Jews today feel over-stretched and over-stressed. At the same time, there are those who simply no longer wish to associate themselves with the cause because it is not popular. We cannot move lightly from cause to cause in the manner of "cocktail advocacy." The denial of rights to Soviet Jews is not diminishing simply because there are fewer manifestations on their behalf. The rights of Syrian Jews are no less important just because little is being done to improve their lot. The rights of Ethiopian Jews are not assisted by any misleading information that is disseminated with regard to their condition. And the rights of Israel are not secure when people want to distance themselves psychologically from Israel because it is isolated in the community of nations.

It is critical for us to assume responsibility by redefining ourselves, not as victims of Jewish history or human history, but as actors capable of doing something about it;

not simply as witnesses—as important as it is to bear testimony—but as advocates who will defend the cause. At times such as these *qui s'excuse s'accuse*, who remains indifferent indicts himself or herself. A world which will not be safe for democracy will not be safe for Jews. We therefore have a commitment to preserve the democratic process wherever we are. More importantly, a world which will not be safe for Jews will not be safe for democracy.

What does it mean to be a Jew today? To see, to understand, to affirm; always to act as legatees, heirs of a great Jewish past with all the power of Jewish memory, Jewish values, and Jewish history, and no less so as trustees—as people who carry in their own hearts and minds the Jewish future. To be a Jew today is to remember that there is a Jewish state—and a Jewish people—which is an antidote to Jewish powerless. As Edmund Burke said, ''The surest way to ensure that evil will triumph in the world is for enough good people to do nothing.'' There are enough good people to stand up and be counted without looking around to see whoever else is standing. Precisely at times when the cause is unpopular, when people are not standing, we must adopt and internalize the motto of the Israeli soldier: *Acharai!* ''Follow me! I will stand and I will be counted, however unpopular, however prejudicial it may be to my person or to my profession, and regardless of what the costs are!'' If we do this, we will be not only good Jews but good Canadians. Israel, in the last analysis, is a metaphor for human rights, a litmus test for democracy. As it goes with Israel, so will it go with the rest of us.

V
ISRAEL

Israel and the
United Nations
Yoram Dinstein

An overview of the history of the first three and a half decades of the United Nations would demonstrate that its main achievement has been sheer survival. The fact that the organization has managed to remain alive after thirty-seven years of trial and error is an attainment of no small consequence, particularly if one bears in mind that its predecessor, the League of Nations, did not survive (in practice, as distinct from theory) for more than twenty years. The United Nations, so far, has outlasted the League of Nations. The question, however, is whether one can guarantee that the United Nations will continue to exist at the end of the century.

The United Nations of 1982 is not the organization conceived at the San Francisco Conference of 1945. For one thing, the founding members of the United Nations are now in a decided minority. The current total of member-states is 157, as compared to 51 at the outset. There is a constant proliferation in members—a veritable population explosion—within the organization. Every year more and more states join the organization, while representing less and less territorially, economically, and demographically.

Furthermore, the original basic concept of the United Nations has proved unrealistic. The San Francisco Conference was convened in April 1945, while the Second World War was still in progress. The working assumption then was that the grand alliance between the major powers would continue to function in the postwar period. As a result, the five permanent members of the Security Council were pictured as running the world in concert. Any threat to man-

[136]

kind that might emanate from any source was expected to be met by the Big Five together. There was only one small detail which the founding fathers ignored, namely, the possibility that the Big Five would be entirely disunited and that the threat to peace might even be posed by one of them. By hindsight we now know that the basic concept was flawed from the very beginning.

The trouble lies not only with the basic concept of the United Nations but also with its basic goal. When the organization was created, its main purpose was to put an end to war and to maintain peace. The United Nations' Charter itself, in its first Article, spells out this principal aim. Unfortunately, the goal has not been achieved. In fact, the organization has proved irrelevant to some of the most important wars and warlike situations that have occurred since 1945. If one reads the proceedings of the main organs of the United Nations and tries to reconstruct history on their basis alone, one is apt to reach the conclusion that the Vietnam War was of no consequence to our generation, that the issue of Berlin did not plague the world, and that there was no major conflagration in either Biafra or Bangladesh. In fact, the most important armed conflict which has consumed time, interest, and energy in the United Nations is the Middle East conflict.

Because the United Nations could not pursue the original path envisaged by its founding fathers, the organization has, in a sense, been detoured in the general direction of a secondary aim, namely, upholding certain political, social, economic, and cultural goals of mankind. These goals have become—faute de mieux—the effective purpose of the United Nations. Since it cannot deal with war and peace, the organization deals with other matters.

There have been three distinct periods in the history of the United Nations. The first period was the era of the ascendency of the West in the organization. The original fifty-one members were essentially American and western European, with a small minority from Eastern Europe and other countries. Subject to the use and abuse of the Soviet veto during

[137]

the first decade or so, it was the West, more particularly the United States, that set the tone and determined the direction taken by the United Nations.

The second period covers the time when the United Nations started to expand. For close to ten years the original number of member-states remained almost frozen: it grew from fifty-one to sixty, and then stopped. Only when a Big Power package-deal was reached in 1954 did many more states manage to get in. Then the dam practically burst, and almost any state could join. The second period is characterized by the addition of numerous member-states from all quarters, particularly from Africa. The African countries joined in force in the sixties. Subsequently, the whole balance of power started to tilt. In the mid-sixties, not only was the West divested of its ascendency in the organization, but it already had to worry about getting the required one-third of the vote to block important General Assembly resolutions that it did not like. Still, throughout the sixties, the West could, if it so desired, thwart hostile resolutions. It could not always adopt its own resolutions, but it could prevent the adoption of resolutions that it found unacceptable.

Then came the third period, when the less-developed countries, to all effects and purposes, took over the organization. Today, they not only constitute the majority, but they have the necessary two-thirds of the vote to overrule any Western objection in the General Assembly. As a result, one no longer hears about debates in the General Assembly over the issue of whether a given question is "important," in the vocabulary of the Charter (and would therefore demand a two-thirds' majority), or an ordinary question (and would therefore only need a regular majority). Such debates have become redundant or moot. In any event, the less-developed countries have the required majority.

Unfortunately, in the club of states called the United Nations, many of the new members are not used to the traditional rules. They are playing a parliamentary game without worrying about parliamentary niceties. Consequently, the new majority is prepared to adopt any resolution that will suit its purpose. The infamous General Assembly resolution equating Zionism with racism is the ultimate demonstration that the current majority in the General Assembly is not restrained by respect for the interests or the values of the minority.

It must be borne in mind that the United Nations does not mirror the real balance of power in the world. Even in terms of power politics, the glass building of the United Nations does not reflect the rays of light, but deflects them. When one is inside the building, one is under the impression that the Federal Republic of Germany is equal to Grenada, that Dominica is equal to India. Indeed, these four countries have the same power in the organization. But, needless to say, when one takes a step outside the glass walls into reality, one becomes aware of the facts of life. It so happens that, in real life, the Federal Republic of Germany is much more important than Grenada. It so happens that Dominica is hardly noticed on the map geographically, and scarcely counts economically or politically compared with India. Considering that the real balance of power is not reflected in the organization, and that there is less to the majority than meets the eye, there is no reason why the minority must bow to arbitrary resolutions adopted by the General Assembly.

If there have been three periods in the history of the United Nations, there have been five in the history of the relationship between the organization and the State of Israel.

The first period was 1947–1948. It started before the creation of the State of Israel and continued briefly thereafter. That was a period of enthusiasm by Israel, its inhabitants, and its supporters all over the world for the organization. The United Nations in those days was regarded by Jews everywhere as almost a deus ex machina. The apex of that period was the famous partition resolution of November 29, 1947, when the General Assembly, by a two-thirds' majority, recommended the partition of Palestine with the establishment of a Jewish state as well as an Arab state and a *corpus separatum* in Jerusalem.

[139]

Following the resolution, a civil war between Arabs and Jews commenced in Palestine. Then, when the State of Israel came into being on May 15, 1948, the neighboring Arab states invaded Israel. Here arose the greatest challenge to the United Nations. Many people tend to forget that important watershed date: May 15, 1948. It was the occasion of the first armed attack, the first flagrant act of aggression, in in the post–Second World War era. What was the United Nations supposed to do? The answer is to be found in the Charter. It is spelled "collective security." The Security Council should have decided to condemn the aggressors and to mobilize armed units of the various member-states in order to stem the tide of aggression. But what happened in fact? Nothing, absolutely nothing. Israel had to fight for itself, while the United Nations was debating the question at some length, occasionally adopting resolutions calling upon the parties to impose a truce. The United Nations even appointed a mediator, and then an acting-mediator. But it did not do what it was supposed to have done. Thus, the State of Israel was not established by the partition resolution. The partition scheme remained in the 1947 volume of resolutions of the General Assembly. The state was created by ordeal of fire on the battlefield, and it paid a very high price. Israel lost six thousand men, women, and children in its war of independence, with a total population of 600,000. One per cent of the total population died in the war.

This was when a period of disenchantment with the United Nations started. At this stage it was merely disenchantment, the feeling that something went wrong, that the United Nations was not the panacea, that it would not solve all the problems. Nevertheless, there was still recognition of the importance of the United Nations and of its tremendous potential.

The disenchantment continued and even mounted in the early fifties, when the United Nations began to adopt resolutions condemning Israeli reprisal actions against neighboring Arab countries, while ignoring completely the original acts of sabotage that had triggered the retaliation. Israeli resentment gradually grew because the United Nations' resolutions were increasingly one-sided. Nevertheless, during that period we can also put our finger on the last, if not the only, pro-Israeli resolution ever carried in the Security Council. It was adopted on September 1, 1951, in the matter of the Suez Canal. In it, the Security Council endorsed the Israeli contention that the so-called blockade of the Suez Canal by Egypt was unlawful.

Then came the third period, commencing in the mid-1950s and ending in 1967. This was a period of disappointment, as distinct from mere disenchantment, with the United Nations. It was brought about by a material change in Soviet policy. Until the early fifties, the Soviet Union supported Israel to some degree: had it not been for the Soviet Union, there would have been no partition resolution in 1947. But in the early fifties the Soviet Union changed its policy in the Middle East. As of that time, it has supported the Arab cause to the hilt, without any reservation. On the other hand, Western support of Israel has always been based on the principle of limited liability. That is to say, support, yes; but up to a point, not beyond. Hence, resolutions in the Security Council could either be pro-Arab or not be adopted. If they were pro-Arab, a compromise with the West could be reached. But if they were pro-Israeli, the Soviet Union would veto them. When the case was glaringly in favor of Israel, the result usually was a standoff and no resolution at all.

Then came 1956, and as a result of the hectic activity of the then-secretary general of the United Nations, Dag Hammerskjøld, backed by the United States, Israel had to pull out of Sinai. When Hammerskjøld reached the deal that paved the road for Israeli withdrawal in 1957, it was based on certain assumptions and expectations as to Egyptian conduct. From the outset Egypt failed to keep its part of the bargain (by sending its army into the Gaza Strip), and the disappointment in Israel grew. But in 1967 the disappointment turned into distrust of the United Nations. Between 1957 and 1967, the United Nations' Emergency Force (UNEF) patrolled the area. The shield of the United Nations was supposed to protect both parties. The expectation was that UNEF would play the role of a fire brigade, doing its best to prevent or extinguish fire. The fire brigade was there for ten years, as long as there was no fire. Yet, once fire appeared to flare up, the secretary general of the United Nations, U Thant, decided to pull the fire brigade out. As far as Israel was concerned, UNEF no longer stood for United Nations' Emergency Force. It stood for United Nations' Emergency Farce. Israel discovered that it could not rely on the United Nations.

Finally, the situation changed in the seventies, as an outcome of the assumption of complete control of the United Nations by the present majority. The General Assembly has simply become a political tool in the hands of the Arabs against Israel, and the Palestine Liberation Organization, as an "observer," started to wield more power in the organization than Israel did as a member-state. Thus, the fifth period, of Israeli defiance, has begun. Israel's attitude is no longer disenchantment. It is no longer disappointment. It is no longer distrust. It is defiance. From the standpoint of Israel today, the United Nations will do its worst, and Israel will do its best. The position of Israel is: damn the United Nations and go ahead! Consequently, the United Nations in many respects has·become irrelevant to the Middle East conflict.

It has been indicated above that the most important conflict which has ever been deliberated at length and in depth in the United Nations is the Middle East conflict. Perhaps as many as one-third of all the meetings of the Security Council have been devoted to the Middle East. This is due to the fact that the United Nations was very relevant to the conflict. By the same token, the conflict was very relevant to the United Nations. Indeed, a number of dates and events relating to the Middle East are landmark dates and watershed events in the evolution of the United Nations.

Take, for example, the partition resolution. It reflects the first major attempt on the part of the United Nations to settle a territorial conflict. There have been other cases since, but none before 1947. Then, as mentioned, take the very important decision that was not taken, in May and June 1948. For the first time the United Nations failed in its main duty of checking aggression, and that failure was a precursor of things to come. Then, in 1956, came the establishment of UNEF, the first United Nations' Emergency Force (which was different in many respects from the preexisting conglomeration of forces fighting in Korea). Similar United Nations' forces have in the meantime been created. One of them in Sinai (after the Yom Kippur War) with the same acronym, others with different names, for example, in the Congo and Cyprus. But all of them have been based on the pattern of the original UNEF.

Despite the close links that have traditionally existed between the United Nations and the Middle East conflict, the late seventies were characterized by the substantial irrelevance of the organization to the conflict. The proof of this irrelevance can easily be detected in practice. The peace treaty between Israel and Egypt, concluded in 1978, was negotiated without the help of the United Nations. In fact, the organization refused to help in the implementation of the treaty, and the second UNEF ceased to exist when it appeared that the force was likely to promote the cause of peace. The peace treaty may not be an ideal document. But by becoming a tool of the "rejectionist front" in the Arab world, the organization has lost its former usefulness as a neutral umpire.

Indeed, by playing a one-sided role in the context of the Middle East, the organization risks its very survival. The United Nations may find itself today in the same position that the League of Nations reached in the mid-thirties. If one reads the vast literature on the subject, one discovers that already in the mid-thirties many people felt that the days of the League of Nations were numbered. Evidently, many other people objected vociferously and passionately, suggesting that the League of Nations was indestructible. The League of Nations did, however, come to an end. This is an historical fact. Today the time is ripe to consider the possibility that the days of the United Nations, too, are

[143]

numbered. Personally, I believe that if the United Nations will not mend its ways; if there will not be an end to the United Nations' chatter and a return to the United Nations' Charter; if the United Nations will not reestablish responsibility within its organs; if the actual political power existing in the outside world will not be reflected inside the organization; then the United Nations is doomed. I do not claim to be a soothsayer, and I certainly do not wish the United Nations to follow in the footsteps of the League of Nations. But we must face reality.

The only way, in my opinion, for the United Nations to remain alive as an organization is for it to change. It could change in a number of ways. One way is to amend the Charter, yet the Charter's amendment does not appear to be in the political cards. Another possibility is that the procedures of the United Nations will change informally, and there will be a transition to the politics of consensus. In the League of Nations every important resolution, even of the Assembly, and not only of the Council, required consensus rather than a majority vote. This could be the trend of the future. Indeed, there is now a very important United Nations' conference going on, on the Law of the Sea, in which the principle of consensus has so far prevailed. Whereas it makes life very hard for delegates, consensus politics guarantees that once decisions are taken, they will not be simply ignored.

The alternative is to maintain things as they are. That, in my opinion, will bring about the ultimate disintegration of the United Nations. There is no doubt that the public in many Western countries is already, in some measure, disillusioned with the United Nations, and this disillusionment appears to be on the increase. Public opinion is known to have forced Western governments to alter their foreign policy in the past. And withdrawal by the United States and other Western countries would seal the fate of the United Nations.

I happen to be the chairman of the Tel Aviv United Nations' Association. I believe in the Charter of the United Nations, and regard the possible demise of the organization as a tragedy. But it is not enough to be in favor of an organization in order to avoid its demise. All those interested in the survival of the United Nations must raise their voices in unison with a view to pressuring the United Nations to mend its ways. In a sense, the United Nations must be saved from itself.

ALIYAH AND LESSER
REFLECTIONS
Emil L. Fackenheim

Among the many things brought out into the open by the United Nations' Zionism-racism resolution is the fact that to be confused about the meaning of Zionism is already to be victimized by its enemies.

Zionism is the proposition that Jewish homelessness must be brought to an end.

Prior to the Holocaust a decent anti- or non-Zionism was possible. The Orthodox could believe that only the Messiah had the authority to end Jewish homelessness, while the liberals, the present writer included, could believe that there was no Jewish homelessness left in the enlightened parts of the world, and that the unenlightened remnant of the world would soon become enlightened. After the Holocaust, there is no such thing as a decent anti-Zionist.

Had there been a Jewish state at the time of Nazism, it would have flung its gates open to Jews fleeing while flight was still possible, and tried to bomb the railways to Auschwitz at the time of the apocalypse.

Incredibly, there exists the obscene fact of post-Holocaust antisemitism. It exists in Russia and Poland. It exists in lesser forms almost everywhere else except in the democracies, increasingly few in number. It exists in the Arab world, despite the recent expensive Iraqi ads, saying to Iraq's 125,000 Jews brutally expelled: come back, all is forgiven.

Jewish homelessness has not come to an end. Hence the deliverance of the captives is a principle which no longer brooks postponement or compromise, whether from a religious or secularist point of view. Hence, even if he lives in a free country and does not consider himself personally homeless, every decent Jew must be a Zionist. So must every decent person. So must every decent Arab. Zionism says nothing which denies Arab rights, including the right of self-determination.

Zionism today consists of the unequivocal support of two principles: the autonomy and safety of the State of Israel, without which Israel could not hope to end homelessness for Jews wherever it exists; and the law of return, without which the Jewish state would become a selfish entity which, having ended homelessness for some, would shut the doors to others. The proposition that Jewish homelessness as such must be ended (instead of just for some Jews) would be betrayed.

Every decent person must be a Zionist. At least if he is a Jewish Zionist, he chooses second best if he does not go on Aliyah himself.

There may be and doubtless often are excellent reasons why a Jew chooses second best. It is second best all the same.

This is true even if in the Diaspora he becomes a great Jewish scholar and in Israel he becomes a kibbutznik ploughing a field.

For Israel cannot end Jewish homelessness unless there are those who dedicate to the vitality of the home itself, not just their money, their political support, the brilliance of their intellect, but existence itself.

It should be obvious that as long as Israel is still under attack, it would be quite indecent for any Jew in the safety of the North American Diaspora to compare his Zionism with that of Israelis who, simply by being in Israel, are under the threat of terrorism, to say nothing of war. But even if, as one must fervently hope, true peace should come to the Middle East, Diaspora existence would continue to be second best. Coming as it did after the greatest catastrophe in Jewish history and one of the greatest in all history, the re-

[147]

birth of the Jewish people after death itself is an act which should, and perhaps one day will, be an inspiration to all mankind. To be a direct participant in this rebirth and the growing pains which will last for a long time is, at this moment in Jewish history, an opportunity for which future Jews may well envy this generation, just as we envy those who were in the company of Rabbi Yohanan ben Zakkai.

WHY DO WE HAVE Hope?
Walter F. Mondale

I am deeply grateful and honored to receive this degree—grateful that you should have thought of me as its recipient, and honored because I know the greatness of the university that bestows it.

In many ways, this university contains all the elements that are so remarkable in Israeli life. Recorded in your library is the memory of the Jewish people. Unlocked in your laboratories are the secrets by which arid regions bloom. Behind your sharing of knowledge with less developed countries is the compassion of this nation. And mirrored in your students—in their handling of studies and jobs and the defense of the nation all at once—is the drive, the joy, the faith of Israel itself.

Most of all, it is a tradition five thousand years old, of Jewish dedication to learning, that this university superbly upholds. Teachers who leave the classroom to teach on the front are completely devoted to the ideals of the classroom. Soldiers who become students, reservists who read books, are entirely dedicated to the ideals of learning. A university that has done so much for Israel and the world is one that not only returned, but profoundly deserved to return to this magnificent Mount Scopus. And a people so devoted to the Hebrew University not only support it, but will see that it stays here.

Today we not only celebrate these students, we celebrate a democracy that is working.

If any government could justify supressing dissent in the name of national security, it is the Israeli government. Yet the voices in the Knesset, the free Israel press, the open debate, the rule of law—all are proof that this is a nation deeply committed to civil liberties.

If any people could rationalize the infringement of human

rights in the name of human survival, it is the Israeli people. Yet the new-found home of Jacobo Timerman is one of the world's strongest bastions of human rights.

If any state could be forgiven a lapse in democratic routine because of the constant threat to its existence, it is this state. Yet only yesterday, this nation, which is so young, honored a tradition which is so old, the sacred tradition of free and fair elections.

Of all the possible outcomes from yesterday's elections, the greatest triumph was the triumph of the human spirit. Israel is a sound, faithful, flourishing democracy—and because of that, it is strong. The principle we celebrate today is that the most invincible Israel is an Israel true to its values.

No one knew that better, and no one was a better supporter of Israel, than my friend and mentor, Hubert Humphrey. He once said this about the special bond that connects our two nations: "What I love about Israel so much is that she reveals in her existence what I think are the best objectives of American foreign policy: a people and a country insisting on their right to be free and independent; a people and a country who are willing to use their resources to enrich the lives of their own people; a people and a country who are willing to play a responsible role in world affairs. If every country that we've helped would do as much as Israel, the world would be a happier and safer place in which to live."

The respect and care for Israel which Hubert taught me, I have learned on my own—by walking through the streets of this beautiful city; by listening to Golda Meir describe to me the social justice that drives the Zionist dream; by playing the small part I was privileged to play three years ago in smoothing the way to the Camp David Accords. You can understand this nation by studying its history and reading its writers—and I have. But by knowing its people and sharing their dreams you must love this Israel. And I always will.

Even between two nations as close as ours, there will sometimes be disagreements—if the nations are sovereign.

There will sometimes be debate—if they are democratic. And there are no two nations more sovereign, more democratic, more independent than Israel and the United States.

But no disagreement should be allowed to obscure the fact that from the moment President Harry Truman recognized this state onwards, there has existed a special relationship between our nations. And any American administration that threatens to reassess or reappraise or review that relationship does not understand our historic commitment to Israel. We may disagree about tactics—but never fall out over strategy. We may quibble over the language of diplomacy—but never brandish the codewords of intimidation. We may argue about this or that point—but never dispute what fundamentally counts in American-Israeli relations.

And now I'd like briefly to describe what it is that counts in our relations.

First, there is military security. It is better to deter a war than to win a war. If there was ever any doubt about Israel's defenses, others might be tempted to attack. In order to keep the peace, Israel simply must have the unquestioned military strength to defend itself.

Security is not a pawn to be moved, a chip to be bargained, an item to be negotiated. Security is sacred. If we have a disagreement, let us discuss it—but never stop the flow of materiel which is vital to the security of this nation.

Second: Israel's economy.

Since Israel was reborn as a modern state, you have performed a miracle. You have given a home to hundreds of thousands of people from other nations. You have wrested a living from this once harsh and forbidding land. You have defended your right to be here with invincible might.

All this has cost massive amounts of money, piled up a huge foreign-exchange burden, and fueled a staggering inflation rate. It is only partial help for the United States to lend Israel more money, when Israel cannot handle the debt burden it already has. It is only small comfort for us to give Israel political support, when Israel's economic foundations

[151]

sag beneath it. The United States must not only continue its program of economic assistance, we must start forgiving a much greater part of the loans we make to Israel. And we should start by forgiving the loan we made as part of the 1978 peace package.

The aid we provide Israel is not a kindness—it is profoundly in America's interest. A higher ratio of grants to loans is not charity—it is an investment in our own security. Assistance is not a handout—it is an investment in peace for this part of the world.

Third: terrorism.

Military and economic and energy security is not enough: nations must be free from the threat of terrorism. Our country believes that peace in the Middle East can only come through negotiations—but we must never negotiate with those who believe that murder has a place in international relations.

The United States must not negotiate with the so-called Palestine Liberation Organization (PLO)—we must not recognize it—unless and until the Palestine Liberation Organization recognizes Israel's right to exist and United Nations' Resolution 242.

And there must be an end to PLO terrorism. We must let them know that they will not extort by killing what they cannot get by reasoning. There simply is no room on the West Bank or in Gaza for an independent Palestine state. And we must oppose it.

Fourth: This Special City, Jerusalem.

After the war for independence Hebrew University left this hilltop campus—but did not give it up. Every two weeks for nineteen years a convoy came here and relieved the Israelis who remained on Mount Scopus. The classrooms were empty, but those convoys were a symbol of your determination that some day they would be full again. The Hadassah Medical Center cured no patients, but it stood as a symbol of your hope that someday the wound which had divided Jerusalem would heal—and this city would be whole again.

Now that it is, those who remember the convoys will not

stand for a divided Jerusalem again. Those who once were denied access to the holy places will not be refused it again. Those who returned to Mount Scopus will not be exiled again. We must insist that this sacred city remain united and free for all faiths to enter.

Finally, Israel's sweetest dream—peace, peace with all its neighbors, peace behind secure, recognized, and defensible borders.

I do not need to speak of peace to people who have endured so much war. No one wishes for peace more fervently than those who must pay for its absence with their youth, their money, and their lives. What needs restating here is our belief in the possibility of a general peace. What we thought was impossible has already happened: peace between Israel and Egypt. It was two millennia between the last visit to Egypt by an Israeli head of state and the visit by Prime Minister Begin. Since that visit, we have learned to believe in miracles. And we believe in the miracle of peace between Israel and all its neighbors.

But for the moment the process has stalled. And let no one be deceived: there is no standing still in the matter of peace and war. Already the dangers have mounted in recent months: the missiles in Lebanon, the new weapons of your adversaries, the hardening of hostile opinion, the criticism which mounts as Israel takes actions in her own defense. As time goes on without peace, the dangers to Israel grow. The hour has arrived to act boldly again, and resume the process of peace.

To discover the causes of war and remove them, here at Hebrew University you have created the Harry S. Truman Institute for the Advancement of Peace. It is not to disparage the scholarly efforts of this institute that I say, first of all, there is no plainer, more obvious, more serious impediment to peace than the refusal by your neighbors to recognize Israel, and the unwillingness of your neighbors to live in peace. An absolutely essential step on the path to peace is for Israel's neighbors to follow the statesmanship of President Sadat and Prime Minister Begin, the leadership of the Egyptian and Israeli people, who made peace with each other—because they had the courage to seek it.

No one needs more crises, more blow-ups, more terrorism, more daily threats of war—but they will continue and get worse until the state of war between Israel and her neighbors ceases. There simply is no rational alternative to peace.

Two weeks ago, here in Jerusalem, there concluded perhaps the most moving reunion ever held, the reunion of five thousand survivors of the Nazi death camps. It was like many other reunions: they celebrated their survival. They mourned the missing. They renewed old friendships. They filled each other in on how they had passed the many years apart.

What made it different from other reunions was that though five thousand came, many more had died and disappeared—and six million had perished in the death camps. So of all the activities, the most important was to seek some shred of news about someone you had lost—a brother, a sister, a husband, a daughter. "Ester Fiszgap is looking for any survivor from Brezsc, Poland," read one placard put up in the convention center. Another was: "Anyone who was at Mauthausen in the year 1942 and knew my brother Alexander Kopelmann, please, please contact me."

The survivors have gone home, probably never to hold a reunion again. Life goes on. We argue. We struggle. We debate the wisdom of this tactic or that. But the suffering cries of those placards will echo in our ears forever. They speak of a scar that can never heal, a conscience that cannot rest, a memory that cannot forget. As in the ancient tragedies, they serve as the chorus, telling us the meaning of the drama we are in.

Why do we carry on? The placards answer, because we remember. Why is there an Israel? Because never again. Why do we have hope? Because Israel is forever.

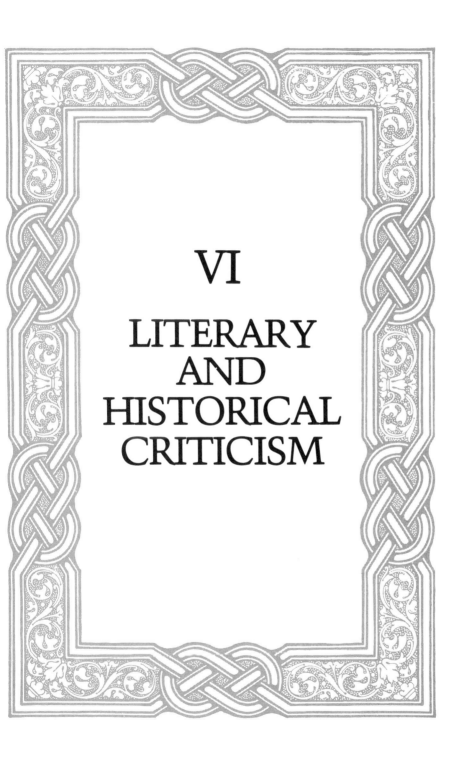

VI
LITERARY
AND
HISTORICAL
CRITICISM

THE AUTHORITY OF THE ETHICAL IMPULSE IN HALAKHAH
Eugene B. Borowitz

A good deal of attention has been given to the turn to Jewish tradition among those who at one time identified the essence of Judaism with universal human ethics. With the loss of confidence in the authority of Western civilization, the possibility arose that classic Jewish teaching might be the best guide to the good life.[1] The question is then often asked, in the all-or-nothing terms beloved by those who like to use intellect coercively, "Why do you not then fully embrace rabbinic teaching as developed over millennia and as amplified in unbroken tradition today?" Much of the response to that query hinges on the place of ethics within Jewish teaching or, to be more precise, on the authority given to the ethical imperative within classic Rabbinic Judaism. (On this term, a euphemism for the unbroken tradition of interpreting the Torah in inherited fashion, see below.)

This issue has been treated most intensively from within traditionalist circles by Aharon Lichtenstein in his widely read paper, "Does Jewish Tradition Recognize an Ethic Independent of Halakha?"[2] Lichtenstein has surely clarified the issue before the community, but in my opinion, has not satisfactorily faced up to the issue troubling many Jews about their heritage.

Lichtenstein focuses on an internal problem of Rabbinic Judaism. It recognizes that its legal procedures occasionally do not directly produce ethical results. It thus includes various measures for overcoming such impasses. He takes particular pains to point out that some of these special processes were actionable, that they could be enforced by a Jewish court. He can then conclude that though Jewish tradition does not recognize an ethic independent of Halakhah, it contains within itself all the ethical resources its notion of God and humankind would expect us to find in it.

The issue of the internal ethical adequacy of Jewish tradition is not a minor one, both for theological and practical reasons. Ethical demands come with an imperative quality. They lay an authoritative claim upon us. If Rabbinic Judaism were to recognize an ethics independent of it, that would be to recognize a second source of authority to the Torah. Or, to say the same thing differently, Jews would have to admit that God had given them only a partial, not a complete, revelation. The former notion conflicts with the common identification of the one God with the one Torah, the latter with the Jewish understanding of the completeness of the Torah revelation.

Practically, too, the notion of an external ethics would raise methodological problems for a contemporary *posek*. His expertise is in Torah. He will certainly recognize the internal ethical impulses and goals in Torah and respond to them as he deems appropriate. Should external ethical considerations be included in determining authoritative Jewish duty, he would have to transcend his received methodology and learning, and become expert in general ethics and its relation to rabbinic tradition. No established institution would easily accept such a radical challenge to its accustomed ways of proceeding.

David Weiss Halivni's statement on the halakhic status of a universal ethics seems more motivated by pragmatic than theological reasons in rejecting the concept of an external morality with authority within Halakhah.[3] Maimonides' famous insistence that Noachides must accept their commandments as revealed by the Torah and not as given by their own reason, while a somewhat different case, is relevant here. Why he should rule this way despite his practical identification of revelation with reason has not yet been made compellingly clear.[4] The pragmatic explanation, in his case securing the ultimate foundation of the social order, is perhaps the easiest to accept, particularly if we are influenced by the "two doctrines" interpretation of his thought. Yet that would require us to accept that, in terms of the higher doctrine, such a sociological "external," if revealed, ethics exists and is authoritative. Our only other alternative would seem to be to take a radically fresh approach to the nonrational or trans-rational aspect of all of his philosophy, a reading often spoken of but not yet done.

Lichtenstein's treatment of the issue, however, proceeds beyond these issues to analyze the way in which an ethical impulse makes itself felt and operates within Rabbinic Judaism. For our purposes, it will help to grant immediately what appears to be one of Lichtenstein's main points: Rabbinic Judaism has a fundamental ethical thrust, not only manifested in the law itself, but most notably in the methods and motives it has for overcoming internal conflicts between its ethical values and its legal procedures. The vulgar contrast made in older Christian polemics between Jewish legalism and general ethics betrays ignorance of Judaism and insensitivity to its own prejudice (in the name of ethics!). Leaving that question, I wish to focus on the problem that I see arising when one speaks about the internal ethics of Judaism as Lichtenstein has done.

Critical to understanding Lichenstein's argument is his special use of the term "Halakhah" (note the capital "H"). He does so in a way different from that commonly found in North American English-language writing on such matters. Through most of his paper he means by Halakhah the totality of the rabbinic tradition. (To conform to his meaning but to avoid the linguistic confusion which can result from his usage, I shall use the term "Rabbinic Judaism" to refer to the same phenomenon.) Lichtenstein's choice of terms is certainly justifiable, but the question posed by many interlocutors asking about an ethics independent of Halakhah often has a somewhat different issue in mind. That is, one regularly sees the word "Halakhah" used as referring to only one part of Rabbinic Judaism, the legal part, as contrasted to *aggadah*, the non-legal part. The *aggadah* ob-

[158]

viously contains much ethical material. To ask about an ethic independent of Halakhah means, then, to ask whether ethical impulses arising outside the law carry full imperative quality either in their own right or, more threateningly, against provisions of the law.

Lichtenstein knows that his usage is somewhat uncommon and on the last two pages of his article makes mention of the more common understanding of the term ''halakhah'' (note the lower-case ''h'').[5] He thinks we would be better off calling *din* what people usually call halakhah. In sum, he argues that this is only a matter of semantics and that, while one may define as one thinks best, the outcome will be the same: Rabbinic Judaism has a vital, effective, internal ethics.[6]

What may go unnoticed as a result of Lichtenstein's unusual terminology is the problem of the several levels of authority within Rabbinic Judaism. Lichtenstein is too careful a scholar not to refer to this along the way, but it does not serve as one of his major foci. The best example of an accurate statement which may perhaps be misleading is found in one of his summary sentences. Referring to various ways of speaking of Jewish tradition, he concludes that it makes little difference as long as we ''issue with the thesis that traditional halakhic Judaism demands of the Jew both adherence to Halakha and commitment to an ethical moment that though different from Halakha is nevertheless of a piece with it and in its own way fully imperative.''[7] The critical yet easily overlooked part of this statement is the qualifying clause, ''in its own way.'' That is, Lichtenstein does not say: ''and commitment to an ethical moment that though different from Halakha is nevertheless of a piece with it and fully imperative.'' No, the ''ethical moment'' that is ''nevertheless of a piece with'' Halakhah is ''fully imperative'' only ''in its own way.'' Just what is that distinctive way? And what are its implications? These questions will be critical to a mind sensitized by general ethics, now seeking to understand how ethics functions within Rabbinic Judaism.

Let us now retrace Lichtenstein's argument insofar as this

[159]

will help us see his answer to these questions. Much of his paper deals with the sort of imperative involved in acting *lifnim mishurat hadin*. Lichtenstein is at pains to point out that this "is no mere option." It has "obligatory character" as shown by the verses Nahmanides uses to ground his argument about it.[8] Obviously, were this matter merely optional, it would not have any serious ethical standing. That it is "obligatory" would seem as good as guaranteed by its being part of the Oral Torah, God's revelation not being a matter of mere play. Our question, however, is just what sort of obligation is involved.

The matter is not settled, as Steven S. Schwarzschild believes, by the term itself. He writes: *lifnim mishurat hadin* is 'within,' not as the usual rendering has it, 'beyond,' the line of the law; i.e., the very term indicates that we are here dealing with a dynamic function that operates within the system."[9] As I see it, Schwarzschild confuses the meaning of the term *din* here. The reference is to the particular legal right which one could now exercise. One is rather directed to restrict one's right in this particular case and not do that which one might otherwise properly do under the law. He correctly reads *lifnim* as "within," that is, not at the limit of what one might do. But that differs from the issue here: the status of this precept as a whole. Does it itself come to us as part of the law, the *din*, or is it in another category (though admittedly part of Rabbinic Judaism and "in its own way fully imperative")? If the reference of the term *din* was the whole legal system and not the specific *din* at issue in this instance, the phrase and its effect would be contradictory. One would be enjoined to act legally—*lifnim mishurat hadin* read as "stay [well] within legal limits"—and yet be told not to do what the law clearly entitles one to do. Lichtenstein apparently does not consider this the meaning of the phrase, and this explains why he struggles to show the imperative nature of the injunction.

To continue, Lichtenstein notes: "With respect to the *degree of obligation*, however, *rishonim* admittedly held different views" (emphasis added).[10] Apparently, only Rabbi Isaac of Corbeille considered it to have the full "degree of obligation." He alone lists the need to act *lifnim mishurat hadin* as one of the 613 commandments. We can understand the issue of degree better if we attend to Lichtenstein's succeeding sentences: "Nahmanides did not go quite this far, as he does not classify *lifnim mishurat hadin* as an independent *mitzvah*, as binding as *shofar* or *tefillin*. However, he does clearly posit it as a normative duty, incumbent upon— and expected of—every Jew as part of his basic obligation."[11]

The treatment of Maimonides' position which then follows is of interest to us, despite the difficulty in giving a consistent interpretation of his position, only because he posits a somewhat different degree of obligation. Depending upon one's interpretation, Maimonides proclaims either a higher or lower level of responsibility than does Nahmanides, but in either case not as strong as that of Rabbi Isaac.[12] Regardless of the interpretation, Lichtenstein is satisfied that a "supralegal ethic" exists within Rabbinic Judaism. What remains unclear is the precise status of the "supralegal," that is, the specific way in which it is "supra" or, alternatively, just how much authority it has and how it is brought to bear upon the full legal requirements of Judaism.

Lichtenstein approaches this issue by inquiring whether *lifnim mishurat hadin* is actionable.[13] He notes that while the Rosh, and therefore probably the whole Spanish school, did not consider it actionable, some Tosafists held such action "could indeed be compelled."[14] He then immediately sets the necessary limits to what might otherwise lead to a gross antinomianism: "Of course, such a position could not conceivably be held with reference to all supralegal behavior. *Din* has many ethical levels; and so, of necessity, must *lifnim mishurat hadin*. Surpassing laws grounded in, say, the concept that 'the Torah has but spoken vis-à-vis the evil inclination' is hardly comparable to transcending those with a powerful moral thrust." This retraction, however, does not lose his point, for he concludes: "Nevertheless, the fact that some *rishonim* held *lifnim mishurat hadin* to be, in principle, actionable, indicates the extent to which it is part of the fabric of Halakha."[15] For our purposes, the very division of opinion and the need to qualify such opinion as coercive indicates that there remains a considerable question about just where this "ethical moment" stands within the Halakhah. And we shall not know very much about its actual ethical status until we know a good deal more about the already qualified way in which it is "fully imperative."

Once again Lichtenstein enables us to clarify an interpretation of Steven S. Schwarzschild's. Citing Hermann Cohen to substantiate philosophically his interpretation of *lifnim mishurat hadin*, Schwarzschild writes, "Equity is not a factor additional to the *jus strictum*, but a judgment-procedure which makes sure that the application of the law in each individual case is proper (i.e., moral); thus all of the law, statutes as well as the procedures, operationalizes ethical values (*aggadah*)."[16] Schwarzschild wants us to consider *lifnim mishurat hadin* as part of *din* and, for Cohenian reasons, necessarily so.

The facts, as Lichtenstein makes plain, are otherwise. Most Jewish authorities do not consider the need to act in this ethical fashion a *din*. And Lichtenstein indicates why. A law, or *din*, which directs one to override the law (for significant ethical reasons) might soon destroy the fabric of the law as a whole and reduce it to morality. As commendable as that might be, Judaism has classically been a religion where morality takes the form of law, not one where moral law effectively dominates the Torah's precepts. Of course, in an ideal Kantian legal system, morality and law would be identical. Cohen has in mind just such a rational ideal. Perhaps Schwarzschild means to argue that in Jewish law an inner essence makes itself seen which corresponds to the ethical ideal and slowly works its way out into reality. In that case, in addition to validating philosophically the notion of essence or ideal, he will have to deal with all the contrary historical data, in this instance, as forthrightly detailed by Lichtenstein. Until then, the famous gap between "religion of reason" and "the sources of Judaism" will continue to loom before the eyes of many contemporary students of the Jewish tradition.

Lichtenstein extends his argument by associating *kofin al midat Sodom* with *lifnim mishurat hadin*, particularly by way of a striking excerpt from the Maharal. He then asks a double question which closely approximates the issue I have been calling attention to: "If *lifnim mishurat hadin* is indeed obligatory as an integral aspect of Halakha, in what sense is it supralegal? More specifically, on the Ravya's view, *what distinguishes its compulsory elements from* din *proper?*" (emphasis added).[17]

He eventually answers his questions, thus apparently telling us what he means later by the ethical moment being "in its own way fully imperative." "It is less rigorous not only in the sense of being less exacting with respect to the degree and force of obligation—and there are times, as has been noted, when it can be equally demanding—but in the sense of being more flexible, its duty more readily definable in light of the existence of particular circumstances." To the average reader, I should think, that provides so many loopholes that it seems to indicate a far less significant sort of imperative. For that reason, I take it, Lichtenstein immediately continues: "This has nothing to do with the force of obligation," though he said the opposite in the prior sentence. And: "Once it has been determined that, in a given case, realization of 'the right and the good' mandates a particular course, its pursuit may conceivably be as imperative as the performance of a *din*."[18] To me that seems to indicate that though the ethical impulse is there, it has much less imperative status than the *din*. It is explicitly termed "less rigorous." Moreover, it only gains "the full force of obligation . . . once it has been determined" that an ethical issue is involved. This determination is not a matter left to the general conscience, but is assigned to competent decisors and permitted to function by them in only a limited number of cases.

Because of this administrative structure, we note that Lichtenstein cannot say more than that, when operational, "its pursuit *may conceivably* be as imperative as the performance of a *din*" (emphasis added).[19]

In a later discussion he indicates that this is the case, for

[163]

he can summarize the dialectic between formalist *din* and contextualist *lifnim mishurat hadin* as follows: "Quite apart from the severity of obligation, therefore, there is a fundamental difference between *din* and *lifnim mishurat hadin*. One, as a more minimal level, imposes fixed objective standards. The demands of the other evolve from a specific situation; and, depending on the circumstances, may vary with the agent."[20]

I do not think anything further in Lichtenstein's paper impinges upon the issue at hand.

Perhaps it will help us to expand a bit the way in which the "ethical moment" in Rabbinic Judaism makes itself felt. It surely is not confined to the notion of *lifnim mishurat hadin*, though this theme constitutes a particularly interesting and even dramatic instance of it. There are a number of other rubrics under which the rabbis act in order to extend or amplify what the *din* requires, so that one may more clearly do that which is "good and right." Joseph Hertz, in *The Main Institutions of Jewish Law*, lists a number of these.[21]

In a recent article, J. David Bleich gives a striking instance of the different levels of rabbinic injunction to action. The case will set into bolder relief the problem of the varying levels of authority within Rabbinic Judaism. Bleich notes that Rashi considers Num. 33:53 merely God's prudent advice to the Jewish people about how they should go about conquering the land.[22] Nahmanides, on the other hand, considers the verse a positive commandment. Maimonides, however, is understood by Bleich as essentiallly agreeing with Rashi.[23] I do not think that Bleich is suggesting that Maimonides considers the advice to Jews about settling on the land of Israel "merely optional," to return to Lichtenstein's formulation. Rather, Bleich here resolves the issue of the "degree of obligation" by invoking the notion of merit, *zekhut*. That is, he suggests that Maimonides believes that while there is no law requiring one to immigrate to the land of Israel, he follows abundant rabbinic teaching in holding that to do so brings one great reward.

The sages often sought to get people to behave ethically

[164]

not as a matter of full legal prescription, but by suggesting that certain acts, while not required, were highly meritorious. These exhortations, too, are part of God's Oral Torah and, therefore, in some sense not "merely optional." But I do not know whether Lichtenstein would consider them within his category of being fully imperative though only in their own way. Bleich does not help us further with this issue, for he notes that "this issue of merit, as distinct from compensation of fulfillment of a Divine commandment, is difficult to elucidate."[24] Again, let me suggest that we shall not properly understand the place of the ethical within Rabbinic Judaism until we clarify the weight of ethical obligations encompassed by such nonlegal rabbinic injunctions to action as that of zekhut, particularly because they so often are used in relation to ethical concerns.

The introduction of the notion of merit, however, has taken us away from Lichtenstein's purpose. While he would not deprecate preaching, education, model-setting, and the like as rabbinically desirable, he recognized that the key issue in this discussion was showing that its proper form was not the relation between a required law and an optional ethics. That would not only fly in the face of the facts as he sees them, but could not suffice as an adequate defense of the ethical impulse in Rabbinic Judaism. With commandment the dominant Jewish religious sense, an ethics that was less than required would hardly have much Jewish status. Then, too, ever since the time of Kant, an ethics which does not take the form of law has hardly seemed to most Jewish thinkers an ethics at all.[25] (I would add that though ethics does not take the form of law in Buber, by being God's own behest it is clearly "fully imperative.") Lichtenstein, therefore, took great pains to show that the ethical thrust in Rabbinic Judaism was a species of command.

The result of Lichtenstein's discussion, however, leaves me, and, I would judge, some considerable portion of the Jewish community, troubled by the balance between the law and its supralegal ethical imperative. The disparity between the different levels of authority restricts the operation of conscience in a way that seems to us unacceptable. No one questions the commanding quality of the law. The ethical normally operates on a different, secondary level, with its degree of obligation not clearly known. The law is authoritative unless occasionally supervened. The ethical must make a case for itself should there be a conflict between them. Even then its legitimacy and functioning will be defined by the legists. The law is clear, with much precedent and institutionalized patterns of procedure. The supralegal functions in a hazy area, with few guidelines as to its proper application and handicapped by needing to make its way against the well-entrenched patterns of community practice, the law.

All this is not astonishing for a legal system. Rather, an open-minded student would probably show great admiration for the Jewish community in creating a legal structure which is so highly ethical. But to one who takes seriously the obligatory character of ethics—whether understood in the Kantian sense of law or the Buberian–Rosenzweigian and perhaps Heschelian sense of personal response to God—a major problem arises. The ethical, which ought to come as a categorical or unmediated imperative, operates within Judaism in a quite qualified, mediated way. A substantial difference exists between a system of action in which ethics is commandingly primary and one in which, though it remains imperative, it can often be a subsidiary consideration. The matter is not merely one for academics to ponder as the continuing agitation over the classic issues of *agunah* and *mamzerut* makes clear.

With some hesitation, permit me to suggest that in claiming a pattern of subsidiary but still "fully imperative" ethics, we seem to contradict our polemical argument against Christianity. Jews have charged that by subordinating works to faith, Christianity seriously compromises the impulse to righteous action.[26] Does not, in the argument we have considered, Judaism do something similar, if not to works of law, then to its own ethical moment?

Let us take the issue presently disturbing a good portion of the Jewish community, the status of Jewish women. Two major lines of thought on this issue seem to emerge. The one finds ethical reason within Rabbinic Judaism for recognizing a problem with the present formulation of the *din* with regard to women, as well as the expectations contained in contemporary Jewish practice. Based on much internal conflict, various authorities seek remedies within the law. On the whole, the more traditionally inclined interpreters who see the problem, though recognizing the ethical need to seek solutions, find that little remedial action can be taken. That is, though the ethical moment has here made itself felt within the system, it is of such limited power in the face of law and precedent that it has no supra-legal effectiveness. Such reasoning has brought some Conservative Jewish legists to challenge this classic balance between law and ethics in Judaism. In this instance, they wish to make the ethical thrust of women's equality in Judaism "fully imperative" and not allow it to function in so qualified a fashion as to rob it of any ability to shape community action. For them, the ethical issue is so categorically felt as to require the vaunted flexibility inherent in Halakhah to operate and accomplish an ethical revision of existing law and practice.[27] They believe, as do many in the Jewish community, that the gap between ethics and law must now be bridged so as to make our understanding of our obligations under the Torah worthy of being called the service of God.

The other line of thought illumines our difficulty even more clearly. Some authorities deny that there is a women's ethical problem at all. That God ordained a different scope of obligation for Jewish men and women is not at all contravened by notions such as God creating humankind equally as male and female, or bestowing these creatures with dignity. The diverse yet allegedly unequal categories of commandment are so well established in Torah teaching that these authorities do not even see an issue. No possibility of an "ethical moment" arises for them. They claim that the so-called ethical impulse behind the women's issue is a Gentile importation into Judaism. Had it not been for the influence of non-Jews, they charge, we

[167]

would not be concerned about this question.

Historically, I think, this judgment is correct. I cannot in this paper seek to determine whether, though the issue was raised by non-Jews, the fresh reading of the rabbinic tradition prompted by them proves that women's equality was all along present in the Torah or whether substantial Jewish basis exists for moving toward it. What we can usefully do here is to inquire about our attitude toward ethics.

The broader theoretical issue concerns the status of non-Torah ethics. Is all that Jews can call ethical fundamentally given in the Torah, or may we ever gain significant ethical insight from Gentiles? Factually, we American Jews should acknowledge that the Gentile notion of universalism and common humanity has reminded us of the Torah's teaching that there is, in fact, but one human family—though some in the Jewish community would as good as say that, although Gentiles remain God's children, they are by God's will inferior to Jews. The issue of democracy takes us a step further. This extraordinary notion, with its corollaries of pluralism and tolerance, did not arise within Rabbinic Judaism. We have yet to hear a good theological argument, as against a pragmatic case, being made within the terms of Rabbinic Judaism to endorse, much less to mandate, the practice of democracy. And this matter would immediately leave the hypothetical realm should the Orthodox parties of the State of Israel come to power.

The more restricted, communal issue concerns the present balance between *din* and the ethical moment within Rabbinic Judaism. To many Jews today, the Torah's ethical behests come with such imperative quality that they can consider them properly heard only when they are accepted categorically. To qualify their functioning as substantially as do the spokesmen of contemporary Rabbinic Judaism cannot be seen by them as other than less than what God now demands of the people of Israel. They therefore cannot consider Rabbinic Judaism, as presently interpreted, God's will for the people of God's covenant.[28]

To be sure, on a vulgar level, almost all human beings prefer personal convenience to heavy responsibility. But not being tainted by original sin, they also have a strong sense of what is good and just. Though it has been difficult to call their attention to it and more difficult to get them to live up to it, many people have acknowledged that slavery is unethical and racial discrimination is immoral. In a similar ethical way they came to realize that keeping Jews from equal rights was unjust. And most Jews who have modernized agree that any proper contemporary sense of the good ought to emphasize the equality of all human beings and, in the present case, to give women the status and opportunities hitherto available only to men. The matter is so compellingly clear to these Jews today—as other matters were in recent generations—that if this impulse cannot function supralegally, that is, to change Jewish law, they will find it necessary, for all their Jewish devotion, to function extralegally.

One reason that they will do so is that they feel they have a more satisfactory understanding of Rabbinic Judaism than it offers of itself. Watching it struggle to confront ethical issues and not be able to move very quickly to resolve them, they do not see it as God's own institution, albeit a human one, for mediating the divine will. Rather, it discloses to them the same traits they find everywhere in thoroughly human institutions. It is regularly more concerned with form than with content, with precedent than present need, with regulations than with persons, with what authorities and peers will say than with what, as best we can tell directly, God wants of us now.

In a prior generation, some such belief caused many serious-minded Jews to make general ethics, rather than Torah, the law by which they lived. Even those of us who know that the universalistic path is unreliable without the corrective guidance of Torah are not willing to forsake the way of ethics entirely for a Rabbinic Judaism which, by construing its ethical concerns as it does, appears to us to vitiate them substantially.

[169]

Notes

1. See my "Rethinking the Reform Jewish Theory of Social Action," *Journal of Reform Judaism*, Fall 1980.
2. Aharon Lichtenstein, "Does Jewish Tradition Recognize an Ethic Independent of Halakha?" in *Modern Jewish Ethics*, ed. Marvin Fox (Ohio State University Press, 1975).
3. "Can a Religious Law be Immoral?" in *Perspectives on Jews and Judaism*, ed. Arthur A. Chiel (Rabbinical Assembly, New York, 1978).
4. For two recent discussions, see Isadore Twersky, *Introduction to the Code of Maimonides* (Princeton, N.J., 1980), pp. 454ff. and Lawrence V. Berman, "Maimonides on the Fall of Man," *AJS Review* V (1980), 3, note 6.
5. Lichtenstein, "Jewish Tradition," pp. 82–83.
6. In his remarks to the December 1980 meeting of the Association of Jewish Studies, J. David Bleich argued in a somewhat similar linguistic fashion. I am grateful to him for allowing my student, Mr. Marc Gruber, to tape his remarks.
7. Lichtenstein, "Jewish Tradition," p. 83.
8. Ibid., p. 71.
9. Steven S. Schwarzschild, "The Question of Jewish Ethics Today," *Sh'ma*, 7/124, p. 31.
10. Lichtenstein, "Jewish Tradition," p. 71.
11. Ibid.
12. Ibid., pp. 71–74.
13. Ibid., p. 74.
14. Ibid.
15. Ibid., p. 75.
16. Schwarzschild, "The Question of Jewish Ethics," p. 31.
17. Lichtenstein, "Jewish Tradition," p. 76.
18. Ibid., p. 77.
19. Ibid.
20. Ibid., p. 79.
21. Joseph Hertz, *The Main Institutions of Jewish Law* (Soncino Press, 1936), vol. I, pp. 379–86.
22. "Judea and Samaria: Settlement and Return," *Tradition* 18:1 (1979), 48.
23. Ibid., p. 50.
24. Ibid.
25. See, for example, the criticisms of Martin Buber by thinkers as diverse as Marvin Fox and Emil Fackenheim in *The Philosophy of Martin Buber*, ed. Schilpp and Friedman (Open Court, 1967).
26. For a recent discussion, see my *Contemporary Christologies, a Jewish response* (Paulist Press, 1980), pp. 127–29; 133–34.
27. See the bold, general statement by Seymour Siegel in "Theology for Today," *Conservative Judaism* XXVIII, no. 4 (1974), 47–48. He had previously asserted these views in "Ethics and the Halakhah," *Conservative Judaism* XXV, no. 3 (1971), and projects them as part of the ideology of Conservative Judaism in his anthology *Conservative*

Judaism and Jewish Law (Rabbinical Assembly, New York, 1977), p. xxiiif. Since then this position has come under increasing attack from the Conservative right-wing as a result of which Siegel was ousted from his position as chairman of the prestigious Rabbinical Assembly Commission on Law and Standards.

28. I have dealt with the liberal Jewish affirmation of personal autonomy despite an increased regard for the guidance of Jewish tradition in chapter 11 of my *Modern Theories of Judaism* (Behrman House), forthcoming. A fuller statement of my views of the proper process of liberal Jewish decision-making will be found in my paper, "The Demands of the Autonomous Jewish Self," soon to appear in a collection of conference papers sponsored by the National Jewish Resource Center and the Center for Judaic Studies of the University of Denver.

THE MAIMONIDEAN MATRIX OF RABBI JOSEPH B. SOLOVEITCHIK'S TWO-TIERED ETHICS
Walter S. Wurzburger

Rabbi Soloveitchik's philosophy revolves around the primacy of the Halakhah. Because Halakhah figures as the revealed will of God, all other considerations are subordinated to its dictates. This approach to Halakhah is typical of Orthodox thinkers. But for Rabbi Soloveitchik, Halakhah's role is not limited to providing evaluative standards; instead, it functions as the matrix of his entire philosophy.

One may, therefore, seriously question whether one is at all justified in employing the term "ethical" within the context of such a thoroughly theocentric system, where the property of being commanded by God is the only relevant criterion for determining the validity of any norm. After all, *Chukim*, positive laws obeyed solely on the basis of their being commanded by God, enjoy no less authority than so-called ethical laws, which, apart from the authority deriving from their being commanded by God, can also be buttressed by appeals to reason, conscience, or moral sentiment. But since in such a monistic system the property of being commanded by God is both a necessary and sufficient condition of normative significance, one is hard-pressed to assign any real significance to the ethical qua ethical.

To complicate matters even further, Rabbi Soloveitchik displays a somewhat ambivalent attitude toward secular ethics. Occasionally, he points to the development of ethical norms as a legitimate manifestation of human creativity, which itself forms an integral part of the human quest to impose order upon the raw data of our experience, in keeping with the divine mandate "to conquer the universe."[1] At other times, however, he calls attention to our inability to ground ethics in reason.[2] In his view, any attempt to establish a purely secular ethics is doomed to failure. It is, however, not quite clear whether in his opinion, the failure of secular ethics is due to its inability to provide the kind of incentives and motives for ethical conduct which religion can supply; or to the intrinsic limitations of secular ethics which preclude the construction of an adequate system; or to the one-sidedness of a success-oriented secular ethics that fails to account for the dimension of the "ethics of humility," which, according to Rabbi Soloveitchik, represents one of the indispensable components of morality.

The ambivalence encountered in Rabbi Soloveitchik's thought can in large measure be attributed to the fact that the various components of his "system" are not in a state of equilibrium, but in constant dialectical tension. Because he is willing to reconcile himself to the irreducibility of this tension, he is under no pressure to force disparate experiential data into a procrustean bed for the sake of forming a neat and coherent system. Instead, he unabashedly advocates a pluralistic, multi-tiered ethics, eschewing the pitfalls of a reductionist approach, which in the interests of neatness and economy glosses over the disparities and incongruities that abound in the human condition.

The emphasis upon the irreducibility of dialectical tensions, which are grounded not in socio-cultural factors but in the very nature of the human condition, permeates not only Rabbi Soloveitchik's ethics, but all facets of his philosophy. To resort to the typology of "The Lonely Man of Faith,"[3] Adam I and Adam II represent two disparate components of human nature which account for the dialectical tension within man. Reflecting the distinctive features assigned to them in the respective chapters of Genesis, Adam I, as portrayed in Genesis, chapter 1, creatively utilizes his reason and imagination to subdue the forces of nature and harness them to his purposes. Adam I engages in

[173]

the process of "filling the earth and conquering it" in order to realize his potential as a creature bearing the image of God, the Creator. By exercising dominion over the forces of nature, man not only asserts his dignity but responds to the mandate of becoming a co-creator with God, who relegated to man the task of helping perfect the universe.

In striking contrast with the Promethean myth, which disparages human creativity as an arrogant intrusion upon the divine realm, the Bible encourages man to employ his rational faculties to mold his environment in accordance with his needs. In the biblical conception, man is not intended to be a passive victim of circumstances or conditions. The function assigned to him in the divine economy is to achieve majesty by dint of his skill, resourcefulness, and creativity. Hence, science and technology reflect not human hubris, the improper arrogation of powers reserved for a higher being, but the fulfillment of a divine imperative mandating "conquest" of the natural universe.

But there is another facet of human nature where scientific triumphs or technological accomplishments play no role whatsoever. Success in manipulating the universe cannot assuage the existential loneliness of Adam II, who even under the idyllic conditions enjoyed in the Garden of Eden must come to grips with the fact that "it is not good for man to be alone" (Gen. 2:18). But in the final analysis, it is only through formation of a covenantal community with God that Adam II's sense of isolation can be overcome. Unlike Adam I, who seeks dignity through control over his environment, Adam II yearns for redemption through self-surrender and self-sacrifice.[4]

Halakhah, in Rabbi Soloveitchik's opinion, recognizes the legitimacy of the two separate domains.[5] Since the dialectical tension between Adam I and Adam II is inevitable, Halakhah makes no attempt to resolve it, but seeks to provide a normative framework designed to make man function as a citizen of two worlds—the majestic as well as the covenantal community.

Similar considerations rule out the construction of any homogeneous ethics that would accommodate the re-

[174]

quirements of the disparate components of human nature. In Rabbi Soloveitchik's opinion, in order to be adequate, ethics must involve continuous oscillation between the ethics of victory and the ethics of defeat.[6] Purely rationalistic ethics as formulated by Kant or Hermann Cohen is marred by one-sidedness. While taking account of the human quest to impose rational structure upon the world of experience, it is totally oblivious of those dimensions of the human personality that strive not for autonomy, mastery, and control, but for redemption through self-sacrifice.

In the light of Rabbi Soloveitchik's ethical doctrines as set forth in his recently published "Majesty and Humility,"[7] we must reject Professor Lawrence Kaplan's thesis that, according to Rabbi Soloveitchik, only ritual *mitzvot* qualify as sacrificial acts which, because they are performed in humble submissiveness to an incomprehensible divine will, involve the covenantal community.[8] Ethical *mitzvot*, on the other hand, supposedly address themselves exclusively to man qua member of the majestic community, since ethical norms express the majestic human quest to impose rational order upon conduct. But such a sharp line of demarcation between the ethical and the ritual spheres can hardly be maintained on the basis of the opinions expressed by Rabbi Soloveitchik in his "Majesty and Humility." As the very term ethics of defeat suggests, the need for humble submission to an unfathomable divine will characterizes not only the ritual sphere, but applies to the ethical sphere as well.

In fairness to Professor Kaplan, it should, however, be pointed out that he offered his interpretation of Rabbi Soloveitchik's doctrine long before the appearance of "Majesty and Humility," which in our opinion is so crucial for an understanding of the latter's position. We must also concede to Professor Kaplan that the specific illustrations provided for his ethics of humility in the essay "Majesty and Humility" really involve *Chukim*, ritual laws, not ethical requirements. But Rabbi Soloveitchik's repeated emphasis upon the inadequacies of a one-sided, success-oriented ethics further confirms our opinion that for Rabbi Soloveitchik the ethical domain involves both the majestic and the covenantal communities.

It has been suggested that Rabbi Soloveitchik's conception of the dialectical tension arising from man's ontological status mirrors the tensions between the neo-Kantian (Adam I) and the existentialist strands (Adam II) of his thought. In Professor Kaplan's view, the emphasis upon human creativity which predominates in the "Ish Hahalakhah"[9] and which characterizes the typology of Adam I can be traced back to the impact of Hermann Cohen's neo-Kantianism.[10] The influence of existentialist thinkers, on the other hand, supposedly makes itself felt in his Adam II, who, à la Kierkegaard, surrenders in a spirit of sacrificial submission to an unfathomable divine will. Professor Kaplan contends that a gradual shift can be detected in Rabbi Soloveitchik's thought, with existentialist elements acquiring increasing prominence.[11]

Actually, this is a misconception that has arisen largely because of historical accidents relating to the publication of Rabbi Soloveitchik's writings. For many years, "Ish Hahalakhah" was his only major contribution to religious philosophy that was accessible to the general public.[12] Moreover, without the balance provided by some of his later writings, the thrust of his thought lent itself to misunderstanding. Regrettably, some interpreters were not aware that an early draft of his existentialist "Ubikashtem Misham" was already completed by the time "Ish Hahalakhah" had made its first appearance.[13] Small wonder, then, that in many circles the impression prevailed that Rabbi Soloveitchik's description of Halakhah as a discipline calling for the exercise of activity, spontaneity, and innovativeness, rather than blind submission to the divine will, betrayed the influence of Hermann Cohen, to whom the "given" was merely a question posed to the human mind.

Similarly, Rabbi Soloveitchik's enthusiasm for science and technology was seen as evidence of Hermann Cohen's influence, especially since Rabbi Soloveitchik's views on this issue diverge so much from those prevailing in his early environment. To cite a telling example: from the premise that man is mandated to emulate his Creator, he draws conclusions which have little in common with those inferred by his ancestor, Rabbi Chaim of Volozin. The latter, employing Kabbalistic categories, was concerned with an entirely different sort of creativity. For him, the study of the Torah and the performance of *mitzvot* were deemed creative acts because, in keeping with the doctrine that "stirrings below precede stirrings above," they initiate chain reactions extending to the highest reaches of being. Human creativity manifested itself in the creation of spiritual values which affect the relationship of God to His world and are instrumental in helping bring about the reunification of the Holy One Blessed Be He and His Shekhinah.[14] When human creativity is interpreted in such pietistic fashion, it obviously cannot provide religious justification for science and technology. What mattered to Rabbi Chaim was not the empirically observable consequences of human actions, but their supernatural repercussions.

In contradistinction to this approach, which even nowadays permeates the "yeshivah world" and results in total indifference to scientific pursuits, Rabbi Soloveitchik extols the merits of whatever activities enlarge the human capacity to exercise control over the environment and to achieve the dignity due to man as the bearer of the image of God.[15] Science and technology no longer are dismissed as purely secular enterprises. They are cherished as invaluable instruments facilitating the religious quest of imitating the creative "ways" of the Creator.

There can be no doubt that this openness to science represents a major shift from the ethos and value system of Eastern European Orthodoxy. But we must not jump to the conclusion that this transformation was due to the influence of Hermann Cohen. Perusal of the "Ubikashtem Misham" clearly reveals that Maimonides (especially in relation to the apparent conflict between the first and second chapters of *Hilkhot Deot*), rather than Cohen, provided the matrix for the development of Rabbi Soloveitchik's philosophy. In this context, it should also be borne in mind that, as Aharon Lichtenstein has pointed out, Rabbi Soloveitchik

[177]

had originally planned to submit a dissertation on Maimonides, not on Hermann Cohen.[16] Rabbi Soloveitchik was forced, however, to abandon the project because no member of the Philosophy Department in Berlin possessed sufficient expertise to supervise such a thesis.

It must, however, be admitted that some aspects of Rabbi Soloveitchik's own highly original approach to Maimonides, which in turn provides the basic foundation of his entire religious philosophy, can in some measure be traced back to Cohen's insistence upon the predominance of Platonic elements in Maimonidean ethics.[17] Rabbi Soloveitchik subscribes to Cohen's basic premise that, notwithstanding the prevalence of Aristotelian notions and categories in his ethics, Maimonides could not accept the basic premises of Aristotle, which relegated ethics to an inferior branch of knowledge. In the Aristotelian scheme, ethics figured as a prelude to politics. As a low-grade science, its function was to provide practical guidelines, useful for the attainment of personal or communal well being, but unworthy of the high status commanded by a theoretical science. But for Maimonides, ethics transcends teleological or eudaemonistic considerations. Acquistion of virtue is not merely a prudential requirement, but a religious obligation (in other words, *imitatio Dei*).[18] Moreover, the concluding chapter of Maimonides' *Guide of the Perplexed* treats moral virtue not merely as a means to an end, that is, knowledge of God, but as an integral part of the *summum bonum*.[19]

Although Rabbi Soloveitchik agrees with many features of Cohen's approach, there are vital differences. Of special importance are their divergent views concerning "middle road" ethics. Cohen had contended that only the ethics of the pious really qualified as genuine religious ideals. Whatever features of the Aristotelian golden mean Maimonides had incorporated into his *Hilkhot Deot* were dismissed as totally incompatible with the ethico-religious ideals that reflect the ultimate thrust of Maimonides.

In Cohen's view, the standards contained in the ethics of the wise are merely counsels of prudence which fail to satisfy the higher requirements of a religious ethics based upon *imitatio Dei*. Hence, according to Cohen, there are strata of Maimonidean ethics which are mere "survivals" of a prudential ethics; they should be overcome and transcended in the quest for religious ideals.

Rabbi Soloveitchik categorically rejects this doctrine. He shares Shimon Rawidowicz's view that the middle road cannot be dismissed as the intrusion of Greek elements upon biblical morality,[20] especially since Maimonides explicitly mentions the middle road as one of the features included in "Walking in His Ways."[21]

The ethics of the wise, not merely the ethics of the pious, constitutes *imitatio Dei*, because for Maimonides it is indispensable to *Yishuv Haolam*, the settlement of the world. Cultivation of traits of character that are required for the proper functioning of society ceases to be merely a prudential dictate of social utility. It is transformed into a religious imperative which is based upon the obligation to pattern ourselves after the model of the Creator. In keeping with this interpretation, Maimonides allows no dichotomy between a religious and supposedly secular (Aristotelian) ethics. Rather, there are two separate strands of religious ethics which are in a state of dialectical tension. If my thesis is correct, it can be put schematically: the ethics of the wise represents *imitatio Dei* on the part of Adam I (the majestic community), whereas the ethics of the pious reflects the quest for redemption through self-sacrifice characterizing Adam II (the covenantal community). But, according to Rabbi Soloveitchik, both ethics seek to appropriate divine moral attributes. Adam I emulates divine creativity. Through his acts of renunciation and withdrawal, Adam II imitates the divine *Tzimtzum*, self-contraction, which Kabbalistic doctrine regards as the precondition of the act of Creation.[22] Significantly, Maimonides, in chapter 2 of *Hilkhot Deot*, advocates extremism rather than the middle road precisely in those areas that come under the purview of the ethics of humility.

To be sure, it is no simple task to satisfy the claims of two distinct levels of ethics which at times confront us with conflicting demands. But it should be realized that even without the superimposition of an ethics of the pious, the ethics of the wise would still be plagued with all sorts of moral ambiguities and dilemmas. There is no formal principle that can be invoked to determine the precise nature of the golden mean. Aristotle already noted that guidance on matters pertaining to virtue can be provided only by the experience of individuals who excel in practical wisdom.[23] What renders the task of determining the requirements of the middle road even more difficult in the Maimonidean system is the fact that for him the conception of the middle road is dynamic rather than static. Whereas for Aristotle the golden mean is patterned after the Greek ideal of balance attained in a state of equilibrium, the Maimonidean religious ideal of the middle road reflects creative tension arising from oscillation between polar values.[24] Maimonides, like Aristotle, was unable to furnish a satisfactory definition of the desirable traits of character. It is only through the imitation of the proper model, the Torah scholar, that we can develop the intuitive faculties needed for the formation of proper ethical judgments.[25]

To be sure, the addition of another tier (in other words, the ethics of the pious) to the structure of morality further exacerbates the difficulties. If decision-making at the level of the ethics of the wise is beset by problems, they become compounded when we must wrestle with the additional question whether, in a given existential situation, we should invoke the standards of the ethics of the wise or those of the ethics of the pious. But these added difficulties amount merely to differences of degree, not of kind. As we have noted previously, because it must accommodate numerous conflicting values, the entire ethical domain is replete with moral ambiguities and dilemmas. Unfortunate though this may be, there is no magic formula that can be applied to settle conflicting ethical claims.

Our analysis so far has proceeded on the assumption that Rabbi Soloveitchik's ethics of majesty (Adam I) is the equivalent of Maimonides' ethics of the wise, while the ethics of humility (Adam II) is the counterpart of the ethics of the pious. But it must be admitted that for all their plausibility, these assumptions are beset by serious difficulties, inasmuch as Rabbi Soloveitchik maintains that the dialectical tension between Adam I and Adam II is at least in principle capable of resolution. Extraordinary individuals, such as the Patriarchs, find it possible to live simultaneously in the majestic and redemptive communities.[26] But it is difficult to envisage even the theoretical possibility of acting simultaneously in accordance with the requirements of both the ethics of the pious and the ethics of the wise since, by definition, the ways of the pious deviate from the middle road.

Notwithstanding the seriousness of this problem, there is no question that Rabbi Soloveitchik totally disagrees with the thesis of Hermann Cohen and Steven Schwarzschild, who reduce the ethics of the wise to a second-class ethics, which is intended merely as a stepping-stone to the higher plateau of the ethics of the pious.[27] According to Rabbi Soloveitchik, the dialectical tension between the two indispensable elements of religious ethics, both of which reflect polar phases of *imitatio Dei*, does not disappear even in the ideal situation.

To be sure, in any given situation we cannot be certain whether we should act in accordance with the standards of the ethics of the wise or those of the ethics of the pious. But uncertainty and ambiguity characterize the entire ethical domain. There are numerous instances when conflicting moral claims leave us no alternative but to rely on our admittedly exceedingly fallible intuitions for guidance in ethical decision-making.

There is a corollary of our analysis with important ramifications for contemporary moral issues. Since, according to our interpretation of Rabbi Soloveitchik's ethics, the dialectical tension between the two types of ethics is inherent in the human condition itself, the ethics of the wise can never be totally transcended. Hence, Rabbi Soloveitchik is bound to reject the utopian, messianic ethics of Hermann Cohen, which contributed so much to the latter's utter disdain for Zionism. Professor Schwarzschild, following in the footsteps of Hermann Cohen, went so far as to identify Maimonides' ethics of the pious with messianic ethics which, in his opinion, ideally should totally supersede the ethics of the middle road.[28] This messianic perspective accounts for Professor Schwarzschild's aversion to the "militarism" of the State of Israel, which obviously does not conform to his standards of a utopian, messianic ethics.

Fortunately, Rabbi Soloveitchik's ethics is far more realistic. He would oppose any form of pacifism that would deny the legitimacy of Israel's policies to secure survival, if necessary, through reliance on military means. In his view, it would hardly make sense to apply to an unredeemed world the kind of moral norms that are suited to a perfect, redeemed world. Nonresistance to evil, be it on the individual or the collective level, can hardly qualify as a moral desideratum. To invite the liquidation of the State of Israel through the advocacy of a radical, utopian ethics would be utterly incompatible with the requirements of an ethics that mandates continuous oscillation between the claims of majesty and humility.

To be sure, even for Rabbi Soloveitchik, the messianic doctrine is not just an eschatological article of faith, but possesses ethical significance.[29] It is the matrix of the ethical postulate to strive for everything possible to help bring about the realization of the messianic goal. But this kind of messianism has nothing in common with utopian ethics. It rather reflects the realism of a Maimonides, according to whom the need for a state will not wither away completely even in the messianic era.[30] Not the abolition of power but its exercise in accordance with ideals of the Torah is the ultimate objective of the ethico-religious thrust of halakhic Judaism.

Notes

1. Joseph B. Soloveitchik, "The Lonely Man of Faith," *Tradition*, Summer 1965, p. 15; idem, "Majesty and Humility," *Tradition*, Spring 1978, pp. 34–35.

2. Soloveitchik, "Ubikashtem Misham," *Hadarom*, Tishri 5739, pp. 25-26; Joseph Epstein, ed., *Shiurei Harav*, pp. 47-48, 60-63; Abraham R. Besdin, *Reflections of the Rav*, pp. 104-5.
3. Soloveitchik, "The Lonely Man," pp. 11-20.
4. Ibid., pp. 23-25.
5. Ibid., pp. 50-51.
6. Soloveitchik, "Majesty and Humility," p. 36.
7. Ibid., p. 26.
8. Lawrence Kaplan, "The Religious Philosophy," *Tradition*, Fall 1973, p. 58.
9. Soloveitchik, "Ish Hahalakhah," *Talpiot*, 1944, pp. 651-735.
10. Kaplan, "The Religious Philosophy," p. 44.
11. Ibid., p. 59.
12. Soloveitchik, "Ubikashtem Misham," pp. 1-83.
13. Ibid.
14. Chaim of Volozin, *Nefesh Chaim* 1, no. 4.
15. Soloveitchik, "The Lonely Man," p. 15-16. See, also, David Hartman, *Joy and Responsibility* (1978), pp. 198-231.
16. Aharon Lichtenstein, "R. Joseph Soloveitchik," in *Great Jewish Thinkers of the Twentieth Century*, ed. Simon Noveck (1963), p. 285.
17. Hermann Cohen, "Charakteristik der Ethik Maimunis," *Jüdische Schriften* III (1924), 221-89.
18. Maimonides, *Mishneh Torah, Hilkhot Deot*, 1:5, *Sefer Hamitzvot, Mitzvot*, Aseh 8.
19. Maimonides, *Guide of the Perplexed*, III, p. 54.
20. Shimon Rawidowicz, "Perek Betorat Hamussar Larambam," in *Sefer Hayovel Lichvod Mordekhai Menachem Kaplan* (1953), p. 236. But there is a pronounced difference between Rabbi Soloveitchik's and Rawidowicz's views, inasmuch as the latter regards the "middle road" as an inferior brand of religious ethics, which serves merely as the gate to the higher ethics of the pious.
21. See my "Alienation and Exile," *Tradition*, Spring-Summer 1964.
22. Soloveitchik, "Majesty and Humility," pp. 35-36; 48-50.
23. Aristotle, *Nicomachean Ethics*, Book III.
24. I have elsewhere discussed Rabbi Soloveitchik's view that for Maimonides the "middle road emerges as the resultant of an ongoing creative tension"; see Maimonides, *Guide of the Perplexed*.
25. Maimonides, *Mishneh Torah, Hilkhot Deot*, 6:2.
26. Soloveitchik, "The Lonely Man," p. 52.
27. Cohen, "Charakteristik"; Steven S. Schwarzschild, "Moral Radicalism and 'Middlingness' in the Ethics of Maimonides," *Studies in Medieval Culture*, pp. 65-92. While not going quite as far as Schwarzschild, Rawidowicz also essentially adopts this approach; see Rawidowicz, "Perek Betorat," p. 236.
28. Schwarzschild, "Moral Radicalism," pp. 81-83.
29. Soloveitchik, "Ish Hahalakhah," pp. 722-23; idem, "Ubikashtem Misham," p. 39.
30. Maimonides, *Mishneh Torah, Hilkhot Melakhim*, chapter 11.

FRANZ WERFEL'S LOOK AT GENOCIDE
Gregory Baum

In her writings Hannah Arendt has repeatedly claimed that the Jews lack political wisdom; they do not recognize the danger in which they live, and when it finally dawns upon them, they do not adopt sound political strategies to wrestle against it. Hannah Arendt had in mind, primarily though not exclusively, the Jews in Germany and German-speaking lands prior to the victory of the Nazi movement. In this article I wish to show that whatever the foresight of the Jews may have been, one person, Franz Werfel, the famous poet, playwright, and novelist, had already in the early thirties a clear sense that the Nazi movement was giving birth to a new antisemitism, one that would lead to the genocide of the Jewish people.

In his novel, *The Forty Days*, which interprets the Armenian genocide at the hands of the Turkish government during the First World War, Werfel addressed himself quite unmistakably to the rise of Hitler and the Nazi party in Germany.[1] His analysis of the evil passion that led to the mass murder of Armenian men, women, and children, with the intention of making their race disappear from the face of the earth, suggests to the reader that Werfel is establishing a comparison with the Nazi movement of his day. In my opinion, in writing his novel Werfel also wanted to raise the question of the powerlessness of the victims. "Are we really helpless? Must we really hold out our heads to the noose in silence?" he makes his hero say. Gabriel Bagradian, the assimilated Armenian, becomes organizer, strategist, and military leader to defend the population of a dozen villages in the western part of Armenia, near the Mediterranean coast, at the foot of Mount Musa Dhag. He directs their forty days of resistance on Musa Dhag.

The Forty Days was recommended to me quite recently. A public meeting described as "An Evening against Genocide," organized by the Toronto branch of the Council of Christians and Jews, brought together concerned citizens to examine the social forces that lead to genocide and to stir up commitment to oppose these forces wherever they show themselves. Among the speakers was Professor Vartan Gregorian, an American of Armenian origin, who presented an analysis of the Armenian holocaust.

The entire Armenian population, more than a million and a half people, were forcefully deported by government decree, sent on foot into the desert planes of Mesopotamia, and left to die under the torture of thirst, hunger, exhaustion, and despair. For reasons that are difficult to explain, the world never fully woke up to this genocide. It occurred in the years 1917–1918, while the war was still raging, when the countries of Europe were preoccupied with their own struggle for survival. Since Turkey lost the war and became a small Asian nation with its dreams of empire totally destroyed, no one seemed to talk any more of the genocide. To this day books on modern history hardly mention the event. The great encyclopedias make a few references to it. In Turkey the historical facts have never been acknowledged. The planners of the Armenian mass murder were the founders of modern Turkey: they are greatly honored in their country. The great pain of the Armenians who survived in the Diaspora was, and still is, that the mass extirpation of their people has gone unrecognized in the world. In this context, Professor Gregorian said that he was happy to speak in the presence of so many Jews. Why? Because a great Jew, Franz Werfel, was the only major author who broke the silence and told the awful story to the world. And he told this story precisely because he was Jewish. He discovered in the genocidal crime inflicted on the Armenians a type or model for understanding the danger which threatened the Jews of Germany and German-speaking lands.

I had heard of *The Forty Days*, I knew that it was about the mass murder of the Armenians, but I had never read it. I decided to read it then. The book touched me deeply because it gave such a vivid picture of the plight of the Armenians and of their heroic resistance on Musa Dagh. But I was especially touched because through this extraordinary story Werfel addressed himself to the plight of the Jews in Germany. I read the book as an appeal to Jews to organize their defense and an even stronger appeal to Christians to stem the tide of racial hatred. Was this really Werfel's intention? Or did I project my own ideas into his head? The biographical studies I examined made only the briefest remarks, relating the writing of *The Forty Days* to the contemporary political situation. In 1929 Werfel had traveled to the Middle East, and in Damascus he had come upon several crippled children who worked in stores manufacturing carpets. When he asked who these young people were, he was told they were survivors of the Turkish mass murder of the Armenian people. He shuddered. Later he decided to write a novel about the Armenian tragedy. He consulted British and French archives, he immersed himself in historical studies. It is my opinion that he also wrestled with the meaning of the Nazi movement, which at that time was gaining an ever greater following in Germany.

The strongest evidence for Werfel's political intention is found in the vigorous conversation between Enver Pascha, the Turkish dictator, "the new war-god," and Dr. Johannes Lepsius, the German Lutheran missionary who pleads the cause of the Armenian people. But before examining this extraordinary scene, I must explain how the reader is introduced to the Armenian story. Gabriel Bagradian, the hero of *The Forty Days*, is an Armenian in Paris, married to a young French woman, whom he loves dearly and through whom he loves French culture and French life. Gabriel comes from a family of wealthy merchants. His grandfather had become very successful. His company in Istanbul had grown into an international operation with branches in the capitals of Europe. Despite his wealth, the grandfather remained attached to his homeland, in western Armenia, near the Mediterranean coast, at the foot of Musa Dagh. There he builds his mansion. There he retires.

Gabriel was brought up in this house, but at the age of

twelve he leaves with his family for France, where he was to spend twenty-two years of his life. Gabriel becomes a Western intellectual, a scholar, a writer, a man at home in the French environment. Since his older brother looks after the family firm, the family decides that they do not need Gabriel's help. Gabriel admits to himself that he looks down on his older brother. He loses touch with him. He thinks of him as "the Oriental" or "the Businessman," even though he realizes that it is the family's money that provides his own income and makes possible his life of study, writing, and leisure.

When his brother falls ill in Istanbul, Gabriel decides to visit him. With his wife and his young son, he leaves Paris, but when he gets to Istanbul he learns that his brother, whose illness has worsened, has decided to return to the family home at the foot of Musa Dagh. When Gabriel and his family arrive there, just as the war is being declared, they find out that his brother has already died. But now they are trapped. France and Turkey are at war, and since Gabriel still has a Turkish passport, he must stay. It is then that he gradually discovers the plot of the Turkish government to humiliate the Armenian people. Slowly the features of the government's genocidal policy are revealed.

The ideology of the Turkish government embodies the secular philosophy and political will of Turkey's Westernizing party, the Committee for Unity and Progress, which had opposed traditional Ottoman society with its link to the Caliphate and Islamic religion. The revolution of 1908 had allowed the so-called Young Turks to come to power. Because their founders were mainly from Saloniki, they thought of themselves as European. They wanted to introduce progress in Turkey in imitation of the industrialized, colonial powers of Europe, especially France and Germany. After the revolution of 1908 they had signed a pact with the Armenian people which expressed promises of mutual support, but the government had repeatedly betrayed it. The Young Turks resented religion, they opposed the old ways, they wanted a country unified in the spirit of nationalism and utilitarian modernity, capable of becoming a Western-style colonial power in Asia Minor reaching all the way to India.

Werfel introduces the reader to devout Moslem personalities who have nothing but contempt for "the Atheists" at Istanbul. They regard them as brutal and immoral men, dressed in Western clothes, opposed to religion and virtue, who at that moment need racial hatred of the Armenian people for the realization of their ambitious political purposes. The Turkish people are a kindly people, the Moslems say. They occasionally lose their temper and commit violent acts, as do at times the Armenians, but they basically respect human life because they believe in God. God has created people. People are holy. The atheistic government at Istanbul has become utilitarian; they have no moral sense: they are unbelievers.

Werfel realized of course that the new Turkish ideology combining nationalism and progressivism was quite different from the spirit of Nazism. The nationalism of the Nazis was hostile to Western rationalism; it sought to ground itself in myth and destiny, and appealed to the ancient, pre-Christian symbols of the Germanic past. There is no strict parallel between the Young Turks and the Nazis. Werfel emphasizes that the spirit of the Young Turks was profoundly at odds with the spirit of the Turkish people—in Werfel's eyes with the spirit of any people. The organized hatred that leads to genocide is never supported by ordinary folks. It is always produced by the calculated decision of a small elite.

The spiral of increasing discrimination against the Armenians reaches a high point in the town of Zeitun. The government-inspired repression becomes so provocative that a few acts of enraged violence occur. The desired occasion has arrived. As a reprisal the government decrees the expulsion of the population. What takes place is the dress rehearsal and first act of the entire genocidal operation, planned by the government. Tens of thousands of people, the entire Armenian population of Zeitun, are chased along the road into the endless desert where they suffer death, after the merciless tortures of exhaustion and despair. After

Zeitun, those who want to know realize what the government has decided to do. Genocide has been decreed.

It is at this point that Dr. Johannes Lepsius, Lutheran missionary from Germany, appears in Istanbul to have an interview with the dictator, Enver Pascha, the leader of the Turkish people. Lepsius loves the Armenians. He worked among them as a missionary. The ancient Armenian church and the new Protestant communities founded by German and American missionaries got along peacefully. The atmosphere of hostility and suspicion in Turkey prevented the hostility and resentment that usually characterize the relations between an ancient church and the sects introduced by foreigners. The Armenians were united. They had adopted Johannes Lepsius as one of their family. He knew them well. It was true, of course, that the Armenian community was significantly different from the Turkish population. The Armenians were Christians. That fact alone set them apart. They had their own language, their own customs, their own organizations. They had close international contacts, which the Turks on the whole did not. A significant section of the Armenian people lived in Russia beyond the Turkish border in the Caucasus. And the Armenians of the Diaspora in Europe and the Americas remained in touch with their families in the old country. These international connections were now made a reproach to them. The government claimed that Armenians could not be good Turks, they could not become ardent nationalists, and because of their contacts with Russia and the West, they could not be trusted, especially in time of war.

Johannes Lepsius had arrived in Istanbul from Potsdam in Germany, where he now lived. Enver Pascha had consented to an interview. Lepsius, with the backing of German church groups and secular organizations, intended to clarify the intentions of the Turkish government in regard to the Armenians. He wanted to engage in a political argument with the dictator. If Enver Pascha insisted on continuing his genocidal policy, Lepsius was ready to organize protests in Germany and appeal to the Reichstag and the emperor for intervention. But since Germany needed its Turkish allies to carry on the great war in the Mediterranean, it was uncertain whether the German government would be willing to protest against the Armenian genocide.

The conversation between Pascha and Lepsius is crucial for the understanding of the entire book. Werfel shows here that within this leader, with his gentle, disciplined, almost boyish looks, there is hidden, beyond the utilitarianism of national ambitions, something altogether different, something satanic, a senseless, irrational hatred of another race, without any utilitarian justification. This satanic passion emerges only at the end of the conversation. At first, Enver Pascha appears as a reasonable person. He invokes a principle that has presently become important in Latin American countries and even in Western nations, the doctrine of "national security." He argues that "the Armenian question" needs settlement. While the Turkish revolution was at first friendly to the Armenians, Turkey has since been betrayed by them many times. The Armenians do not support the new Turkey. Now that the war is going on, the presence of these Armenians becomes a risk to the nation. They have displayed subversive tendencies, they become army deserters in great number, they staged an open revolt at Zeitun, they keep up their connections with Russia and the West. Either the Armenian question is solved once and for all, or the entire country will be swept into chaos. For this reason the government has decided on a policy of resettlement. The protection of national security entitles the government to take such harsh measures, measures that are not normally adopted in modern countries.

Lepsius knows that Pascha is lying. There is no evidence whatever for widespread disloyalty of Armenians. Most of them are mountaineer peasants and craftsmen. A significant minority belongs to the middle class as merchants and professionals. The Armenians supply a comparatively high percentage of doctors, lawyers, engineers, and managers in Turkey. Lepsius knows that the incident at Zeitun was not an Armenian revolt: it was a provocation staged by the Turkish government to justify the first act of their genocidal policy. Lepsius also realizes that while the government documents speak of "the resettlement" of the Armenian population, what is actually meant is their mass murder. He knows the parts of Turkey in which the genocidal policy has already been applied and the other parts where terrified Armenians are still waiting for their death. He reveals his knowledge to the dictator and pleads with him not to continue the genocidal action. Lepsius quotes his sources of information to Enver Pascha. Among them, he mentions Mr. Morgenthau, the American ambassador. Here comes one of the few references to Jews in the novel. The dictator discredits Lepsius's sources of information. "Mr. Morgenthau is a Jew," he says. "And Jews are always fanatically on the side of minorities." Lepsius does not give in. The horrors of the deportation policy are too well known. What is taking place is mass murder in the desert.

At this point the dictator invokes again the doctrine of national security. He says this to Dr. Lepsius: "Germany has few, or no, internal enemies. But let's suppose that, in other circumstances, she found herself with traitors in her midst—Alsace-Lorrainers, shall we say, or Poles, or Social-Democrats, or Jews—and in far greater number than at present. . . . Would you consider it cruel if, for the sake of victory, all dangerous elements in the population were simply herded together and sent into a distant, uninhabited territory?" Sentences such as these make it apparent that in writing *Forty Days* Werfel did think of the emerging Nazi movement and that he foresaw that what it aimed at was the genocidal destruction of the Jews. Lepsius replies: "If my government behaved unjustly, unlawfully, inhumanly ('in an unChristian way' was the expression on the tip of his tongue) to our fellow-countrymen of a different race or different persuasion, I shall clear out of Germany at once and go to America." This curious sentence makes sense only if we suppose that Werfel is thinking of his own days, when victims of Nazi oppression sought refuge in America. For why would Lepsius, in the middle of the First World War, refer to America in this context? Enver Pascha replies this to him: "Sad for Germany, if many other people there think as you do. A sign that your people lack the strength to enforce its national will relentlessly." This is the language of Hitler. The anachronism of the conversation becomes evident. Lepsius tells the dictator that his policy is not really aimed at protecting Turkey against an enemy within, it is rather "a planned extirpation of another race."

In the person of the German missionary, Werfel himself is arguing with the dictator who has decreed the destruction of the people. Lepsius urges that the Armenians have been such loyal Turks, that they have done so much for Turkey, that "they represent the most progressive and active section of the Ottoman population, [and] had for years made efforts to lead Turkey out of its old-fashioned, simple methods of agriculture into a new world of up-to-date farming and building industrialization." In fact, the Armenians do so much for Turkey, they are so intelligent and hard-working, that some people have become resentful of them—a resentment born of sloth. Enver Pascha replies that it is this very intelligence that makes the Armenians dangerous. For what Turkey plans to become is a disciplined modern nation, an empire, equipped to play in Asia the role the great Western nations play in Europe and in their colonies. We need the heroism of the Turkish people, their dedication, their sense of being called to empire, the conviction that they are meant to be rulers—and a certain kind of intelligence undermines such greatness. Enver Pascha becomes more passionate now. He reveals his dream of domination. Lepsius sees in him the resentful power-seeking of a spoiled child, "a childish anti-Christ."

The German continues: "You want to found an empire, Excellency. But the corpse of the Armenian people will be beneath its foundations. Can that bring you prosperity?" At the end of his strength, Lepsius insists that it is not too late to rescind the decree of deportation from the sections of the country that have not been touched, including the western region near the Mediterranean. Lepsius intends to mobilize public opinion in Germany and address himself to the Reichstag and the emperor, unless Enver Pascha decides this very minute to discontinue his genocidal policy and make peace with the remaining Armenians. "There can be no peace," Pascha allows himself to say in a moment of passion, even though he quickly resumes the disciplined mask of the politician: "there can be no peace between human beings and plague germs." Lepsius is struck with horror. He realizes that he has glimpsed the core of the dictator's heart, his inhuman hatred, a satanic element. He manages to utter, "So you openly admit your intention of using the war to extirpate the Armenian people." Lepsius is shattered. Beyond usefulness, beyond the lust for power, beyond the logic of empire, and beyond the imagined threats to national security stands a profound hatred that is connected to these, but has a life of its own. From it derives the inspiration for genocide. Lepsius looks at the disciplined dictator, gentle, boyish even, offering deliverance and glory to his people: behind "the arctic mask" he recognizes a human being who has overcome moral sentiment, moved beyond all guilt and qualms of conscience, acting out of "the strange, almost innocent naiveté of utter Godlessness."

After the interview Lepsius sees the mass murderer, Enver Pascha, move from his office where they talked through the halls of the War Ministry. He observes how this small, demonic creature is perceived by the men who work at the desks as possessing messianic power. He is their leader, they follow his orders, he will build a new Turkey for them. As he walks through the corridors looking at his staff, the mass murderer says to himself that already in the fall, he will be able to give his men the good news: "The Armenian question has been resolved."

This conversation makes the entire novel a story about genocide, with a particular message to the Germany of the early thirties. Against world opinion, and against the opinion of many German Jews that Nazi antisemitism was a *Kinderkrankheit*, a children's disease, eventually to be left behind, Franz Werfel read the signs of the times correctly. He detected that behind the rational arguments for a new Germany, imbued with a national purpose, purified of foreign elements, there stood something infinitely worse, a pathological will of a dictator, his satanic, irrational, genocidal hatred of the Jews, a position in the long run destructive of Germany itself.

What is Werfel's message to the Jews in the German-speaking lands? He wants to inspire them to find strategies to defend themselves. When the Armenians at the foot of Musa Dagh discuss their future, a priest utters these words: "We are helpless, we must bow our head. We may perhaps be allowed to cry out." Gabriel rebels against this attitude. Werfel suggests that his identification with European culture has made him different from the people in whose midst he now lives. "Are we really helpless? Must we really hold out our heads to the noose in silence?" he asks his fellow Armenians. The major part of the novel deals with Gabriel Bagradian's ingenious effort to organize the population of the villages, set up with them an armed camp on Musa Dagh, and defend their life and their honor under the most difficult conditions for forty days, until, exhausted and devoid of resources, they are ready for death from Turkish arms. Then a miracle happens. The French and English fleets arrive at the shore, they bombard the villages along the coast, and under this pressure the Turkish troops decide to withdraw. The Armenians from Musa Dagh are rescued; Gabriel is not.

It is my opinion that the main message of the novel was addressed to the citizens of Germany and the German-speaking lands, especially those who regarded themselves as believing Christians. Werfel seems to plead with them to join Dr. Lepsius in the struggle against the forces that lead to genocide. Werfel has an idea, not commonly held by social scientists but often defended by religious thinkers, that the waning of religion, the decline of faith in the God of the Bible, has made modern civilization vulnerable to a new barbarism. Without the acknowledgement of God and the recognition of their own finiteness, people easily deliver themselves to their impulses and their strangest and most destructive passions. Without faith in God, the neighbor ceases to be neighbor and becomes an object to be manipulated, disposed of, and, if need be, destroyed altogether.

Werfel's trust in the power of the Christian religion to save Western civilization from barbarism, a theme that runs through a number of his novels, seems strange when one recalls that in the early thirties the Catholic Church stood on the side of Fascism in Italy and supported reactionary parties in many parts of Europe—in Spain, Portugal, and even Austria, among them. In Germany, it is true, because of its particular history as a minority, the Catholic Church stood at the center and to the left-of-center of the political spectrum. The German Lutheran Church entertained a more conservative vision of society. It was certainly not inconceivable that the Christians in Germany would decide to stand together on the grounds of their common moral heritage and create an alliance against the evil forces of Nazism. Werfel may have believed that there was still the opportunity to act politically. He may have been in touch with Christians in Germany, Protestant and Catholic, who vehemently opposed Hitler and Nazi ideology. From history we know that such a mass resistance did not materialize. Still, Werfel's political sense and his analytical powers enabled him in the early thirties to recognize the logic of genocide built into the Nazi movement and to look into the pathological heart of its founder and führer. This was an achievement. The message of the novel is undoubtedly that the genocidal passion and the execution of mass murder through a trained elite and obedient paramilitary forces can take place anywhere where people are touched by the spirit of modernity and submit to the irrationalities of their leader.

Notes

1. *The Forty Days* appeared in German in 1933, and in English translation in 1934. Ed.

AHAD HA-AM AND LEOPOLD ZUNZ: TWO PERSPECTIVES ON THE *WISSENSCHAFT DES JUDENTUMS*
Alfred Gottschalk

When *Wissenschaft des Judentums* was founded in the 1820s, it entered the historical scene with a singular purpose which does not prevail in today's scholarly studies. Specifically, Jewish *Wissenschaft* did not originate from the mere desire to clarify and understand nor from the timeless wish to know or to improve on knowledge already gained. Rather, it came into being to take care of certain conditions in the life of Jews, namely, to help overcome difficulties which had arisen in the post-Mendelssohnian period when Jews went through the process of leaving the ghetto and entering modern society. Life carries with it both essential and accidental accretions, the organically genuine and the foreign elements that are acquired on the long march through the millennia. The scholarly study of any people's history and creativity separates the genuine from the false, the permanent from the passing. This was the faith of the ideological theorists of the early 1800s and Leopold Zunz, the founder of *Wissenschaft des Judentums*, shared it.

He and his colleagues at the *Culturverein* established modern Jewish studies. Operating within the framework of general scholarship, they used its methods in order to secure Judaism and, after having secured it, to guarantee its continuous validity. In this sense, the *Zeitschrift* of the *Culturverein* stated:

[T]he establishment of a science of Judaism seems to be a necessity of our age. . . . It is manifest everywhere that the fundamental principle of Judaism is again in a state of inner ferment, striving to assume a shape in harmony with the spirit of the times. But in accordance with the age this development can only take place through the medium of science.[1]

In other words, Judaism had to be scientifically certified. In that shape it could enter the modern world and withstand all efforts to expel it.

Wissenschaft des Judentums would also have an influence on the individual Jew. It would draw from Jewish tradition a body of valid Jewish knowledge from which he could shape his Judaism. It would provide him with a Judaism based on, and generated by, the Jewish past, but scientifically filtered and defined so as to result in concepts which conformed to the texture of the modern mind. (As a brief aside, it might be interesting to point out that where, today, the term "tradition" comes easily to mind and pen, in the early days of *Wissenschaft* the corresponding word was "past," *Vergangenheit*.) Using contemporary terminology one might say, with a slight degree of exaggeration, that *Wissenschaft* was regarded not only as a process enabling modernity, but also as an instrumentality for Jewish survival.

It is not difficult to see that this view still prevails. More than ever before, Jews are being admonished to study. Adult education, as presented by almost every synagogue, certainly almost every Conservative and Reform one, is often offered as an academic course and not merely as a pleasant literary pastime for the layman. Our congregations now invite professors for a weekend and call them—the designation is extremely revealing—"scholars in residence." The study of Judaism is regarded as one of the most important activities that a Jew can engage in as a Jew. Next to the distinctly religious activities of a Jew, it appears as one that contributes to making a nominal Jew into a "practicing" one. Often, in fact, Jewish study becomes a surrogate for religious activities and the sole, or strongest, expression of a person's Judaism. Thus, we have the Jewish layman who participates, in a mediated way, in Jewish scholarship, and such participation is recognized as a valid form of Jewish living, of Jewish "existence."

There is no parallel to this condition in the Christian world. The Christian religionist is not being told that his knowledge of the history of Christianity or of the philosophy of Thomas Aquinas adds to his religious standing as a Christian. There are almost no churches which cultivate, for their congregants, Christian studies in the way that synagogues organize Jewish studies. All of this underlines how *Wissenschaft des Judentums*, particularly where it took the place of traditionalist Jewish learning, reached far beyond the circle of scholars. Judaism did not draw a demarcation line between academic endeavor and the layman's interest in its results. In fact, it often appeared that the emotional and religious involvement of the Jewish layman in the findings and formulations of *Jüdische Wissenschaft* were stronger than those of the scholars themselves.

Like any other Jew who had been brought up exclusively on biblical and talmudic knowledge and the traditional ways of Jewish learning, and was eager to escape from them into the wide, glorious world of modern culture and literature, Ahad Ha-Am used Jewish *Wissenschaft* as a tool for his "liberation." From that encounter stems his lifelong attitude toward it—one marked by diminishing attraction and increasing critique. Though he once regarded it as an indispensible instrumentality for the acquisition of much-longed-for learning, he very soon arrived at a rejection of some of its central concepts. He believed that the scholarly approaches to which it was accustomed led to assimilation and, in his biting critique, he emphasized that *Wissenschaft* had failed adequately to comprehend the Jewish national element as it reflects itself in the Bible and in the early periods of Jewish history. He lumps together the German school of *Wissenschaft* and *Haskalah*, the Jewish enlightenment that bore the stamp of Russian and Galician Jewry. Both, he points out, neglected to focus on the genius of Hebrew culture when they set out to modernize Judaism.

They made no attempt, he says, to recognize the land of Israel, the Hebrew language, and the people of Israel as Jewish national elements organically bound together in an integrated Jewish ideology. Ahad Ha-Am was a cultural Zionist. He did not believe in traditional Judaism; neither did he believe in the kind of Judaism which the Reform Movement had shaped. Yet, some of his concepts, such as "the mission of Israel," derived from the ideology of the Reform Movement which he criticized without mercy, and other concepts, such as the "need for renewal," were genuine to the pragmatic utterances of the early school of Jewish *Wissenschaft* which he denounced with equal vigor. His "spiritual Zionism" propounded the perennial "essentiality" of Israel.

In many respects, Ahad Ha-Am's denunciation of Jewish *Wissenschaft* was unfounded or unfair. When Zunz outlined the range of Jewish history, he laid considerable emphasis on the *factual* data that are contained in it and that characterize it: on the way that Jews lived, on the manner in which they were constituted in history, on the kinds of cohesion which determined the character of their living together. He includes, among others,

> the position of the Jew in world history; their former and present position, political *and* spiritual [*sic*]; tracing them back from their respective present places of residence to their old community [*sic*], . . . physical conditions, their causes and consequences, . . . inner constitution, political or communal. . . .[2]

And so he continues, through fourteen paragraphs. All of this material was either unknown to Ahad Ha-Am or disregarded by him, and it goes a considerable way to defuse his censuring of Jewish *Wissenschaft* for its excessive inclination to depoliticize Jewish history.

Furthermore, at least as far as intent goes, there are obvious parallels between the *Wissenschaft* that Ahad Ha-Am criticizes and his own writings, in which he wove together a tapestry of ideology where seemingly contradictory threads were held together by his nationalist orientation. According to him, the national spirit of Judaism was still in a state of evolution. The people's spirit had atrophied in the Diaspora and its lack of dynamism had created a spiritual crisis which had to be resolved before the future of Judaism could be secured in the modern world. Propelled by such thought, Ahad Ha-Am concentrated on an ideology of renewal. This is the ever-recurring theme of his writing.

Yet, unlike other theorists who put the problem of the Jew before the problem of the survival of Judaism, he

> put redemption into the center of the nation's thought, not because of external persecution, divine visitations, or evil decrees, but simply because he could not conceive of an honorable existence for the image of God in exile. . . . You might call it the transmigration of the idea of "the Shekinah in exile," the realization that there is no power of resistance without the revival of the Shekinah, the spirit, the soul—call it what you will—and that there is nothing more important than building this power of resistance within ourselves. . . . [He] was interested in all Jewish problems of the spirit. He saw Eretz Israel as the embodiment of the prophetic vision, but only in the sense that it was to serve as a spiritual center.[3]

An argument can be made that Ahad Ha-Am's tendency toward spiritualization is no weaker, and is, possibly, stronger than Zunz's. Zunz, both as a theoretician and a practitioner of Jewish *Wissenschaft*, is close to the realities of Jewish history, yet Ahad Ha-Am never recognizes this, although he sometimes does use the findings of Zunz. Also, in his beginnings and in some of his main works, such as *Die gottesdienstlichen Vorträge*, Zunz demonstrates his strong awareness of the "national" quality of Jewish literary and cultural productivity—another facet of early *Wissenschaft des Judentums* which Ahad Ha-Am overlooks.

For example, the philosophy of history which Zunz took over from the Historical School enabled him to regard the Jews as a peculiar "historical entity recognized by world history." Jewish history and Jewish literature are not identical with the general world spirit; they form a particular entity of that spirit, reflecting Judaism as an organic whole. Jewish literature is an organism in its own right; it is "the literature of a nation." Jewish literature does not have an accidental arbitrary origin; it is no "idle oratory, no haphazard writing," Zunz states, referring to prophetic literature and the Haggadah. As for the Midrash, its productions "are utterances of an activity founded in the life, the ideas, and the interests of the Jewish people in which the people, so to speak, has always collaborated." The outstanding works of the Halakhah, as well as of the Haggadah,

> like the Law and the prophets, are national writings, confronted with which the later generations almost voluntarily gave up their autonomy; they became the property of all, results of a millennial development, monuments of the nation's life and products of its most significant minds.[4]

Other statements by Zunz make us wonder about the one-sidedness of Ahad Ha-Am's polemic against him. Here are a few additional samples. "Constitution and priesthood guarded in the Hebrew state the Law and the Ark of the Covenant, the visible foci of the nationality." When the Jewish state ceased to exist, Jewish nationality did not cease to exist. Though Jewish "autonomy" was destroyed, Jewish "nationality found its center in the Holy Scriptures." The "Synagogue" did not replace nationality, it became its "sole bearer." If prophecy had been "an unconditional expression of national life," such was also the character of the Haggadah. In Zunz's term, "the Jewish writers were *National-Schriftsteller*, national writers, and *Volkslehrer*, teachers of the people." When Jewish literature spoke of the rabbis as "our teachers" or "our sages," it was to mark them as authorities in national literature. Zunz was aware that Jewish history was a sequence of foreign influences trying to repress the national element, but he believed that the efforts toward "the preservation of national literature" never ceased.

It certainly cannot be part of this paper to probe more deeply into the ideology of Zunz. But one more point should be made because it also applies to Ahad Ha-Am. It is extremely difficult to pinpoint what Zunz understood by "nationality" and what were its essential ingredients. This problem exists not only in the Jewish realm. Any kind of *Volksgeist* or national genius becomes highly elusive when one sets out to define it. Ahad Ha-Am himself tried different approaches in order to define the unifying element of Jewish culture. Less than Zunz's, his definitions derive from varied sources, in fact from varied philosophies.

> In a nation's culture [Ahad Ha-Am explained in one of his essays], there is something which has a reality of its own: it is the concrete expression of the best minds of the nation in every period of its existence. The nation expresses itself in certain definite forms which remain for all time, and which is no longer dependent on those who created them, any more than a fallen apple is dependent on the tree from which it fell.[5]

Such a statement may apply, of course, to a great many concepts of culture and, au fond, it does nothing more than state that culture may be examined as to its psychological genesis or evaluated according to its objective worth. Or does it mean that in a people's history there are creative periods when its genius is active and its spirit productive, and others when creativity is lacking or at a low ebb, and the nation rests on, or luxuriates in, the creative periods of the past? There appear to be in Ahad Ha-Am's writings sufficient instances to warrant such an approach. He holds that the biblical period was such an era of creative power and he seems to feel that this creative power continued to communicate itself in later periods. In fact, he says, "the Bible, Talmud and *Shulhan Arukh* are simply three different steps in the process of the development of one essence—the Jewish national spirit—in accordance with the circumstances and the requirements of different epochs in history."[6] This *Volksgeist* permeates the entire existence of the Jewish people. Suffusing every aspect of life, this spirit, "a national ego on the analogy of the individual self," represents the creative force of the people and is a manifestation of its will to live. Ahad Ha-Am conceives the national organism and its propelling force in Spencerian terms. Analogous to no other physical organism, the Jewish national organism is governed by a natural basic drive which he calls *ha-kium ha-leumi*, the national instinct for self-preservation.

This concept is interesting for two reasons. First, into the organic philosophy of the Historical School, which Ahad Ha-Am seemed to share with the early *Wissenschaft des Judentums*, it introduces nineteenth-century Spencerian philosophy, a kind of developmental materialism which is found in many of the naturalistic *Populärphilosophen* of the second half of that century. This addition eliminates, or certainly substantially weakens, the influence of the philosophical idealism which Geiger and others adopted in their development of *Wissenschaft des Judentums*. That idealism blended with religious thought without major difficulties; Spencerian evolutionism did not. In fact, it usually led to a break with religion and such a break also occurred in Ahad Ha-Am's thought. The transcendent God was replaced by the national will to live, and Jewish ethics, no longer divinely inspired, is merely an outcome of the Jewish nation's natural perception of the moral sense.

Once Ahad Ha-am arrived at this definition of the Jewish *Volksgeist*, it carried him toward significant conclusions. The Jewish national spirit is the instrumentality which will bring about the revival of modern Jewry by impregnating "the heart" of the present generation with the true and potent impetus of national determination. It is this spirit which he found in the truly Jewish creativity of the past and which, he maintained, was the sole legitimate motivation of Jewish activity in the present, that becomes a criterion for measuring the national value of current Jewish phenomena.

One of the items thus examined and measured was Jewish *Wissenschaft*. Research for its own sake did not interest Ahad Ha-Am. For him it was plain luxury, and only scientific work produced in immediate consonance with "the Jewish national spirit" was recognized by him. Applying this yardstick, he postulates that only literature written in Hebrew can be regarded as national literature of the Jewish people. Generally, he accepts *Haskalah* literature and the preceding literature of the Chasidim. Specifically, however, he is highly critical of both. He laments that *Haskalah* literature had become a haven for dullards and mediocrities who slavishly imitated and translated inconsequential material. Its products were imports and not original to the Jewish genius. It was a purveyor of foreign ideas, badly presented in style and form, and incapable of appealing as something intrinsic to Jewish life and characteristic of it.

Part of this criticism was deserved, and is due to Ahad Ha-Am's own exemplary standards of literary style. But another part of it is due to his dogmatism and his historical myopia. These are particularly evident in his critique of Moses Mendelssohn's translation of the Bible into German and of the subsequent endeavors of the early practitioners of Jewish *Wissenschaft*. Ahad Ha-Am entirely overlooks the fact that Mendelssohn, Orthodox and traditional Jew that he was, rejected assimilation. He has no place for it in his philosophy and he rejects it on numerous occasions in his writings and letters. Mendelssohn's aim was to purify the language of his contemporary Jews, to improve their vernacular, and to educate them to use pure Hebrew and a pure German, instead of the mixture of both which was then current. Ironically, Ahad Ha-Am, the Hebraist who insisted on the classic excellence of the language, never realized that Mendelssohn's purposes and his own with respect to the Hebrew language were the same.

Ahad Ha-Am saw *Haskalah* and *Wissenschaft des Judentums* in a strange relationship. According to him, the positive efforts of German *Haskalah*, as well as the critique emanating from it, led to the overthrow of the strongholds of the nation, uprooting not only the primitive beliefs and outworn customs of religious Judaism, but damaging the very center of what had constituted Jewish national life and unity. As he states it, this destruction created a void which some filled by building great synagogues and preaching

vacuous sermons, while others, the "bigger men," turned
to Jewish *Wissenschaft* in an attempt to overcome the
shortcomings of *Haskalah*. He characterizes the literature
resulting from this attempt as analogous to a piece of
writing in which the preface is full of praise and reverence
for Israel and its national traditions and heritage, while the
body of the work, the scientific parts, digs into the works of
mere commentators and punctuators, dealing with lifeless
liturgical compositions and other arid materials without
which the world would have been not a bit poorer. He con-
temptuously condemns the followers of *Wissenschaft des
Judentums* for having been content with "tombstones and
synagogue chants."

This critique did not die with him. *Wissenschaft des
Judentums* is still being blamed for the excesses of some of
its proponents and the dull exercises of some of its less inspired devotees. As a rebuttal to this argument I refer to the
penetrating introduction which Gerson D. Cohen contributed to the twentieth volume of the Leo Baeck Institute
Year Book. In his essay, entitled "German Jewry as Mirror
of Modernity," he stresses the historical legitimacy of
Wissenschaft des Judentums.

> Critical scholarship became the first significant effort at a
> meaningful Jewish response to a wave of Jewish defection
> in the nineteenth century and to the intellectual climate
> that had made traditional form and theory obsolete. This
> effort at regeneration and reaffirmation of the Jewish
> legacy became the outstanding and characteristic feature
> of German–Jewish leadership of every hue and cast
> (p. xxv).

More specifically:

> If Judaism was to develop and gain a fresh relevance for
> contemporary Jewry, it could do so only by developing in
> the spirit and by the laws of its own inner history. Hence,
> each school of scholar-theologians—Reform, Historical,
> Orthodox—sought to pinpoint and describe the structure
> of rabbinic faith and literature, and thereby to gain not

[205]

only new insight into the sources themselves but the foundations for legitimatizing their respective religious responses to the contemporary world. No one school attained a monopoly on excellence in this area of research. The study of post-Biblical literature and religion was illuminated by brilliant fruits of research from the pens of leaders of all three tendencies in German Jewry (p. xxvi).

And summarizing this:

German-Jewish scholarship was a massive effort at reinfusing vitality into what many Jews had come to regard as a fossil that was totally irrelevant to contemporary spiritual life. In the reconquest of the past and in the mastery of the dynamics of history—of law, liturgy, philosophy—the scholars hoped to provide the rationale and motivations for adherence and the guidelines for a spiritual rebirth and future creativity. Zunz never pretended otherwise (p. xxvii).

Contrast with this view the judgment of Ahad Ha-Am:

One of the founders of the movement of *Wissenschaft des Judentums*, Zunz saw in it only [*sic*] the opportunity of converting the nations to a more friendly attitude towards Jews and to establish the great ideal of those days—equal rights.[7]

The attitude of Ahad Ha-Am toward later phases of *Jüdische Wissenschaft* is equally narrow and lacking in historical understanding. He knew Jewish *Wissenschaft*. He quoted it when it suited his purposes, but he had no eye for the historical circumstances which made it develop in different modes and different directions. In fact, it seems that Ahad Ha-Am had little genuine historical sense. His own criteria for Jewishness, the presence of the innate Jewish will for survival, the Hebrew language, were yardsticks set once and for all time, and the land of Israel, as a national goal, is for him more strongly idea than historical pressing reality. It is understandable that as a political thinker and pamphleteer he was not primarily interested in the advance-

[206]

ment of scholarship. Considering that he relentlessly pleaded for the elimination of Jewish illiteracy among the Jews of his time, the reception which he granted to the first modern Jewish encyclopaedia comes as a surprise. He regarded as a lasting reproach and a national disgrace the fact that the large American-Jewish encyclopaedia, which appeared in the years 1901–1906, was written in English instead of in Hebrew.

Wissenschaft des Judentums is a historical science. Its founder, Leopold Zunz, influenced by modern scholarship as it had developed since the beginning of the nineteenth century, had put that mark on it. Zunz himself was fundamentally a *Literarhistoriker*, a literary historian, who traced the development of literature through history and showed its dependence on historical conditions and circumstances.

For Ahad Ha-Am, the Bible was the blueprint of the evolution of Jewish national existence. Criticism of a radical nature would revise the lines of that blueprint, blur its outlines, and undermine its authority. For this reason, he had little taste and no use for modern biblical studies and, rather, relied on the *textus receptus*, untouched by alien revisionism. Thus, to his strong doubts about the validity of Jewish *Wissenschaft* he added an even stronger rejection of modern biblical studies. This negativism with respect to two comprehensive attempts at bringing about secure knowledge in two main fields of Jewish learning, Bible and Jewish history, facilitated his unmethodical way of handling ideas. He was no systematizer, he was an essayist—a first-rate one—and a political ad hoc pamphleteer—though one of enduring effectiveness. He selected, shuffled, and put together concepts that suited his politics and were conducive to expressing the political message that he had for his contemporaries.

Zunz's historic achievement was that he opened the doors to the Jewish past. His philological studies of literature were designed to lead toward genuine history, rebuild the past as it really was and connect it to the Jewish presence, for Jewish literature offers the best access to Jewish history and most adequately reflects its spirit. Some of those who followed Zunz engaged in theologizing that history. Ahad Ha-Am recognized this, intuitively so, and was moved by his dissent to reject the entire concept. But did he realize that he himself did not engage in genuine history either? To apply a modern term, does it not appear that Ahad Ha-Am's writing and conceptualizations move straight into "political theology"?

Notes

1. The programmatic article in the *Zeitschrift* was written by Immanuel Wolf, a member of the *Culturverein*. The quotation is from the English translation by Lionel E. Kochan, "On the Concept of a Science of Judaism (1822)," p. 204, which appeard in *Year Book II* of the Leo Baeck Institute (London, 1957), pp. 194–204.
2. *Gesammelte Schriften* (Berlin, 1875), vol. 1, p. 137f.
3. Chaim Nachman Bialik, "On Ahad Ha-Am," *Jewish Frontier* (November, 1964), 16–17.
4. Fritz Bamberger, "Zunz's Conception of History," *Proceedings of the American Academy for Jewish Research*, vol. XI (1941), p. 17f.
5. Ahad Ha-Am, *Selected Essays*, trans. L. Simon (Philadelphia, 1912), p. 259.
6. *Kol Kitvei Ahad Ha-Am* (Tel Aviv, 1956), p. 272.
7. Ibid., p. 178.

DAS FALKENBERG'SCHE GEBETBUCH: A BIBLIOGRAPHIC ADVENTURE
Lou H. Silberman

Some years ago I was approached by a graduate student in the Department of German in Vanderbilt University, who wished to discuss a dissertation proposal to be presented to that department. She was interested in a subject that would touch upon Jewish literature in Germany in the early Hitler period, and was seeking suggestions. We discussed several possibilities and came to focus on one. Was it possible to base a dissertation on an examination of the volumes that had appeared in the series, *Bücherei des Schocken Verlags*? To answer that question I suggested she survey the titles of the series and look through our holdings in the Divinity Library of Vanderbilt University. We had managed to collect all of the volumes, beginning with our original holdings in the Ismar Elbogen Collection, to which we had added volumes acquired from the libraries of the late Rabbi Dr. Karl Rosenthal, who had served as rabbi of the Jüdische Reformgemeinde of Berlin and then at the congregation in Wilmington, North Carolina, and of the late Professor Gerd (Gad) Frankel of the faculty of George Peabody College for Teachers in Nashville, Tennessee.

In sending her to look through the volumes, I made one request: would she save any papers she found inserted in them. I had long since discovered that Professor Elbogen used his library as a filing cabinet, so I was anxious to collect whatever I could. As it turned out, the only significant piece came not from a volume in his collection, but from the Rosenthal Library.

The double volume, *Das Jahr des Juden*, 55–56, by Moritz

Zobel, published in 1936, yielded a letter written on the letterhead: Mitteilungen/der Jüdischen Reformgemeinde zu Berlin/Geschäftsstelle der Jüdischen Reformgemeinde: Berlin N 24, Johannisstrasse 16—Fernruf: D1 Norden 5150. It is dated Berlin, den 27, Januar 1936, and is addressed to Herrn/Rabbiner Dr. Karl Rosenthal/Berlin NW.87/Holsteiner Ufer 20. It reads: Sehr geehrter Herr Dr. Rosenthal!/In der Anlage senden wir Ihnen das soeben er-/schienene Falkenberg'sche Gebetbuch, Abendgebete, mit der Bitte/um Besprechung für die Mitteilungen./Mit freundlichem Gruss. The signature is not legible. On the left side, toward the bottom, the term ''Anlage'' appears. There are some penciled names at the side, among them, ''Falkenberg.'' I assume these refer to the reviews Rosenthal wrote for the Mitteilungen.

Here, then, began the adventure that was to lead me, not only to the book, but, much later, to the role Jonas Plaut, father of Gunther Plaut, played in the life of the congregation from which the as-then mysterious Falkenberg'sche Gebetbuch emerged. My curiosity was piqued. What was the Falkenberg'sche Gebetbuch? I turned to Jakob J. Petuchowski's definitive volume, *Prayer Book Reform in Europe: The Liturgy of European Liberal and Reform Judaism*, published by the World Union for Progressive Judaism in 1968, but found no entry. Then it was not a Reform prayer book? Yet the alternative, that it was a traditional prayer book, seemed unlikely. So I dashed off a letter to Petuchowski: what did he know of the book?

The same afternoon, visiting the Divinity Library on another matter, I was again bitten by curiosity. Yet neither the catalogue of the Klau Library of the Hebrew Union College—had it been there Petuchowski would have known it—nor the catalogue of the Judaica Collection of the New York Public Library was of help. Nor, for that matter, was the Divinity Library catalogue. As I turned to leave, the voice of scholarship—or was it the echo of Jacob Z. Lauterbach's admonition: ''Go look on the shelves!''—rang in my ears. So I went to look on the shelves. I have a good visual image of the Judaica Collection so I had no difficulty in locating the liturgy section. But was I to take every book whose title was not stamped on the spine off the shelves? Then serendipity intervened. There, on one shelf, was a handful of small volumes with unmarked spines. I picked up one and read at the top of the title page: Abend-gebete/für/Sabbat und Festtage. The bottom third read: Gebetbuch der Liberalen Synagoge Berlin/Herausgegeben von der Liberalen Synagoge Norden in Berlin/Aus der Sammlung DIE GEMEINSCHAFT/Hefte für die religiöse Erstärkung des Judentums/Zweite veränderte und ver-mehrte Auflage/des "Freitagabend-Gebets"/1935. Was this the Falkenberg'sche Gebetbuch? Page 6 relieved me of any doubt, for the Vorrede, dated Berlin, Chanukka 1935, was signed, Hermann Falkenberg.

I returned to my study and wrote another letter to Petuchowski, relating my find. Several days later I had his reply. He had learned of the book after the publication of his study. In a review published in a bulletin of the congregation in Bulwayo, Rhodesia, the reviewer had noted the absence of any reference to it. In his reply to Petuchowski's query, he indicated that he did not possess a copy. Thus, until the copy in the Vanderbilt Divinity Library turned up, Petuchowski had no idea whether or not an example was in existence.

Relying on Petuchowski's wide canvass of the field, I have not rechecked other library holdings except for the Leo Baeck Institute in New York. It does not have a copy, but it has—although at the time of my inquiry I did not know it—a copy of the first edition, noted obliquely on the title page. Of this, more below. At the same time I checked in Kiryat Sefer but found no entry. Therefore, on the assumption that the Vanderbilt copy may be the only recorded one of the second edition, and that the Leo Baeck Institute copy may be the only one of the first, it seems wise to describe them and report as well something about Die Gemeinschaft and the synagogue, Berlin Norden.

As indicated above and as will be discussed in some detail below, the first edition was found by Fred Bogin, reference librarian of the Leo Baeck Institute Library, as the result of a search made in response to my inquiry. Its title page reads at the top: Das/Freitagabend-/Gebet/. At the bottom the following: Die Gemeinschaft/Hefte für die religiöse Erstärkung des Judentums/Herausgegeben von der Liberalen Synagoge Norden in Berlin/Nr. 10 (Chanukka-Heft/Berlin, 18. Dezember 1927). It is a booklet of sixteen pages, bound in dark-blue heavy paper, with the text beginning on page 3. It was published, according to the colophon on page 16, by Itzkowski and Co., Berlin N24, Auguststr. 69. The German text is printed in Gothic type. On page 16, there is a reference to the Notenbeilage. This was published in number 9, with a title page reading: Gesänge/für den/Freitagabend-Gottesdienst, and six pages containing the melodic line and texts—transliterated—for the following items: Wie schön sind deine Zelte; l'cho daudi; bor'chu; sch'ma; emess'; mi chomaucho; adaunoj jimlauch; w'schomru. About two-thirds down page 3 is the rubric Predigtlieder and then (a) way'chullu; and (b) Du hast, o Herr. This is followed by Kiddusch, with the note (auch für die häusliche Feier) and finally Schlussgesänge, adaum aulom; w'hojo.

The order of service in this first edition is as follows:

1. Gemeindegesang-Ma tauwu (i.e., Wie schön . . .);
2. Einleitungsgebet des Predigers;
3. l'cho daudi (indicated for Vorbeter and Gemeinde). The text is printed in Hebrew and provides in addition to the refrain, three verses. It is followed by a German translation.
4. Der Psalm des Sabbats [Ps. 92], with Hebrew and German texts;
5. Vorspruch des Predigers:
6. Kaddisch der Leidtragenden, with the Aramaic text and a German, partially paraphrastic, translation;
7. Abendgebet, beginning with bor'chu and the response, marked (Gemeinde), together with Hebrew text and a German translation of the first benediction. The second benediction is reduced to the opening line of 'ahavat' olom in Hebrew, followed by a German text without a concluding eulogy;

[212]

8. Sch'ma: Hebrew text of Deut. 6:4–8, marked (Vorbeter und Gemeinde); the response is omitted. The second and third paragraphs are omitted except for the concluding verses, Num. 15:39–41. A German translation is provided and the biblical sources are noted.

9. Emes weëmuno, marked (Gemeinde), follows in a very abbreviated Hebrew text that leads into mi chomaucho, marked (Gemeinde) as is adaunoj jimloch. The reader is assigned malkhutkha and vene'emar. This, too, is provided with a German translation with alternating paragraphs marked (Gemeinde) and with the biblical sources noted.

10. Haschkiwenu has both a full Hebrew and German text but v'al y'rushalayim is omitted.

11. W'schomru occurs in both Hebrew and German. Both are marked (Gemeinde) and the biblical source is noted.

12. Das Hauptgebet-Stilles Gebet. The first three benedictive are given in traditional form but the addition in the second benediction reads: mashiv ha-ruah umorid ha-tal v'hageshem. There are, as to be expected in a liberal prayer book, some variations in the intermediate benedictions for the Sabbath and in the first of the concluding benedictions, retze. The German translation is on the facing pages. The rendering of the conclusion of the second benediction is noteworthy: "Du schaffst, das glauben wir, ewiges Leben."

13. Predigtlieder as found in the Notenbeilage with the addition of "Schirm und Schutz in Sturm und Graus" for Chanukkah.

14. Vorlesung aus der Bibel.

15. Predigt.

16. Kiddusch in its traditional form with a German translation.

17. Schlussgebet des Predigers.

18. Olënu in German, reduced to three biblical verses, Deut. 4:39; Exod. 15:18; Zech. 14:9; with an in-

troductory verse taken from the traditional text and the concluding verse repeated in Hebrew.

19. Elauhaj n'zaur, the traditional conclusion of the tefilla—Hauptgebet, in a German version that quotes Pss. 72:12; 19:15; Job 25:3.
20. Schlussgesang.

There are three notes on the last page. The first indicates that the preacher's opening and concluding prayers should, together with the biblical reading and the sermon, form a conceptual whole. The second suggests that the introductory and concluding songs, as well as the Predigtlieder, should vary. The third refers to the Notenbeilage and states that the participation of the congregation in the singing is presupposed.

The second edition, whose discovery set off the search, is a slender volume bound in medium-blue linen, opening in the fashion of a Hebrew book. The title, *Abendgebete*, is stamped in gold, slightly above the center of the cover that has a stamped double-ruling around its four sides. It is printed on manufactured paper with no detectable watermark and is saddle-stitched in 11 gatherings of 8 leaves, a total of 88 leaves, 176 pages, IV–XVI, 1–159. It is 19 centimeters tall. On page [II], toward the bottom, the printer's mark is found: Druck von M. Lehrberger & Co., Frankfurt A.M. Pages [III] and IV contain the table of contents:

INHALT:
I. Abendgebet

III. Häusliche Feier

Page [111] provides the title page for the remainder of the volume: Abendgebete/für/Sabbat und Festtage/Gemeinde-Gesänge. These begin on page 113. Page [131] bears the title: Gesänge/für die/Besonderen Feiern, which begin on page 133. Page [147] reads: Gesänge/für die/Häusliche Feier. These begin on page 148.

This volume indicates the development of the congregation and its liturgical interests. It deserves careful study and comparison with the Einheitsgebetbuch that appeared in 1929. The music, too, may be of interest, as it may or may not relate to the work of the important synagogal composers of the time. Above all, the Vorrede of Falkenberg suggests something of the times in which it appeared: ''In schwerster Zeit erscheint dieses Buch. In einer Zeit, in der nach der Meinung selbst mancher unserer engeren Freunde alles nur für die Hebung wirtschäftlicher Nöte eingesetzt werden sollte. Aber von jeher war es Sorge und Stolz Israels, die seelischen Sorgen über materiellen zu stellen. Das innere Fundament der Menschen zu festen, ist die ebenso grosse wir [= wie] schwere Aufgabe der Zeit. In bangen Stunden sucht die Seele Frieden in der Geborgenheit des Gotteshauses und des Gebets. Dieses Buch ist in seinem

Bereich bestimmt, den Weg zu führen aus der Unruhe der Welt in die Weihe religiöser Vertiefung."

One final note concerning the book before turning to a consideration of the congregation that brought it forth. At the end of the Kurze Einführung that is an introduction to the history and content of the evening liturgy of the synagogue, acknowledgement is made of the assistance of Professor Ismar Elbogen (from whose library the Vanderbilt copy came) and of Franz Rosenzweig in the matter of the German renderings: "Die Bearbeitung des deutschen Teils lehnt sich an einigen Stellen an die Übertragungen von Franz Rosenzweig an, der die Arbeit unseres Synagogue oftmals durch seinen Rat und seine Hinweise gefördert hat, und dem wir auch über seinen Heimgang hinaus Dank schulden." The German version of Hammawdil is Rosenzweig's, appearing first—as Professor N. N. Glatzer wrote to me—in the Festschrift for Rabbi Nobel of Frankfurt.

Our concluding questions concern those whose prayer book this was and who, in the face of the times, produced it with such evident devotion. What was the Liberal Synagogue, Berlin Norden? When did it come into existence and why? Who were its leaders? Where did it meet? What was its end? Some answers to these questions, except the last, are to be found on the pages of *Die Gemeinschaft*. But what was it? At the beginning of my search, I consulted the lists of German-Jewish periodicals found in the *Jüdisches Lexikon* and in the Leo Baeck Institute Year Book, volume 1 (1952), but to no avail. It was not noted. Why, is not clear. Fred Bogin, reference librarian of the Leo Baeck Institute in New York, to whom I am indebted for his thoughtful assistance, suggested in a letter dated March 25, 1980, that it may be because it was the publication of a synagogue. By that I assume he meant, in-house. The Institute has a bound volume containing numbers 1–15, from September 19, 1925, through December 7, 1928. Number 10, as noted above, is the first edition of the prayer book and is bound out of order to accommodate to the fact that it is a Hebrew book. In addition to the bound volume, the Institute has numbers 19–20 and 21–22. The latter is dated November 1933. Mr.

Bogin wrote on February 13, 1980, that the library records the periodical as having "appeared from 1925 to 1933(?)" in numbers 1–22. However, as can be seen from the title page of the second edition of the prayer book, it too belonged to the collection *Die Gemeinschaft*. It is not numbered, however, and there is no way, at the moment, of determining whether any numbers appeared between 22 and its publication.

The origins of the congregation are described in the first issue of *Die Gemeinschaft* (September 19, 1925), in an article by Falkenberg, who seems to have been the moving spirit of the group, entitled "Unser Gottesdienst." He wrote that the first service was held in November 1923 under the auspices of the "Ortsgruppe Norden des Liberalen Vereins," because at the time northern and northeastern Berlin had no "gottesdienstlichen Veranstaltungen für liberal denkende religiöse Juden" (p. 6). The service was held in the inspiring (stimmungsvollen) synagogue of Auerbachsches Waisenhaus, Schönhauser Allee 162. Incidentally, the orientation of the synagogue was north-south because it was not originally intended for that purpose, but was to be a meeting hall.

At this point the connection between the Plaut family and the congregation begins to emerge, for Jonas Plaut was the director of the home that was as well the location of the family residence. The relationship was, however, more than physical contiguity. At the Kol Nidre service on September 22, 1925, Director Plaut delivered the sermon, and again on the eve of Rosh Hashanah and on Kol Nidre 1926, he was the preacher. In addition, he was a member of the board of the congregation, apparently from its beginning, and numbers 1, 2, and 4 of *Die Gemeinschaft* contain a history of Das Auerbachsche Waisenhaus written by him. On page 5 of number 7, there is a picture of the synagogue, which was on the third floor of the building.[1] In numbers 21–22 (November 24, 1933) Plaut published an article dealing with the decade of the congregation's existence.[2]

To return briefly to the origins of the congregation as reported by Falkenberg: it was noted that in addition to Friday evening services, held at 7:15 for the convenience of business people, but also to accommodate the home celebration of the Sabbath, festival evening services were instituted, as well as service, both evening and day, for the Holy Days. In the beginning (1923), attendance was uncertain, but a corps of regular worshippers developed. In 1925, at Passover, Dr. Martin Solomonski was appointed rabbi. At that time the need for a prayer book reflecting the interests and desires of the congregation made itself felt. Although the order of service followed that of the "Berliner Gebetbuch für die Orgelsynagogen," yet changes were introduced. The most important was the reading of the Torah before the sermon, "sodass diese ihre naturgemässe Stellung gewissermassen als Schrifterklärung und als Schluss und Höhepunkt des Gottesdienstes erhält." Further, the reading of the scrolls on the evening of the festivals—Song of Songs on Passover, Ruth on Pentecost, Ecclesiastes on Tabernacles—instead of, as traditionally, at the morning service, was introduced. As for morning services, when such were held, Falkenberg wrote: "Beim Morgengottesdienst haben wir uns bewusst von der Liturgie der Orgelsynagogen entfernt."

Reading through *Die Gemeinschaft*, one realizes that there is quite enough material to construct a fuller picture of the development of the congregation and of its wider influence, but such must be left to another time and to other hands. It was but by chance that it became my obligation to restore, briefly and partially, the fading past. What began as a bibliographic chase has ended as more, a Festgabe to an old and cherished friend, recalling an episode in the life of his family that may have otherwise been lost.

Notes

1. The synagogue was directly above the apartment of the Plaut family.
2. A record of the synagogue service and the institution in which it was housed may be found in Gunther Plaut's *Unfinished Business* (Toronto, 1981).—ED.

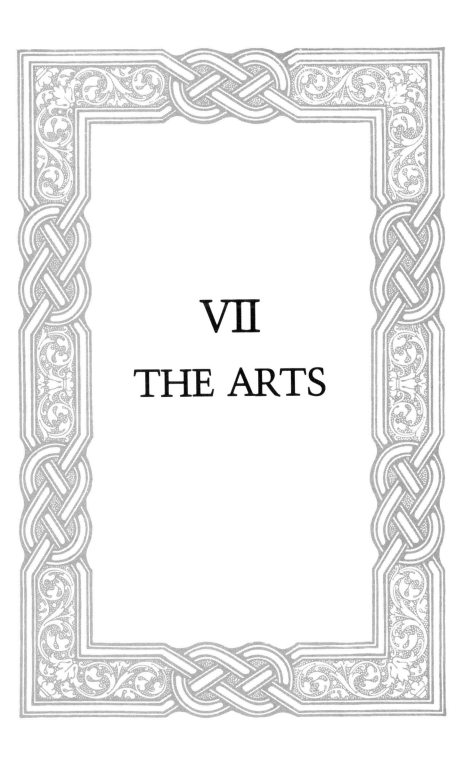

VII
THE ARTS

ART AND SOCIAL CHANGE: TWENTY YEARS IN THE LIFE OF THE MINNESOTA MUSEUM OF ART
Malcolm E. Lein

An art museum appears to the outsider as a kind of awesome ivory tower. Its offerings are often cached in phrases not casily understood and too frequently made more obscure by purveyors of the "painted word," described by Tom Wolfe in his book about curators and critics. However, the tower itself remains no less beautiful or serene. But inside, life among museum workers differs little from the rest of the working world. There are the same dreams and disappointments, successes and failures, selflessness and self-interest—everything one finds in any other place and in much the same degree.

This article, highlighting a portion of the history of one such ivory tower, the Minnesota Museum of Art in St. Paul, was written in response to Dr. Jonathan Plaut's invitation to contribute to the book being published as a tribute to his father, Rabbi W. Gunther Plaut. It focuses on the period from 1947 to 1966, during which an unknown local art school and gallery progressed to a museum, whose exhibitions were circulated by the United States' government throughout much of the world. Interest lies not so much in the change as in the obstacles and the unique course that was charted. This is written to serve also as a narrative supplement to material for the Archives of American Art. It will fill gaps and provide insights and explanations about many aspects not obvious in formal documents. Our policies and experiments, obstacles and successes—as a late entry into the museum field—could prove useful to other groups or cities with lofty aspirations. The problems will be much the same.

Gunther Plaut, a member of the museum's governing body throughout most of the critical period covered here, and now an honorary life trustee of the museum, headed the board for many of those formative years. His philosophy, his political instinct, and his grasp of operational needs played a major role in the development of the institution, and so they have particular significance to this book honoring his seventieth birthday. For those of us who worked with him, it was a great privilege. We extend to Rabbi Plaut our appreciation and congratulations.

The first phase of the history of the Minnesota Museum of Art began with a kind of artificial insemination of art-genes in 1927 and continued through a twenty-year period of gestation and adolescence. The attending midwife was duly recorded on the certificate of birth as the Board of Control, made up of a mixed group of interested socialites, the expected dilettantes and quasi-intellectual observers of "modern" art. All moved in a polite circle of respectability on the fringe of the power structure of the old city. None commanded substantial influence.[1]

Incorporated as the St. Paul School of Art on the first of November of that year, it was the formal successor to more than thirty years of varied art activities. The roster of board members then and in the years that followed included important citizens: "old-family" names, prominent ladies, foundation officials, senior executives of successful businesses, as well as Warren Burger, a lawyer who would later become chief justice of the Supreme Court, and Elmer L. Andersen, a future governor. But the most important element essential to the success of every art museum was lacking in St. Paul from the start: the presence, leadership, and support of at least one serious collector with affluence and influence, and the willingness to use both. Nevertheless the institution survived.

Following its birth, the infant struggled through early childhood unendowed and inadequately supported. The school, philosophically sound and administered by compe-

[223]

tent professional artists and teachers, barely made it through the depression years on the sustenance furnished by the well-meaning board. Inadequately housed in rented quarters, it offered a bohemian atmosphere and a sense of patronage of the arts to its loyal corps of volunteers. Their efforts eventually bore fruit. In 1939 a fifty-year-old brownstone mansion in the passé sector of the city was given as a permanent home. The name was changed to the St. Paul Gallery and School of Art. A modest fund of about $30,000 was raised to remodel the building.

The old mansion, although not very suitable for use as a museum, afforded rougly 20,000 square feet of floor space to house an art school and exhibitions of mostly avant-garde painting shows from New York. The future was generally viewed as unpromising.

The board, dominated from the beginning by political conservatives unable to develop a real financial commitment by the community, chose not to follow an alternate course which could have provided a more solid foundation: support by the Work Project Administration's Art Program of the late thirties and early forties. Any reminder of Franklin D. Roosevelt was not welcome in most social circles in St. Paul.

The Second World War was probably a disguised blessing as far as the St. Paul Gallery and School of Art was concerned, because of the changes that came as a result. The kind of institution that it was intended to be could not be achieved without substantial financial support. There was still no friend of the institution who possessed the means, interest, and dedicated leadership to work the miracle that would be necessary.[2] Inevitably, the change began. In the mid-forties the head of a small manufacturing company became president of the board. He was succeeded by the head of another local manufacturing company who was to emerge as an important political figure in the state, ultimately to be elected governor.

As late as 1946 the institution's tangible assets totaled less than $50,000; its annual operating budget for that year was under $15,000. There were separate heads of the art school, the administration, and the gallery, all answering independently to the board.

William L. West, the president of the board elected in 1947, was a Harvard Business School graduate with a self-assured manner and piercing eyes, which looked through heavy, wire-rimmed glasses, too late for an earlier fashion and too early for that which would follow. He followed in his family's tradition of concern and responsibility for community affairs. Those before him had concentrated on social welfare. He turned his attention to the struggling semblance of an art institution, badly handicapped by the advent of the war, but which he believed to be worth saving as a necessary asset to the city.

West's family background, the social climate of St. Paul, and the Harvard Business School gave him little understanding of the avant-garde movement in the arts. The loyal devotees who appeared at the opening tea for each monthly art exhibition had equal difficulty understanding his view that the coal bill and sound financing took precedence over the lofty philosophical concerns of the more culturally inclined. Out of necessity, volunteers, including board members, had been intimately involved in routine operations and administration. Confusion could hardly be avoided. Incoming correspondence was filed by subject; outgoing correspondence according to the author; and telegrams, incoming or outgoing, filed under ''T.''

A paid head of staff was obviously needed. The Search Committee, appointed by the president to find a director, turned for advice to the brilliant though controversial director of the Walker Art Center.[3] His recommendation was seconded by a number of others on the local scene. Their nominee: a thirty-three-year-old newcomer to St. Paul, back from five years in the army, a colonel in the Corps of Engineers. Trained as an architect, interested in art, and intrigued by the challenge, he stated his terms: to be solely responsible for all aspects of operation; to continue his own business interests along with his teaching at a local college; and to stay for no more and no less than three years. He chose to ignore the sage advice of an older, wiser, and exper-

[225]

ienced observer of the St. Paul scene, who said: "St. Paul has a long record of enthusiastic beginnings in the arts, much lip service, but no real suppport. You can never change the pattern!"[4]

The board accepted and Malcolm E. Lein took over on August 1, 1947. The board breathed a sigh of relief, continued business as usual, and only partially faced the real problem. Two months later the glistening white paint on the front door of the staid old Summit Avenue mansion, turned art gallery and school, hinted that a new day had come. There would be worse to follow. The traditional May Rummage Mart, a fund-raising event which, in reality, was a kind of fashionable gathering over lunch to launch the sale of cast-off finery, shuddered under the impact of a sale of used cars in front of the building.

The four-person staff in 1947 was actively supplemented by large numbers of volunteers, trim and attractive Junior Leaguers, close friends of the new director, and assorted hangers-on. Neither formal guidelines nor policies had been established by the board, but the traditions that had grown out of another time and kind of leadership were rooted deeply enough to cause irritations quite like poison ivy, which is hard to keep under control and harder to get rid of.

The civic-minded devotion of the stalwarts who had kept the gallery and school alive during the war continued for the most part. They had recognized the need for a broader view, some positive new focus, and a single directing head. With understandable concern because of limited resources, they nevertheless would risk the consequences of the new three-year commitment. Yet the St. Paul Gallery and School of Art still retained its curious blend of enthusiastic optimism and an unrealistic attitude toward the arts. And no one involved could then guess what storms the future would bring.

Buoyed by blind optimism, but balanced by pragmatic idealism, a Five-Year Development Plan defined specific objectives: first, annual financial support from the city government and greatly increased public contributions; second, an exhibition program that would attract national attention (that would, in other words, draw the circle larger, for a prophet is without honor in his own country); third, a fireproof building with proper climate control for art works.

There were longer-range goals, too: start a permanent collection (a name on a brass plaque is a powerful incentive to awaken support—if you would be remembered, look to the arts); create an adequate endowment fund (a necessary prerequisite to a lasting future, as well as a subtle persuader of prospective donors concerned about the museum's financial stability); and, finally, add illustrious names to the board roster, individuals used to handling substantial assets who would inspire confidence in those same potential donors.

That first step in the early 1950s—the attempt to woo financial support from a city plagued by its own serious money problems—challenged the staid traditions of the board. New leadership was needed.

When Gunther Plaut was asked if he would be willing to head the board,[5] St. Paul wealth was concentrated among Republicans, Catholics, and Presbyterians; political power among Democrats and Labor; financial power among the old families and the banks. Dr. Plaut pondered the question. "It is not just that I am a Jew. I am a rabbi—a Jew among Jews. . . . And I do not want to preside over the demise of a museum." But in the end, he agreed. His election, an unusual action among art museums of that day, gave enormous impetus to the move toward a new era for the institution.

In the early 1950s there was very little lifeblood in the form of money to keep St. Paul's few art organizations alive. Gunther Plaut's decision to head the St. Paul Gallery and School of Art in those bleak years was of monumental importance. He was a persuasive spokesman. Although a newcomer to St. Paul following his years as an army chaplain, he became a major force in the community. For the museum, his breadth of vision and innate sensitivity to the arts were vital in the implementation of bold new programs proposed by the staff. To the Labor-dominated City Council

[227]

his role inspired confidence in the political wisdom of committing city funds to an art institution; and for an organization still dependent on massive volunteer support, he was a brilliant advocate and example.

Concurrent with the effort to obtain city support for the museum was a ground swell of activity directed toward some form of joint effort to seek funds for the arts on a broad basis. With active participation by the Junior League, a modest contribution from a local foundation, the blessing of the city fathers, and endorsement by the city's musical organizations, a somewhat dubious and reluctant Science Museum joined the effort. An Arts and Science Council was established. In the beginning its purpose was to raise funds. That it would stray from that purpose was realistically foreseen as a serious threat. But there was then no adequate alternative.

The three years which had been envisioned for completion of those optimistic early objectives, and which was the basis of the commitment by the new director in 1947, had long since passed when pieces began to fall into place: annual support from the city began in 1952; an issue of city bonds was passed in 1953, which included funds for a building in the downtown area to house the art museum (then called the St. Paul Art Center), a theater, and the Science Museum; a very important art work, Degas's "Femme à sa toilette," was given to the Permanent Collection in 1954; and the Arts and Science Fund Drive, beginning in 1959, would triple the amount of contributions that the member groups had been able to raise individually.

Only in retrospect does it all appear simple. It had been a painful Herculean effort made possible only through a skilfull blending of varied objectives and conflicting interests. The Citizens' Committee, charged with planning the new Arts and Science Building, was dominated by the publisher of the paper, a recently returned under-secretary of the treasury in the Eisenhower administration and the president of a railroad. At a meeting in the prestigious boardroom of a bank, a city councilman also serving on the committee was unruffled by his colleagues or the surroundings.

He commented: "I always told you it would be Labor that would bring culture to St. Paul."[6] The remark was in large measure correct.

Meanwhile, the staff of the museum had been developing plans for a program which would carry out the objective of achieving national recognition. With no large funding available, it would necessarily be an exercise in lifting oneself by one's own bootstraps. A national craft competition, "Fiber, Clay, and Metal," was launched in 1952, the culmination of a decision in 1948 to commit the bulk of staff, exhibition, and educational resources to an integrated program focusing on the reviving national interest in the hand-crafts. In the Twin Cities other art organizations ignored the crafts; nationally, too, the field was open. A small organization, with substantial volunteer help, could execute a major national competition and exhibition for a fraction of the cost of a single major painting show, which at best would be a watered-down, "me-too" version of what the large museums could do better. Nor was there distinction to be gained by simply renting the traveling exhibitions which had been organized by others.

That successful first show, followed by a national tour to a dozen other art institutions, formed the cornerstone of the museum's program for nearly a decade. It also established the basic theme for the museum's later interest: exhibitions and purchases in the art of the Orient and in Primitive Art.

In order to add a Fine Arts' complement to the crafts' program, another biennial national competition—"Drawings USA"—was launched in 1961. Each of the two competitions drew several thousand entries, with every state represented; each exhibition was then circulated to another twelve to sixteen museums and universities throughout the United States. Their importance in turn led to international circulation of the museum's exhibitions to Eastern and western Europe, Central and South America, Mexico, Australia, and the Far East. The aim for national prestige exceeded its goal. International recognition became a rewarding by-product.[7]

By the mid-fifties the basic building blocks for the future

were in place. A new building was assured; the city was giving annual financial support; the Arts and Science Council was established with joint fund-raising in the offing; national recognition had been achieved. But local prestige was more elusive. The Endowment Fund and Permanent Collection, although making progress, needed broader support. That, in turn, depended upon the confidence that would come with a prestigious board.

One of the keys to the revitalization and expansion of the museum until then had been its "working Board of Directors"—young, committed, upward-bound, and civic-minded citizens. Now it was proposed to create a separate and independent Board of Trustees, elected by the directors, to be responsible for the museum's permanent assets—the building, collection, and endowment. The Board of Directors would continue to be responsible for administration and operation.

The plan for the "dual board," although logical in that it offered the sole way to obtain the best of both worlds—young workers and affluent elder statesmen—did not enjoy Gunther Plaut's enthusiastic support. A remark by the treasurer on the issue, when it was coming up for final consideration by the board, indicated the president's enormous influence and persuasive power: "Gunther may lose this battle. The odds are even. Everyone is against him."[8]

The proposal for the Board of Trustees was approved, its responsibilities defined. Within weeks it was operational, its membership reading like a roster of St. Paul aristocracy and power. The foundation for a major collection and endowment was greatly strengthened. Although he could foresee potential problems (quite accurately, as it turned out, but not for the reasons or in the way that were anticipated), Gunther Plaut accepted the decision and used his skill to help implement the proposal.

A few collections spring full-blown, like Athena from the head of Zeus. Most start modestly, however, often with dismal credentials. A large early gift to one of America's greatest museums consisted of hundreds of drawings bearing the names of famous artists of several centuries past—

unfortunately fakes.[9] A Midwest museum, which would ultimately earn national distinction, was for many years laughed at discreetly because of the important names on many of its paintings—attributed incorrectly.[10] The profession itself, more than most, does not look kindly on fledglings learning to fly. Nor is it inclined to act helpfully. It is a snob profession. As with all snobs, any of its own questionable origins are casually swept under the rug and easily forgotten.

Endowment funds, too, are likely to start unpretentiously. Both the Permanent Collection and the Endowment Fund of the Minnesota Museum of Art had been started in the late forties.[11] With occasional gifts and bequests they grew slowly but steadily. When the Board of Trustees was established in 1958 the total value of the museum's assets was still very modest. Nevertheless, the new trustees treated their charge with serious and deliberate concern. Important policies were adopted. Endowment Fund principles provided that income could be used only for the Permanent Collection. Purchases for the collection would be made only in specialized fields, although all gifts of art works—without strings attached—would be encouraged and accepted. Exhibition and program emphasis would be integrated with the needs and interests of the collection. Well-designed publications reflecting the collection and the exhibitions would serve as useful promotional pieces for potential friends and donors in distant places, who might never visit the museum itself. The principal target area for the source of gifts was seen as being beyond Minnesota, rather than in St. Paul itself. Tough and experienced trustees, such as Walter Trenerry, personal lawyer for the head of 3M, and Allan McNab, former director of the Chicago Art Institute, added credibility and stature.

The strategy paid dividends beyond expectations. With the museum's move to the new building in late 1964, its potential expanded enormously. The years of waiting had been frustrating, but they gave time to plan, to arrange for multi-million dollar exhibitions, to prepare the foundation for future gifts to the Permanent Collection. For those who had participated in the long struggle, the success of that first full year in the new building was deeply gratifying.[12]

The second phase of the history of the Minnesota Museum of Art came to an end in 1966.[13] The effort to create a museum where there was no indigenous demand had been as unorthodox as it had been difficult. It often appeared that an art museum in St. Paul was less than welcome. Each success seemed to inspire an undercurrent of opposition. But in spite of the early unfavorable environment, the momentum which had been developed continued, and finally brought unprecedented support. The museum acquired its own separate building as a Permanent Collection Gallery. The collection, building, and Endowment Fund grew at an average of $600,000 per year, mostly from gifts, eighty per cent of them from outside St. Paul. By the end of the 1970s assets approached $8 million, the Endowment Fund $2 million, and the annual operating budget $750,000.

But the foundation for the surprising success that was to come had been laid in those critical and stringent years of the fifties and early sixties. On August 1, 1961, a Civic Recognition Dinner was held in St. Paul to honor Gunther Plaut for his many accomplishments. High among them was his leadership of the Minnesota Museum of Art, the success which it had even then achieved, and the bright future which lay ahead. He had indeed made sure that he would not be the one to preside over its demise.

Notes

1. Minnesota's Twin Cities of St. Paul and Minneapolis developed in the nineteenth century as an adjunct to Fort Snelling, a frontier

military outpost. St. Paul, the more dominant during early years, became the capital of the state and an important railroad, lumber, and wholesale-trade center for the northwest. However, by the 1920s Minneapolis was significantly larger and more influential. An article about the Twin Cities in *Fortune* in the mid-thirties focused mainly on Minneapolis, its aggressive leadership and accomplishments, while characterizing St. Paul as the staid Boston of the Midwest.

2. By the Second World War the great fortunes amassed by early St. Paulites were largely in trust for their heirs. Members of the "old families" were notably absent from leadership roles in the city. A Minneapolis survey, completed in 1964, to determine the potential for financial support of the arts noted a dozen Minnesota sources able to give a million dollars or more; two-thirds were in St. Paul. At about that same time a Minneapolis newspaper, in an article about its "twin-sister city," commented that "nothing happens in St. Paul without the blessing of Louis Hill," the grandson of railroad tycoon James J. Hill.

3. The director of the Walker Art Center, from 1939 to 1950, was Daniel S. Defenbacher.

4. Statement by Wilhelmus B. Bryan, dean of Macalester College, St. Paul. In 1947 Minneapolis was home to a distinguished and well-endowed art museum, a nationally acclaimed symphony orchestra, and the influential Walker Art Center; in the early sixties the Guthrie Theater would become its fourth major cultural asset, as well as its financial responsibility. In 1947 St. Paul had no significant or solidly established cultural organization.

5. Dr. Plaut became a member of the board in 1949 and served as its president from 1952 to 1959.

6. Statement by Frank Marzitelli, city councilman. The committee also included Herbert Lewis, *St. Paul Dispatch*; Julian Baird, First National Bank; John Budd, Great Northern Railroad; and several others. The committee succeeded in having the 1953 issue of city bonds provide funds for an Arts and Science Center in St. Paul. The center was not completed and opened until late 1964.

7. In 1959 the United States Information Agency (USIA) commissioned the museum to organize a major exhibition of contemporary American crafts to be sent for two years to Europe, including the Iron Curtain countries. The premier showing was held at Mount Zion Temple in St. Paul, where Dr. Plaut served as rabbi. In 1963 the USIA again commissioned the museum to organize a craft show for circulation in Australia and the Far East; and in 1977 it commissioned the museum to organize the exhibition, "Fifty Years of American Drawings, 1927–1977," to be shown in Europe and in South and Central America. The success of the museum's exhibition exchange-program was an important factor in the decision by the Soviet Union to include the museum in St. Paul as one of six American museums to present its monumental and landmark showing of "Soviet Arts and Crafts," in 1972.

[233]

8. Statement by Richard Heller, Treasurer, Board of Directors.
9. Metropolitan Museum, New York City.
10. Walker Art Center, Minneapolis, Minnesota.
11. The first gift of art works came as a bequest from George Lindsay of St. Paul in 1946, but a permanent collection was not officially established by the board until 1956. The Endowment Fund was started by a gift of approximately $5,000 from Mrs. Arthur Savage of St. Paul, in 1947.
12. The museum's Annual Report for 1965–1966, published in its *Bulletin*:

> The annual meeting was held on November 16, 1966. The start of a new year is a time to look back as well as forward. In the case of the St. Paul Art Center [changed to the Minnesota Museum of Art in 1969], it is particularly noteworthy since the most spectacular year in its history just closed. Though important in itself, perhaps the greatest significance is that it gave a preview of the great potential that can be realized for St. Paul in the years ahead. The following letter from director, Malcolm Lein, is included as a report of the year's activity and progress [the letter was written to John Harvey, art critic, *St. Paul Dispatch*, at his request]:
>
> Dear J. H.
>
> It is enlightening to look at the forest rather than the trees to answer your question about progress during the past year. The perspective gained is rewarding. With pride in the accomplishments, appreciation to the community for its support, and thanks to my staff for their efforts, I pass on to you an abbreviated version of Museum history for 1965–66.
>
> 1. Money in itself does not ensure quality. But quality always costs money. The availability of the necessary funds and our location in fireproof and well-guarded facilities have made it possible for us to include magnificent exhibitions in our schedule. Out of nineteen this year, there were three major shows, each of multi-million dollar valuation.
>   a. Jerome Hill: Painter, Film Maker, Collector
>   An exhibition of great breadth showing the range of talents and interests of a 20th-Century Renaissance Man well known for his Academy Award-winning film.
>   b. The Robert Edward Peters Collection: Reached a new segment of the Twin City area population with attendance of 20,000 per month, an all time building record.
>   c. Age of Belief: Rare ecclesiastical paintings and sculpture from the 12th to the 17th centuries; first in a series of loans from the Harding Museum of Chicago. . . .
> 2. Our third biennial presentation of DRAWINGS/USA brought 4,000 entries from every state. Within three weeks after being offered as a loan exhibition to other museums, it was solidly booked for two years after its close in St. Paul. It will be shown in 16 other institutions. News releases about DUSA reached 800 publications in the United States.

[234]

3. The Museum's Drawing Collection received further national recognition, typified by a request from IBM to show a representative group of 55 drawings at its distinguished 57th Street IBM Gallery in New York City. The show was extensively reviewed including nearly half a page of coverage and reproductions in the erudite Christian Science Monitor of 13 September 1966.

4. The importance of a close working relationship between industry and the Museum was demonstrated by the February exhibition, Communication Through Art and Industry, sponsored by 3M, and featuring a series of full-size color reproductions of some of the great works in the Museum Collection. The exhibition was later shown in New York City, and plans are now being made to show it next year in Dusseldorf, Germany.

5. Approximately 1,300 students were registered in the School. There were classes in drawing, painting, sculpture and crafts for all ages, with professional and avocational students ranging from four to ninety-four. Tuition income reached a record high.

6. Our earned income reached an all-time high of $76,136. The cost of operating and maintaining the building and providing guard service is paid by the city. The Arts and Science Fund provided an allocation of $64,681 toward the cost of exhibitions and educational programs. With some necessary pruning and the application of stringent economies and careful management we adhered to the Museum's traditional ''modus operandi'' of keeping expenses below income.

7. The exhibition of contemporary American handcrafts, FIBER/CLAY/METAL USA, organized by the Museum at the request of the U.S. Information Agency, continues on tour in the Far East. Most of the works included are from the Museum's own collection, the foremost of its kind in the U.S.

8. The State's Art Council announced a grant to the Musem to further an expanded educational Tour Program for children and adults. Primary focus is the Junior High School age level, a group not now being served by other Twin City museum programs.

9. The Board of Trustees was not only expanded but it also assumed a more active role, particularly in regard to the development of the Collection and the Endowment Fund. New Trustees include Thomas Ellerbe, Jerome Hill, Mrs. John Musser, Miss Katharine Ordway and Robert Edward Peters. Walter Trenerry was elected Chairman. Over-all development dramatically reflects the effective interest of the Trustees.

   a. There were approximately 1,000 new acquisitions for the Permanent Collection, with particularly strong gains in the Museum's fields of emphasis: Sculpture, drawings, crafts and oriental art. Using income from the Endowment, the Museum contracted to purchase the extensive Konantz-Benton-Minnich Collection of oriental art, including a superb group of costumes and textiles, sculpture, paintings and crafts. Robert Sarnoff, Board Chairman of RCA, New York City, gave Klaus Ihlenfeld's major sculpture, Cluster of Butterflies. Edward Weiss of Chicago presented a large sculpture by Abbott Pattison. Other major gifts include a pair of George Inness paintings from Mr. and Mrs. Carl Schuneman, Sr.; an extensive collection of Oriental art from Mrs. Bernard Blum; Japanese Prints from Mr. and Mrs. Louis W. Hill, Jr.; a Bernard Reder bronze from Mr. and Mrs. Phillip A. Bruno of New York City; and a group of 19th century paintings from Robert Edward Peters, who also announced that he has willed his collection, valued at more than two million dollars, to the Museum.

b. The most extensive single gift this year was the bequest by the noted sculptor Paul Manship, who was born in St. Paul, of half of his works. More than 200 pieces were included. The remaining items went to the Smithsonian Institution. A memorial exhibition of his work will open in January 1967.

c. The year's success can perhaps best be visualized in terms of the growth of permanent assets. The value of all contributions to the Endowment Fund and the Permanent Collection during the past year is approximately equal to the total dollars given for all purposes from all sources: . . . city, Arts and Science Fund, foundations and individuals . . . during the entire preceding 39 years since the Museum was incorporated.

In short, this was indeed a year of great achievement. The extraordinary growth and momentum are a stimulating challenge to the future. On behalf of the Trustees, Directors and a grateful community, I want to extend our deep appreciation for your interest.

13. The purchase of the Konantz-Benton-Minnich Collection for $50,000 in 1965, the bequest of the Paul Manship Collection in 1966, and the promised bequest of the Peters Collection that same year were forerunners of major developments that would highlight phase three of the museum's history: a $200,000 anonymous gift to the endowment fund; the announcement that Katharine Ordway of New York City planned to leave her collection to the museum in St. Paul where it had been exhibited in 1968; the name change to the Minnesota Museum of Art, reflecting the broadened interest and support far beyond that known by the small provincial art center of twenty years before. The interest of major donors and the expansion of the Permanent Collection dictated the need for space to house the collection beyond the limited facilities in the Arts and Science Center. With the assurance of $1 million from three trustees toward a $6 million goal, the museum won the support of the City Council and the federal government's General Services Administration to give the recently vacated old Federal Courts Building to the city for the art museum. However, by 1971 it was clear that the Federal Courts Building proposal faced insurmountable obstacles other than money. Consequently, in 1972, with a challenge grant of half a

[236]

million dollars from Miss Ordway, the museum raised the funds needed to purchase and remodel a 1931 architectural gem, of about 30,000 square feet, as a Permanent Collection Gallery ideally located across from the City Hall. The new building, along with the $2 million Endowment Fund achieved by the end of the decade, promised the stability and financial foundation that every art museum hopes to achieve.

Meanwhile, the downtown business center of the city was being rejuvenated. Outside investment capital, revived business interest, and government and private construction combined to reverse the stagnation and decay of more than thirty years. A greatly expanded Science Museum and a nationally acclaimed chamber orchestra added luster. The St. Paul of the 1980s—although still visibly overshadowed by its twin-sister city—could hardly be recognized as the same staid Boston of the Midwest of *Fortune* magazine fame nearly fifty years before.

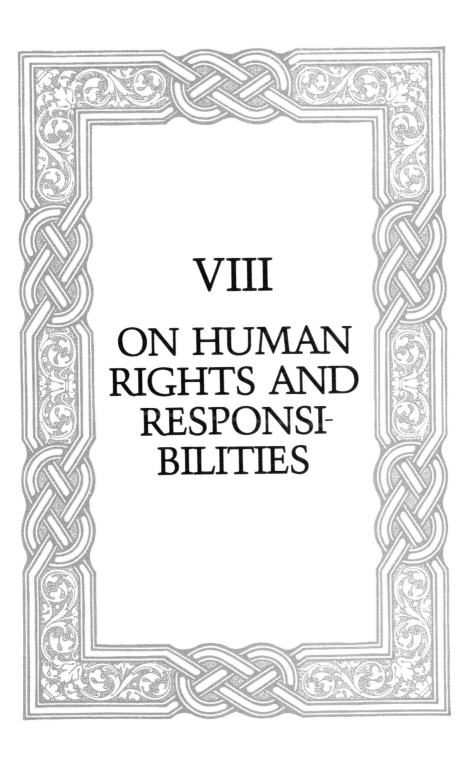

VIII

ON HUMAN RIGHTS AND RESPONSI-BILITIES

Human Rights Under Different Ideologies and Regimes: The Gains and the Limitations
Bhausaheb Ubale

The primary aim of this paper is to examine, from a global perspective, the development of differences in the understanding and practice of human rights under different regimes and ideologies. These differences will be discussed not only in terms of the political and institutional rationale that have been advanced to sustain them, but in relation to the United Nations' goal to promote a universal value-consensus in the area of human rights. The last part of the article will examine the limitations and continuing concerns in the area of human rights, and discuss the meaning and significance of human rights' principles in our contemporary world.

The concept of human rights, or the rights of man, is one that has become firmly rooted in the consciousness of the world society. Yet disputes continue, not only about its true normative reference, but about its practical application in different countries operating often under different ideologies. Nor has it ceased to be an issue of disagreement in religious, political, and moral philosophy. It is agreed, however, that in its origin, the concept was associated with the idea of natural law and, therefore, of the natural rights of man which cannot be taken away from him. But it was not until the last decades of the eighteenth century that the idea took on express formulation.

The goal of human rights is the establishment of a just society. The American and French revolutions emphasized the "inalienable rights" of man, that is, rights considered to belong to the individual under natural law as a consequence of his being human. These two revolutions promoted the concept that the individual must be given maximum freedom of action under a just policy, based on consensus and drawing its legitimacy from the approval of the people. The philosophical justification of the assertion and legal demands of the individual in contemporary Western societies, is, therefore, in terms of human dignity and justice.

Centralist-oriented regimes generally emphasize the power of the state and people's direct relationship with the state. In such regimes, there is a tendency not only toward the growth of centralized, bureaucratic organizations, but of centralization in communication and decision-making. This approach robs the individual of the autonomy which the concept of human rights promotes.

Mobilization and hence totalitarianism is stressed under centralist regimes. These regimes, therefore, generally aim to foster large-scale organizations and all-inclusive, nationwide structures. Under this condition, the notion of limiting the power of the state in deference to individual rights is clearly unacceptable.

Here, then, lies the basis of the divergence in the normative development and practical application of human rights' principles between the Western-bloc nations (mostly capitalist-oriented) and the Eastern-bloc nations (mostly socialist-oriented). In the socialist-oriented regimes, the emphasis is on collective rights and the primary role of the party.[1] Human rights' questions, therefore, are dependent, not on their individual expression, but on their collective articulation by the state in terms of legally enforceable claims in anticipation of individual needs.[2]

The trend toward a universal articulation of common values in the area of human rights, of which the United Nations has acted as a catalyst, did not set in automatically. The Covenant of the League of Nations did not deal with the issue of human rights other than calling for the peaceful settlement of disputes and the need to protect certain minorities. Ancient legal codes for long failed to recognize the area of individual rights and freedoms as protected from state interference. Nor did rulers, often dictatorial, respect the principle of the inviolability of human life, home, and property.

Although certain notable developments had, in the course of time, taken place in Europe and America in support of human rights—the English Magna Carta of 1215, the Petition of Rights of 1628, and the Bill of Rights of 1689; the American Declaration of Independence of 1776 and the Virginia Declaration of Rights of 1776; in France, the Declaration of the Rights of Man of 1789—dictorial regimes' determination to trample human rights on a large scale still flourished in different parts of the globe.

The fact that in the course of the nineteenth and twentieth centuries the entire continent of Europe and, eventually, the Americas, Asia, Africa, and the Caribbean followed the example of the United States and France by adopting bills of rights did not guarantee the institutionalization of human rights' principles within and between nations.[3] Basic differences in concept and approach remained, even among nations that professed respect for those principles.

It was the dictatorship of Hitler, with its implications for world peace, and the war waged against him which convinced the world society of the need for a new approach to human rights' questions—an approach which ultimately resulted in the postwar United Nations' Declaration of Human Rights.

When the war ended, it was inevitable that the world assembly should take new, unparalleled initiatives in the area of human rights. The United Nations' Charter of 1945 affirmed "faith in fundamental human rights, in the dignity and worth of the human person." The Charter stressed at various places the role of the General Assembly in "promoting and encouraging respect for human rights" and in "assisting in the realization of human rights and fundamental freedoms." The responsibility for the guarantee of these rights was vested in the General Assembly and, under the

General Assembly's authority, in the Economic and Social Council.

Through the Commission on Human Rights, a subsidiary body of the Economic and Social Council, an initiative was taken for the first time by the world body to define a catalogue of human rights and fundamental freedoms as a common standard of conduct for all nations. Thus emerged the United Nations' Declaration of Human Rights of December 1948. This declaration was passed without any dissenting voice, ending, as a result, decades of relative international disregard and ushering in a new era of universal human rights' concern and obligation.[4]

The universal Declaration of Human Rights constitutes a major step in the goal to achieve an international perspective on human rights' questions. The clear assumption is that a global value-consensus on the inalienable rights of the individual is both possible and practicable, even in the absence of an enforcement machinery, and even where there are no shared values on the normative dimension of politics.

Among the rights set out in the declaration are the rights to life, liberty, and security of person; the right of equal treatment before the law; the right of freedom from slavery, arbitrary arrest, and inhuman or degrading treatment or punishment; the right to a fair and public trial; the right to freedom of movement and residence; the right to own property and not be arbitrarily deprived of it; the right to freedom of thought, conscience, and religion; the right to freedom of opinion and expression; the right to freedom of peaceful assembly and association; the right to work and freely choose one's employment; the right to form and join trade unions; the right to education and to participate freely in the cultural life of the community.

From a purely empirical standpoint it could be argued that the rights and freedoms catalogued in the Declaration of Human Rights have been respected in many countries more in terms of their breach than in their observance. However, it must be observed that, given the fact that the declaration is not an international treaty but merely a proclamation of "a common standard of achievement," a good deal has been achieved, perhaps much more than was originally hoped for. Many countries, including Canada and its provinces, have incorporated the principles of the declaration into their constitutions or human rights' legislations. Many, again including Canada and its provinces, have created human rights' agencies to promote human rights and enforce sanctions against their breach.

But there are continuing problems and limitations, not only in the normative dimension, but in the practical application of human rights' principles in many states and regions of the world, even among countries that became signatories to the United Nations' declaration and other subsequent conventions on human rights. This is the case even though the United Nations has, from time to time, called the attention of signatory members to the fact that, in the interest of peace and justice in the world, "it is imperative that members of the international community fulfill their solemn obligation to promote and encourage respect for human rights and fundamental freedoms for all without distinction of any kind," and that "gross denials" of human rights . . . outrage the conscience of mankind and endanger the foundations of freedom, justice, and peace in the world."[5]

What, then, are the continuing difficulties in the way of universal human rights' practice? Why has the pressure for human rights' enforcement been met in many countries by cynical responses on the part of ruling governments?

Two major ideological blocs exist—one socialist, the other capitalist. We must, however, be careful that we do not see human rights' breaches purely on the basis of ideological and institutional differences, thereby becoming trapped in what Richard B. Bilder aptly described as a "Sunday School exercise of good and evil."[6] It must be emphasized that breaches have occurred and continue to occur in the two systems of socio-economic organization. To deal with the practical obstacles to effective observance and implementation of human rights' principles in different nations, and under different ideologies, one must first understand the ideological and institutional constraints. The ritual of posturing and political propaganda must be discarded in favor of dispassionate fact-finding.[7] Every local situation must be fully examined to see what the causes of denials of rights are, and what the local expectations might be. Local and national programs on human rights must be looked into to determine their specific merits and shortcomings. It is only from such an understanding that the existing problems can be effectively addressed.

Ideological considerations and institutional constraints apparently contribute to the slow rate of progress in the development of human rights in socialist-oriented countries. At this political dimension, Western and Eastern values have traditionally been competitive rather than reenforcing, each stressing different rights, values, and procedures. This poses a great obstacle to the trend toward a universal articulation of common values on human rights. In terms of the central role of the United Nations, Ernst B. Haas observes: "The future of the United Nations as a catalyst of value-sharing is in the balance, for the character of the eventual synthesis will determine whether we shall have greater universal value-consensus or merely value-conflict among regions, mediated from the Center."[8]

The problem of divergencies in approach as influenced by ideological differences can be illustrated. The Soviet Union, though one of the signatories of the 1948 declaration, has not been able to guarantee key democratic rights to its citizens. The Russian Revolution of 1917, though it emulated the examples of the American and French precedents, turned its emphasis on economic and social rights within the framework of state ideology. On that ground, important political and civil rights, such as freedom of expression and opinion, and freedom of religion, and the right to form independent associations, have been denied.

The dissident movement in Russia and other Eastern-bloc nations has brought to the attention of the world violations of the right to freedom of movement and emigration in these countries. Areas of violations which are not well known in the West include: the rights of citizens to change their place of residence within their own country, and the concept of obligatory internal passport-bearing or residence registration.[9] These restrictions clearly violate the Western notion of freedom in a democracy and the spirit of the 1948 declaration, as well as the various conventions and covenants about human rights signed by the Soviet Union in the post-Stalin years. Purely from the point of view of strict observance, it would seem ironic that the Soviet Union would promote the image of sympathy for human rights abroad, while denying them to its citizens at home.

Emerging societies, mostly from the Third World countries of Asia, Africa, and Latin America, have come to place more emphasis on economic and social rights, to the point of almost total disregard for civil and political rights. They have also used their majority at the United Nations to foster this world view, using the promise of rapid economic and social development as their justification. Many of these countries have had the worst record on human rights. And because these rights are basic to man's aim of achieving respectable human dignity, these regimes have, from time to time, been internally challenged on the grounds of their denial of basic civil and political rights.

Litvinov has well argued that giving priority to social and economic rights over civil and political rights destroys, in essence, the very idea of rights, and that the equal importance of all rights is "confirmed by the continuity of development of social rights from political rights and their interdependence."[10] But above all, such an ordering of rights suggests a lack of faith in the ability of man to make his own decisions and to control his own destiny, unrestricted by totalitarian state powers, whether of the left or of the right.

In the Western-bloc nations, it is easy to assume that everything is alright because democratic institutions have been established stressing the rights of individuals rather than the rights of collectivities. In the West, there is much less commitment to state control and authority. Capitalism, even in its pristine form in the West, emphasized commitment to individualism and personal choices. Individual autonomy and integrity is reemphasized in Western liberalism, which, in essence, holds that individuals have rights that the state cannot invade.

Thus, apart from the social compact that the individual shares with other individuals as a citizen, he is first and foremost a person. But the assumption of total Western commitment to human rights has not been met, as there are continuing specific examples of violation.

First, the observance of human rights in the West is sometimes diluted by national interest and the procedures and requirements of traditional diplomacy. In this context, David Sidorsky maintains that "human rights can seldom be a primary or publicly pursued priority for traditional diplomacy in the contemporary world. It is an issue that tends to complicate relationships with powerful military states, such as the Soviet Union and China, with whom the primary task of the United States is to negotiate a structure of international security."[11]

Sidorsky therefore concludes: "Human-rights goals must usually be pursued quietly in international diplomacy, since no significant sovereign power, whether antagonistic or friendly, could permit open criticism of its internal arrangements without resort to counter-measures."[12] It would appear, therefore, that both in the East and the West, human rights' questions continue to be approached on pragmatic grounds. The same approach is adopted in dealing with human rights' questions abroad.

In the West, a second limitation lies in the very persistence of discrimination in many multiracial societies. The term "discrimination" refers to exclusion or preference usually made on the basis of race, color, sex, language, religion, political or other opinion, national or social origin, property, birth, or other status. In so far as it implies the existence of inequality, it violates the concept of human rights, and has been acknowledged as such by the United Nations.

Discrimination is an area of most immediate concern in many multiracial Western societies. A positive development is the establishment of human rights' agencies or commissions in these societies, specifically charged with

[247]

the responsibility to promote human rights and to enforce the principle of equality of opportunity and rights. The challenge in many of these societies is to increase the investment, human and financial, made in support of these human rights' institutions, in order to help assure their ultimate effectiveness and to move things beyond the level of rhetoric. The norm of equality must be visibly fostered at all levels of society.

A third limitation for a genuine global development in the area of human rights is that the United Nations, as a supranational organization, has no enforcement powers, but only the power of moral suasion. Its decisions are not legally binding on individual states. States undertake an obligation to conduct themselves in a certain way when they sign international declarations, conventions, or covenants, but the United Nations' Charter at the same time upholds the principle of noninterference in the internal affairs of member-states.[13] In effect, member-states have enforced or disregarded United Nations' declarations, conventions, or covenants, of which they are signatories, at their discretion.[14]

There are other limitations at the ideological level which, although they may seem less obvious today, still influence attitudes toward human rights' obligations in multiracial Western societies. Perhaps the most pervasive is the persisting idea of social Darwinism. As a mid–nineteenth-century theory deriving its name from its relationship with the biological work of Charles Darwin, it embodies the idea that the life of man in society is a struggle for existence in which only the "fittest" tend to survive by a process of natural selection.

By implication, social Darwinism justified not only class-stratification (as an outcome of competition in society), but the assumed cultural and biological superiority of certain races. The "unfit" were the poor (considered to be less industrious), as well as subjugated races or cultural groups. To support any social reform for equality and human rights meant, in effect, interfering with natural processes. Although social Darwinism has largely been abandoned in the twentieth century, it has remained the underlying philosophy of racist-supremacist groups opposed to liberalism and human rights.

In spite of difficulties in the way of development of a global system of human rights, the experience of man in the past with dictatorship and man's natural inclination to resist arbitrary powers make it tenable to assert that a logical course for the future is greater determination and commitment on the part of the world society to promote more actively human rights' principles in all areas of the world. It is also the path of peace—as the United Nations has consistently stressed.

In various countries people are still faced with the old question of founding an ideal government. While the sixteenth-century utopian dream of Thomas More might have faded from literary favor, the search of individuals for practical safeguards from the state to protect individual liberty and human dignity continues even in the late twentieth century.

This paper has tried to analyze, from an international viewpoint, the development of universal concern about human rights, the central role that the United Nations has played in this development, and continuing difficulties in the goal of achieving normative global consensus. The pressure to enforce human rights on a worldwide basis has been hampered by the ideological needs of individual states, by national interests and traditional requirements, by procedures of international diplomacy, by the persistence of discrimination especially in multiracial societies, by lack of enforcement powers on the part of the United Nations itself, and by the persistence of the racist and supremacist beliefs based, in part, on the theory of social Darwinism.

The gains and significance of synthesizing human rights' values and promoting them on a global level were discussed. It was also concluded that in the interest of peace, and given man's natural yearning for freedom and justice, the logical route to go in the future is the path of more active promotion of human rights in all areas of the world, in spite of diversity in ideologies as well as in economic and political institutions.

[249]

Notes

1. Thus, whereas the First Amendment to the American Constitution states that Congress shall not make laws abridging the freedom of speech or of the press, the Russian Constitution of 1918 provides that, "for the purpose of securing freedom of expression to the toiling masses," all dependence of the press upon capital shall be abolished and the press itself turned over to the working people and the peasants, who would now control all the "technical and material means" of publication, whether of newspapers, books, pamphlets, etc.
2. Richard P. Clause, "Reliable Information: The Threshold Problem of Human Rights Research," *Human Relations* 6, no. 2 (1977).
3. The dictatorship of Hitler flourished in spite of the fact that the Weimar Constitution of Germany of 1919 had made provisions for political and civil rights. Hitler's regime completely transformed the meaning of civil and political rights to suit its aims and ideology.
4. There were six abstentions and unanimous approval among some forty nations.
5. On the occasion of the twentieth anniversary of the Declaration of Human Rights, in the spring of 1968. On the same occasion, the United Nations stressed that the various human rights' conventions and declarations "have created new standards and obligations to which states should conform," and reaffirmed the principle that the "individual is entitled to maximum freedom and dignity," and that "apartheid, racism and colonialism constitute crimes against humanity."
6. Richard B. Bilder, "The International Promotion of Human Rights: A Current Assessment," *American Journal of International Law* 57, no. 3 (July 1964), 732.
7. Ernst B. Haas, *Human Rights and International Action* (Stanford, 1970), p. 9.
8. Ibid., p. 3.
9. Pavel Litvinov, "The Human Rights Movement in the Soviet Union," in *Essays on Human Rights*, ed. David Sidorsky (Philadelphia, 1979), p. 114. Pavel Litvinov, a grandson of the former Soviet foreign minister, Maxim Litvinov, was a leader of the Moscow democratic dissident community. He was arrested for human rights' activities in the Soviet Union, including leading further protests against the Soviet invasion of Czechoslovakia in 1968. He later became a physics teacher in New York.
10. Ibid.
11. David Sidorsky, *Essay On Human Rights*, p. xl.
12. Ibid.
13. United Nations, *Charter*, Article 2, paragraph 7.
14. Legal scholars have advanced the argument that the human rights' provisions of the UN resolutions do not infringe the Charter's requirement of noninterference in the internal affairs of member-states. Thus, Articles 55 and 56 of the Charter, giving the UN General Assembly jurisdiction over situations involving breaches of

the Charter's human rights' provisions because of imminent or potential threat to peace, are argued to be binding. See Hersch Lauterpacht, *International Law and Human Rights* (New York, 1950), and Ernst B. Haas, *Human Rights and International Action*. However, empirical experience suggests that this argument presently lacks practical utility and feasibility.

REFLECTIONS ON OUR TIME: A CANADIAN PERSPECTIVE
G. Emmett Carter

No one can truly examine with profit the basic human situation without doing so in an historical perspective. Whether it is the fault of my generation, which insisted too much on it, or whether it is simply the type of education which the young are receiving today, nothing seems to turn them off more quickly than to talk about what took place in past times. This attitude may be understandable because we have been bores, but it is also extremely dangerous. How well it was said that he who ignores history is condemned to repeat it. Or, as someone else put it, "experience is a great school, but only a fool knows no other."

I recall, with a great deal of vividness, the Great Depression, which came to us in 1929 and lasted until the beginning of war in 1939. I couple the Great Depression with the Second World War because the same kind of generosity and service to others was evident in both experiences, however unnecessary or frustrating they may have been. In our largely legitimate rejection of the kind of failure in economic planning that brought on the Great Depression. In our hatred of war, we tend to overlook the heroism of those who were affected by both of these events and either to minimize their attitudes and virtues or simply to wave aside the whole situation because it disturbs us. I shall return to these attitudes later.

The war was followed by the prosperity of the late forties and fifties in which we were helping to rebuild a shattered Western world. But even in the fifties there was the worm of discontent. It was characterized mostly by the desire of parents, who had suffered both the depression and the Second World War, to avoid in the lives of their children the heartbreaks which they themselves had been obliged to experience. This reaction was exaggerated and created an attitude of materialism and selfishness, which are the two points that I think are adversely affecting our present civilization. The syndrome was based upon the attempts to secure immediate pleasure and to avoid hardship. It is axiomatic that parents who try to avoid all hardship for their children are condemning them to the greatest of hardships.

This attitude of the late forties and early fifties began to have its fruits in the sixties. The decade was dominated by Vietnam, the revolution in sexual morality, and a universal spirit of anti-authority and anti-establishment in any of its manifestations.

The seventies ushered in a respite. The Vietnam War was over; therefore, the restlessness, not to use a stronger word, of the great republic to our south was curbed. The youth, particularly the young people in our colleges and high schools, seemed to have had enough of rebellion and settled down to a little more positive attitude toward life. But the attitude did not involve to any large degree the return to the fundamental values that had been so predominant in the previous difficulties of the human race in general, and of our own Western civilization in particular. There was the continued absence of fundamental values, and I fear that it still is with us.

Some time ago, while speaking to a graduating class of one of our high schools, I said: "Your valedictorian has told us that you are ready for life. The question I have to put to you is: are you ready for death? By this I don't mean, have you said your prayers? But: do you have values for which you are prepared to die?" I really have to ask myself this question about the whole of our civilization, not only in regard to our youth. Do we have any values left for which we are prepared to die?

In that context I ask a further question: could we fight a war today? I realize that there could be a twofold reply to that question. The first and shrewdest answer would be another question. And the question would be: should we? I would have to answer that if we were to refuse to fight a war on the grounds of true and spiritual pacifism and the absolute refusal to kill our fellow man, then I would have to mark this down as a very real, positive value which, in a sense, *is* fighting a war—fighting a war with ourselves. To refuse to shed blood and thereby to lose one's freedom, economic possessions, and country is a form of martyrdom. But what if we could not fight a war because of indolence, because of lack of values, because we would not put our lives on the line? What then? Not should we, but could we fight a war? Whatever the provocation? I do not pretend to know, but I do ask the question.

Are we then witnessing the collapse of our civilization? Many things point to an affirmative answer. In economics we are spending more than we are earning. In energy we are consuming more than we are producing. In distribution of wealth, more and more is being concentrated into the hands of a few, and we are thereby creating a mass of men and women who are desperate and have nothing to lose by any adventure they may care to undertake.

In industry our work is slipshod and our costs rapidly becoming prohibitive. In both cases an uncontrolled labor situation is threatening to ruin us. To say this does not mean to place all of the blame upon the labor unions. They must bear some of it, but the uncontrolled situation is such for many reasons. Government, management, and ownership must also bear a very heavy burden in this confusion.

We have been brought to this situation by causes that continue to be operative and which are profound in nature. For the same reason no one seems prepared to take realistic remedial action.

I am not referring to the immediate causes, which can be approached by legislation, or economic solution, or nostrums. I refer to the very stuff of life, the philosophy of living—and of dying.

Materialism: this is a catch-all expression. I mean by it that view of life which is concerned exclusively with immediate objectives and goals and aims.

Our view of life has become shortened and blunted. We

are fascinated with and focused upon the here and the now, the bottom line, what we can possess or expend. What has happened to spiritual motivation? The motivation of "it is more blessed to give", "the greater love than this," the very concept of a life beyond this one where true virtue will be rewarded, where sin will be punished, and where the present disparities of life will be forever corrected? Do we really believe in God and in immortality any more? And yet it was that type of spirituality that built our present society. People who were prepared to work for the sake of achievement, of satisfaction in producing the beautiful or the useful, and to please God, because only His goodwill ultimately counts. Try that on a modern labor union—or, for that matter, on a multinational corporation.

Christopher Dawson has brilliantly expressed the thesis that we are living in the post-Christian era and that we are running through our spiritual inheritance at breakneck speed.

Selfishness: this is, of course, the first-born of materialism. If there is nothing of a spiritual nature to man, why, indeed, should I adopt all these absurd notions of putting others before myself? I will offer only two examples.

First, what has happened to patriotism? How sad to hear recently the president of the country that has perhaps the proudest history of selflessness say to his fellow citizens: "Please, wherever you have a chance, say something good about our country?" We don't seem to care any more about anything except ourselves, individually or collectively. We, in Canada, are suffering a crisis of unity and consequently of patriotism. There are a large number of our compatriots who refuse to fly the Canadian flag, who sit sullenly and insultingly during the playing of our national anthem.

This is not the place to analyze that situation. But is it not partly the fault of us English-speaking Canadians, who failed for so long to be proud of being Canadians while we boasted of being anything else but? "I am going home," said an ex-prime minister of Canada, as he left our shores for another land! "How I envy you," replied his successor.

The strange part of it is that we never had so much to be

proud of. We have a magnificent country; we have political freedom perhaps never equalled in history, certainly never surpassed; we have affluence and opportunity and education and social legislation and almost everything conceivable for the good life; and we do little else than criticize and tear down when Canada is mentioned.

My second example is a little less self-evident. It is the unwillingness of our generation to commit itself fully to almost anything. I have placed this under the general heading of selfishness, and it is there it belongs. It is as though the first fruit of selfishness was also self-mistrust. We don't seem to have enough confidence in ourselves to assert, in the famous words of MacMahon, "J'y suis, j'y reste." We don't seem to have sufficient motivation to commit ourselves to a course of action, if necessary, for life. Perhaps the most noble achievement of man has been his ability to give himself, permanently and unwaveringly, in love. The Judeo–Christian concept of the permanence of marriage was the reflection of that ability.

Today, more and more people, particularly the young, are saying that it is folly to commit oneself for life. And when a form of marriage is undertaken, it is frequently with a door left half-open in order to permit a hasty retreat if the going gets tough. The decline in religious commitment has a similar origin.

The same attitude is at the root of the collapse of our moral values, particularly the mores of sexual licence and promiscuity. I don't have to draw a picture. There are enough on the market. But it is being said that sex is for pleasure—my pleasure—and nothing else. It used to be called "making love." Now we call it "making out." It is a most significant expression. Don't get "trapped"—get "out."

I have reflected my fear but not my hope. I have been struck by the motto of the Radcliffe family, the Earls of Derwentwater who were executed as Jacobites in the eighteenth century. It was *Sperare est timere*, "To hope is to fear."

I feel strongly that we must awaken to our peril. But I am

far from giving up hope. I am convinced that our civilization can be saved, but only by a massive return to our basic values and an almost universal involvement by people everywhere. I believe in leadership, and a few years ago I might have based this hope on the appearance and evolution of strong leaders—a few—an elite. I still see that as important, but mostly as a catalyst to arouse and direct the forces of what I will call by the traditional term of democracy—which is still a very good word.

One of the most important and hopeful developments of our time is the evolution in the concept of democracy. I am not sure that we can take all or even much of the credit for this. I believe it has been forced upon us by the rapid growth of the public media, particularly radio and television. Nor do I pretend that we have achieved democracy in its fullest sense, and I am not even sure whether we can achieve it. But one thing is sure: at least in our Western countries, where the concept of democracy has been flourishing after the British style for two hundred years, there has recently emerged a qualitative difference. Radio, television, and, to a lesser degree, the rapid possibilities of transportation, which make the printed word so easily and quickly available, have changed the involvement of the peoples of our countries. We don't have to be students of history to realize that the process of government has almost totally changed in the last thirty or forty years. Vietnam is, of course, a classic example, but Watergate is not any less so. One has to wonder whether the wars of yesteryear, in particular, the Great War of 1914–1918 and, to a lesser degree, the Second World War, could have been fought as they were under the present systems. I doubt it very seriously.

This leads me to my central question which is, whether or not we can survive under the present system and in this period of disaffection. We see the poles I have already mentioned. The first is a situation of spiritual disability in our people. The second is that these same people are made instantaneous judges of the major issues of the world. Our survival and our salvation, therefore, depend upon whether or not enough of our people can become involved in the conduct of the affairs of our country, both nationally and internationally.

I believe that there is no turning back the process of information and public awareness. I am convinced that we often exaggerate on one side or the other the secrecy, or the confidentiality, which is necessary in some cases. But we must face the fact that in our era the public will have almost all of the information available in one way or another. The question before us is what the public will do with it.

The public must develop a more critical attitude toward the media itself. This critical judgment can be developed only in a long, painful process. We must learn to live with the media, and I can see no way of achieving it except through a program of education and awareness that will go hand-in-hand with maturity.

None of the above will have any salutary effect unless the mature and critical judgment, which I am postulating for a society which has not yet evolved, is based upon sound values. To be able to judge with maturity and to criticize in a good and positive sense require a base from which we must operate. Clausewitz has said that the first principle of military strategy is to "secure your base of operation." I cannot offer any other solution for our hope and for our future than that we have people who do possess a base of operation. To use a circular definition: "For life to be meaningful, life must be preserved as having meaning."

If there is no motivation, if there is no long-range vision of the human race with the assurance of an overall plan which I dare to call a divine plan, if there is no altruism and a willingness to give of oneself, then there can be no hope for democracy. We will inevitably come either to self-annihilation or to a form of dictatorship of the right or of the left.

There is no disguising my own philosophy and theology of life. Our civilization was built upon the Judeo–Christian tradition, and it has given form and faith and hope to all of our generations to date. It has purpose. It has strength. And it has the ability to move people to give themselves in a cause that is greater than they.

Even true humanism could at least create a situation in which all of us could exercise our own judgment and our own options in terms of our definitions of values. But there must be a set of principles which are permanent and to which reference can be made in the judgments that each one of us takes.

Participatory democracy does not mean that each one of the citizens of any country takes over the role of government. But it does mean that at least a large number will have the maturity, the courage, and the vision to be able to make judgments not based upon the passing whims of the day, but against a background of values that endure and which are based on something more than the here and now, and it does allow us to give ourselves in the service of others.

THE DUTY TO OBEY THE LAW: A SOCIAL PERSPECTIVE
Bora Laskin

Let me begin by adapting a well-known aphorism to my use —you recall the saying that war is too important to be left to the generals—and I adapt it to say that law is too important to be left to the lawyers, too important even to be left to the law schools. This does not mean that it is not a special art, that it does not require special skills and special training, or that there is an unnecessary elitism involved in restricting representation in the courts to a qualified class. What it does mean is that all of us—lawyers and non-lawyers alike—have a continuing interest in the quality and effectiveness of our legal system, particularly because our form of political organization, through which we give expression and force to our law, is based on public participation in political and social processes, on freedom to debate public issues, freedom to examine and evaluate public institutions, including the courts.

The fact that we, as citizens, have an open-ended right to bring our laws and our legal system under continuing scrutiny imposes upon us a duty, a responsibility, to understand how our system works and the values which give it authority in a democratic state. The social expectation, certainly the preferable approach to public scrutiny and evaluation, is that it will be informed. Not that all members of the public must still their opinions unless they have a lawyer's training, even if not a lawyer's credentials. But even more important than informed appraisal is the social duty to respect the law, to uphold its authority even while seeking to have it changed or amended. Unless this is seen as a social imperative, a protection for all of us as persons living under and within a regime of law, we deny the distinction between lawful social protest and illegal behavior upon

[260]

which our social stability is based. If objection to existing law is itself a justification for refusing to obey it, where do we stop and with whom do we stop? Can we have a selective policy that would admit a privilege of legal disobedience by some but not by others? Or are we to descend into complete anarchy by yielding to everyone the privilege of disobedience whenever the law or any law is considered objectionable? There is no measure by which to determine in advance what are good laws and what are bad laws before we submit to their observance. Is not the only rational rule, commanded by our representative form of government, that we yield obedience, albeit, while continuing with lawful attempts to secure desired changes?

The basic fact of our day-to-day lives is that law is our preeminent instrument of social control. Societies, past and present, have exhibited and do exhibit other forms of social control, such as the church, the corporate enterprise, the labor union, the family, even the service club, each operating upon its membership to a limited degree. All must, however, yield and are obliged to yield—unless anarchy replace political organization—to an overriding state legal system.

No society can survive unless it has institutions or instruments for maintaining public peace, for preserving public safety. This has been evident throughout the continuity of the social history of England, which from the beginning made keeping the peace the focal point of the evolution of its legal system. This was part of our legal inheritance, and the same key concept of keeping the peace is at the forefront of our criminal law. It envisages that there will be agencies and procedures for enforcing domestic peace so that disputes between citizen and state, or between citizen and citizen, disputes that are inevitable in any society, may be subject to final and peaceful settlement.

Of course, these two fundamental conditions of social stability—keeping the peace and the provision of machinery for final and peaceful settlement of disputes—do not in themselves determine the quality of a state. Autocracies, totalitarian countries, have them, no less than do democ-

racies. What then do we claim as being especially characteristic of the quality of our country and of others similarly
organized? One very central feature of our system is the independence of our judges upon their appointment to office,
their freedom from executive direction, their non-account-
ability to the political arm for their decisions. Security of
tenure is one of the hallmarks of this independence, and
another, perhaps a too obvious one, is that judicial decisions do not require executive or political approval in order
to become enforceable. But over and above even this very
central feature of our legal system, the quality of our country (and others organized on similar political principles) is
evidenced by our belief, reinforced by orderly procedures for
change, that our political and judicial institutions must be
open to the advocacy of the widest variety of interests and
demands, so long as that advocacy is asserted within the
law and by orderly procedures.

Inevitably, there will be a conflict among the demands
and the claims and the expectations that are passed for fulfillment. Governments nowadays are beset as never before
by pressure to recognize new interests and to satisfy needs
not hitherto thought or felt to be a public responsibility. A
democracy, a parliamentary system of government, must
do its best to test and weigh conflicting interests and conflicting expectations, and ultimately try to reconcile them
and satisfy them, perhaps by relative adjustment, perhaps
by considering compromise ahead of outright rejection, but
it must, nonetheless, be prepared to risk the political consequences of outright rejection.

This interplay between interest groups and government,
which has been so characteristic of our society, is expected
to take place without breach of the peace, without ruptur-
ing the legal fabric that underlines our social stability. The
fundamental social premise is that after demands and
claims are considered and weighed, there will be peaceful
acceptance of any resulting legislative or judicial decision.
This acceptance does not exclude continued persistence in
peacefully pressing an unsatisfied claim. It may be that the
place to press it is in the political arena rather than in the

judicial. But tolerable though it be in our society to persist if it is done peacefully within the law, what is not tolerable is a resort to illegality when the persistence continues to be unproductive or because expectations are disappointed.

It would be taking a hyphenated view of our political and legal organization to regard the duty to obey the law as resting on legal duty alone, as depending only on the sanction or penalty that is prescribed for breach of a legal obligation. This is, of course, its immediate rationale, but, surely, if it is to have a democratic base, it must rest on a more fundamental conception of social duty, lying behind the law and, indeed, fortifying it. A great American judge, the late Learned Hand, gave short and sharp definition of what I am putting before you by characterizing the law ''as no more than the formal expression of that tolerable compromise which we call justice, without which the rule of the tooth and claw must prevail.''

I have been much concerned, as any legally trained person must be—indeed, as any person devoted to democratic government must be—by accumulating evidence that many in our society, including those who, by reason of their training and their responsibilities, should know better, are untroubled, or appear to be untroubled, in pursuing their objectives though it be in defiance of the law or by means that involve a breach of legal obligation. Defiance of the law is not just another form of social protest which a tolerant society can tolerate. It amounts to a rupture of one of the essential conditions of social stability which I have previously mentioned.

I am familiar with the argument that the law at any given time is an expression of our social order, and, hence, protest against aspects of that order, if peaceful, is a permissible democratic privilege, even though a breach of the law is involved. There is a play on words here that merits only scorn. It is to elevate demonstration and protest above the law, rather than making them subservient to the law. It is as much a distortion as exists when violence is justified because the end or purpose is said to be laudable. Defiance of the law or breach of legal obligation does not become

[263]

respectable merely because it is not attended by physical violence.

It is not too soon for universities to devote some of their resources to educating all their students on the place of law in organized society; to bring them to an understanding of what the rule of law means in a parliamentary democracy; to make them aware of the reliance on law to support our traditional political liberties: freedom of speech and of association, freedom of assembly, freedom of religion and of political creed; to give them an appreciation of the importance of an independent judiciary and an independent bar to the political and social health of our country; to help them to understand the separation of the political and the legal, which is so important in our scheme of government, and, yet, to appreciate the interrelation of the two. It is as important that the liberal-arts and science student be enlightened in these areas as it is that he or she have a knowledge of literature, or of languages, or of mathematics, or of aspects of science. Both the law and the Canadian society in which it operates will be all the better, the safer, and the surer in their commitment to our democratic order if more of us, if most of us if not all of us, know something about our legal system, the institutions through which it works, and the ends which it serves.

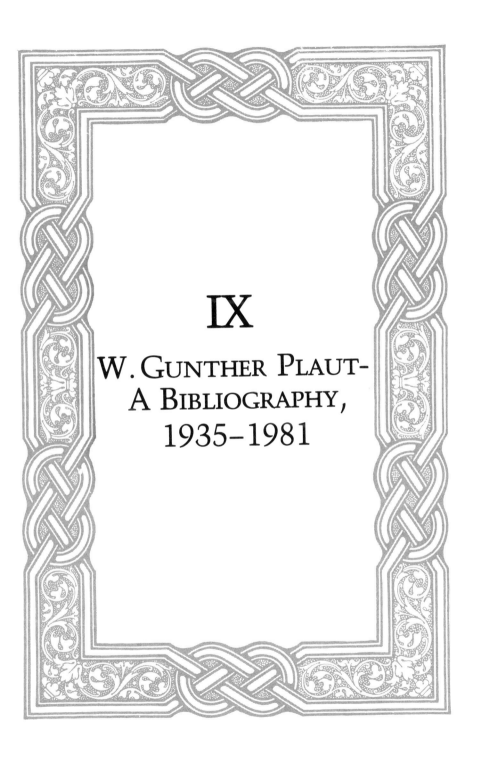

IX

W. GUNTHER PLAUT–
A BIBLIOGRAPHY,
1935–1981

Books

1935 *Die materielle Eheungültigkeit im deutschen und schweizerischen internationalen Privatrecht.* Doctorat dissertation, Dresden, Risse-Verlag, 1935.

1956 *Mount Zion—The First Hundred Years.* St. Paul: Central Publishing Company, 1956.

1959 *The Jews in Minnesota.* New York: American Jewish Historical Society, 1959.

1961 *The Book of Proverbs—A Commentary.* New York: Union of American Hebrew Congregations (UAHC), 1961.

1962 *Judaism and the Scientific Spirit.* New York: UAHC, 1962. (Translated into Hebrew by Peninah Nave. *Ha-yahadut V'ha-madda.* Tel Aviv: Prozdor, 1965.)

1963 *The Rise of Reform Judaism.* New York: World Union for Progressive Judaism, 1963.

1965 *The Case for the Chosen People—The Role of the Jewish People Yesterday and Today.* Garden City, New York: Doubleday and Co., 1965. (Translated into Hebrew by Joseph Emanuel and Gaalya Cornfeld. *Ha-omnam am nivchar?* Tel Aviv: G & L Cornfeld, 1968; translated into French. *Israël, peuple élu?* Paris: Mame, 1967.)
The Growth of Reform Judaism. New York: World Union for Progressive Judaism, 1965.

1967 *Your Neighbour is a Jew.* Toronto: McClelland & Stewart, 1967; Philadelphia: Pilgrim Press, 1968.

1971 *Page Two—Ten Years of "News and Views."* Toronto, 1971.

1974 *Genesis.* The Torah, A Modern Commentary, vol. I. New York: UAHC, 1974.

1977 *Time to Think.* Toronto, 1977.
Numbers. The Torah, A Modern Commentary, vol. IV. New York: UAHC, 1977.
Hanging Threads, Stories Real and Surreal. Toronto: Lester & Orpen, 1978. Published in the U.S. as *The Man in the Blue Vest and Other Stories.* New York: Taplinger Publishing House, 1980.

1981   *Unfinished Business—An Autobiography*, Toronto: Lester & Orpen Dennys, 1981.
      The Torah, A Modern Commentary. Edited by W. Gunther Plaut and containing his commentaries on Genesis (revised), Exodus, Numbers, and Deuteronomy. New York: UAHC, 1981.

CONTRIBUTIONS TO ENCYCLOPEDIAS, ANTHOLOGIES, AND OTHER BOOKS

1939   "Two Notes on the History of the Jews in America": "Early Settlement in Georgia"; "The First Confirmation in America." *Hebrew Union College Annual*, vol. XIV (1939).

1941– *Universal Jewish Encyclopedia.* 10 vols. New York,
1943   1939–1943. Contributing editor, Department of Bible, vol. VI-X. By W. G. Plaut: "Kings, Book of," vol. VI; "Necromancy," vol. VIII; "Nehemiah," vol. VIII; "Numbers, Book of," vol. VIII; "Numbers in Mysticism," vol. VIII; "Omri," vol. VIII; "Red Heifer," vol. IX; "Rosenzweig, Franz," vol. IX; "Ruth," vol. IX; "Shabuoth," vol. IX; "Youth Movements," vol. X.

1950   "Opening Prayer." *Congressional Record*, vol. XCVI, no. 201. December 6, 1950.

1953   "Retreats for Laymen." *CCAR (Central Conference of American Rabbis) Yearbook*, vol. LXXIII (1953).

1955   "The Origin of the Word 'Yarmulke'." *Hebrew Union College Annual*, vol. XXVI (1955). A popular extract of this article appeared under the title "Tracking Down the Yarmulke." *The Jewish Digest*, II, no. 7 (1957).

1962   "The People and the Tent." *CCAR Yearbook*, vol. LXXII (1962).

1965   "The Sabbath in the Reform Movement—Fact, Fiction, Future," *CCAR Yearbook*, vol. LXXIV (1965). Reprinted in Blau, J. L., ed. *Reform Judaism, A*

Historical Perspective. New York: Ktav Publishing House, 1973.

1966 Contribution to *The Condition of Jewish Belief*, A symposium by the editors of *Commentary*. New York: Macmillan Co., 1966.

1967 Foreword to *World Law and World Order*, by Arnold Simoni. Toronto, 1967.

1968 "Councils of Common Concern." *One Church Two Nations*, edited by Philip LeBlanc and Arnold Edinborough. Don Mills, Ontario: Longmans Canada, 1968.

"To Change the Patterns." *Probings*. Toronto: Canadian Mental Health Association, 1968.

"The Halacha of Reform." *Contemporary Reform Jewish Thought*, edited by Bernard Martin. Chicago: Quadrangle Books, in cooperation with the Central Conference of American Rabbis (CCAR), 1968.

1970 "God and the Ethical Impulse." *Judaism and Ethics*, edited by Daniel J. Silver. New York: Ktav Publishing House, 1970.

1971 "Frankel, Hiram D." *Encyclopaedia Judaica*, vol. 7. Jerusalem: Keter Publishing Co., 1971.

"Der Sabbath als Protest." *Kritische Solidarität*, edited by G. Schulz. German version of B. G. Rudolph Lecture, 1970 (for original, see below). Bremen: Verlag Friedrich Röver, 1971.

Editor, *A Shabbat Manual*. New York: CCAR and Ktav Publishing House, 1972.

1974 "Mitzvot: Authority and Freedom, The Problem of the Modern Jew," with Levi Olan and A. J. Reines. UAHC *Centennial Papers*. New York, 1974.

"Preparing for the Seder." In Introduction to *A Passover Haggadah*. New York: CCAR, 1974.

1976 "The Ambiguity of Reform." A Bicentennial Festschrift for Jacob Marcus Rader, edited by B. Korn. Waltham–New York: AJHS and Ktav Publishing House, 1976.

Foreword to *Perpetual Dilemma*, by S. Z. Abramov. Jerusalem–New York: World Union for Progressive Judaism, 1976.

1978   "Canadian Experience: The Dynamics of Jewish Life Since 1945." *Movements and Issues in American Judaism*, edited by B. Martin. Westport: Greenwood Press, 1978.

"The Sabbath as Protest: Thoughts on Work and Leisure in the Automated Society." *Tradition and Change in Jewish Experience*, edited by A. L. Jamison. Reprint of the B. G. Rudolph Lecture, 1970. Syracuse University, 1978.

"The Train Ride." Reprinted from *Hanging Threads. Family Magazine* 3, no. 2 (1978).

"Report on Canadian Jewry." *CCAR Yearbook*, vol. 88 (1978).

Address. In *Convention Proceedings*, Women's League for Conservative Judaism, Biennial Convention, November 15, 1978. New York, 1978.

1979   "The University and Society." *Ideas of the University*, edited by J. Ayre, Pascal, and Scarfe. Toronto: Ontario Institue for Studies in Education, 1979.

1980   "Problems of Migrations and Minorities." *Église et Système Mondial*, edited by A. Jacomy-Millette et al. Quebec: Collection Choix, 1980.

Pamphlets, Lectures, other Separate Publications

1949   *The Real America*. Voice of Religion Series. New York: Joint Commission on Information about Judaism, 1949.

1950   *Young People's Services for Yom Kippur*. St. Paul, Minn., 1950.

1952   *Children's Services for Rosh Hashanah*. St. Paul, 1952. The two Holy Day services were combined into *Children's Services for the High Holy Days*. First printing, 1952; revised, St. Paul, 1958; fifteenth printing, 1970; new revised edition, New York: Ktav Publishing House, 1975.

1954 *Services for School and Family*, with Avraham Soltes and Malcolm Stern. St. Paul, 1954.

1957 *The Cross on the State Centennial Seal*. Sermon preached at Mount Zion Temple, St. Paul, May 3, 1957.

1959 *Out of Zion*. Sermons preached from the pulpit of Mt. Zion Temple, St. Paul, 1959.

1961 *The Hard Way of Reform Judaism*. Three sermons. Holy Blossom Temple, Toronto, 1961.

1962 *Germany Today—A Rabbi Revisits the Land of his Birth*. A collection of articles in the *Globe and Mail*, Toronto, 1962.

Therese Abraham Strauss. Eulogy. Cincinnati, Ohio, August 31, 1962.

Reform's New Frontier. Address to the New England Council of UAHC, November 17, 1962.

New Goals for Reform Judaism. Address at Holy Blossom Temple, Toronto, 1962.

In Sorrow's Hour—A Guide for Mourners. Holy Blossom Temple, Toronto, 1962.

1965 *Color-blind and Border-blind*. Lecture at Metropolitan United Church, Toronto, March 16, 1965.

1966 *Russia is Different*. A collection of articles in the *Globe and Mail*, Toronto, 1966.

1968 *Israel Since the 6 Day War*. Selected articles, Holy Blossom Temple, Toronto, 1968.

1969 *A Time to Reason*. Address to the Canadian Council of Christians and Jews, Toronto, February 22, 1969.

Selichot Service, with Michael S. Stroh. Holy Blossom Temple, Toronto, 1969.

Commentary to Union Prayer Book, with David Polish and Dudley Weinberg. Experimental edition. New York: CCAR, 1962.

1970 *The Rabbi's Role: Divine Ridicule and Human Loneliness*. Address given at the 86th Ordination Exercise at Hebrew Union College–Jewish Institute of Religion, Cincinnati, Ohio, June 6, 1970.

The Sabbath as Protest—Thoughts on Work and Leisure in the Automated Society. Syracuse University, 1970. Reprinted in 1971 and 1978; see entry under "Contributions to Encyclopedias."

1972 *Your Neighbour is a Jew: Reflections on the Possibilities of Dialogue.* Sermon preached at Bloor Street United Church, Toronto, October 22, 1972. Toronto: Canadian District, B'nai Brith.

1972 *Why Be Moral?* Lester B. Pearson memorial lecture at Dominion Chalmers Church, Ottawa, November 5, 1972.

1973 *I Am a Jew.* Speech given at mass rally of solidarity, Royal York Hotel, October 9, 1973. Toronto: B'nai Brith, District 22.
On the Fourth Day of the War. Sermon preached at Holy Blossom Temple, Toronto, November 28, 1973.

1974 *The Conversion Controversy.* Lecture delivered at Holy Blossom Temple, Toronto, February 15, 1974.
Israel, Jews and Canadian Churches. Lecture delivered at Canadian Jewish Congress Plenum, June 17, 1974. Montreal: Canada-Israel Committee.

1975 *Israel Among the Nations.* Montreal: Canada-Israel Committee, 1975.
A Time to Gather—Comments on Our Disposable Society. Yom Kippur sermon preached at Holy Blossom Temple, Toronto, 1975.

1978 *Marion Fainstein—a final tribute.* Toronto, September 25, 1978.

1980 *Dr. Saul B. Fainstein—a final tribute.* Toronto, September 24, 1980.

ARTICLES IN
MAGAZINES AND
NEWSPAPERS

NOTE: Thirty-nine articles which appeared in the *Globe and Mail* between 1962 and 1967 have been reprinted in the collection *Your Neighbour is a Jew* and are not listed in the following. Also not included are the information bulletins which were published, in mimeographed form, by the Canada-Israel Committee, from March 26, 1969, to July 9, 1971. These were extensive news analyses and were usually written by Dr. Plaut. Also not included are the editorials written for the Holy Blossom Temple *Bulletin*, from 1961–1977, a portion of which were published in *Page Two*; as well as articles and editorials —signed and unsigned—in *Affirmation*, which Dr. Plaut has edited since 1980.

The following abbreviations have been used throughout this section: *CJN*—Toronto *Canadian Jewish News*; *GM*—Toronto *Globe and Mail*.

1935   "From Lehranstalt to H.U.C." *Hebrew Union College Monthly*, XXIII, no. 1 (1935), 13–14.

1937   "Vision." A poem. *Hebrew Union College Monthly* XXIV, no. 4 (1937), 6.

"Organisation der Gemeinden." *Gemeindeblatt der jüdischen Gemeinde zu Berlin* XXVII, no. 26 (1937), 1.

"Nationale und religiöse Gruppierungen (Die Struktur des amerikanischen Judentums). *Gemeindeblatt* XXVII, no. 27 (1937), 1.

"Die Erziehung der jüdischen Jugend Amerikas." *Gemeindeblatt* XXVII, no. 31 (1937), 5.

"Jüdische Einwanderung in USA." *Gemeindeblatt* XXVII, no. 47 (1937), 1.

"Moishe Cries Out." A satire on biblical criticism; this article appeared under anonymous authorship. *Hebrew Union College Monthly* XXIV, no. 1 (1937), 15–16.

1938   "Das Einwanderungsproblem in Amerika." *Gemeindeblatt* XXVIII, no. 6 (1938), 1.

"Juden in Cuba." *Gemeindeblatt* XXVIII (1938).

"Testament of Exile." *Atlantic Monthly*, November 1938, pp. 659–60.

1941   "Zionist Coordination Vital." *New Palestine* XXXI, no. 31 (1941), 7–8.

"American Zionist Congress." A communication to

New Palestine XXXI, no. 25 (1941), 31.

1942 "Sermonette." Chicago *Sun*, May 23, 1942.

"Toward a More Integrated Jewish Life." Chicago *Sentinel*, October 15, 1942, p. 9.

1943 "The Printed Word." Chicago *Sentinel*, January 18, p. 9; January 25, p. 9; March 4, p. 9; March 11, p. 9; March 18, p. 9; April 1, p. 9; April 8, p. 9f; April 15, p. 9f; April 22, p. 9; April 29, p. 9; May 6, p. 9; May 20, p. 9; May 27, p. 9; and June 3, p. 9; 1943.

"The Austin (Chicago) Experiment." *The Reconstructionist* IX, no. 1 (1943), 6–7.

"Sermonette." Chicago *Sun*, June 26, 1943.

1945 Editor, *Forward*. A newspaper for Jewish soldiers, published on German soil during the campaign. Six issues (nos. 1 and 2 mimeographed, nos. 3–6 printed; Germany, January 7, 1945–May 18, 1945).

"A Comparison of the Place of the Chapel and the Synagogue." *National Jewish Post* (Special HUC 70th Anniversary Edition), 1, no. 12 (1945), 16–17.

1951 "I-Sight." in *A Set of Holiday Sermons* (New York—UAHC, 5712–1951–1952), pp. 6–8.

1952 "Dramalogues." *Synagogue Service Bulletin* (New York) XX, no. 1 (1952), 8–9.

"Return—A Religious Experiment." *The Reconstructionist*, XVIII, no. 12 (1952), 20–24.

"Statement." *Hearings Before the President's Commission on Immigration and Naturalization* (Washington, 1952), pp. 860–65.

1953 "Children's High Holyday Services." *CCAR Journal*, June, 1953, pp. 10ff.

"A Hebrew-Dakota Dictionary." *Publications of the American Jewish Historical Society*, XLII, no. 4 (1953), 361–70.

"A Jewish Service in Madrid in 1880." Communications to the Editor. *The Reconstructionist* XIX, no. 16 (1953), 32.

1954 "Minnesota Jewry's First Hundred Years." *American Jewish World* (Minneapolis), September 24, 1954, pp. 19–20.

1955 "Aspects of Progressive Jewish Thought." A review.

American Annual Manual, published by American Board of the World Union for Progressive Judaism, May 1955, pp. 62–63.

"Portrait of a Jewish Pioneer." *National Jewish Monthly* (Washington, D.C.), March 1955, pp. 14ff.

1957 "Are Jews Different?" Syndicated by American Jewish Press, *Western Jewish News* (Winnipeg), August 12, 1957; also *The American Jewish Outlook* (Pittsburgh), December 20, 1957.

1958 "The Guiding Spirit of Our Future." A symposium, with Wallace K. Hermes and Gerhard E. Frost. *Minnesota Journal of Education* XXXVIII, no. 7 (1958), 15–16.

"Socio-Psychological Aspects of Reform Judaism." *CCAR Journal*, January 1958, pp. 17ff.

"An Interview with Moses Mendelssohn." *Commentary* XXV, no. 5 (1958), 428–30.

"Should Jews Seek Converts?" *United Israel Bulletin* (New York) VII, no. 12 (1958), 4.

1959 "Four Languages of Man." *American Jewish World*, April 24, 1959, pp. 15ff; also, *The Southern Israelite*, Passover 1959, pp. 45ff; *American Jewish Outlook*, April 24, 1959, Sect. 1, pp. 17ff; *Western Jewish News*, Passover 1959; *The Jewish Independent*, Passover 1959, Sect. 2, pp. 4ff.

"Daily Services in the Reform Synagogue." *CCAR Journal*, April 1959, pp. 14ff.

"A Voice from the Grave—A True Story." *Jewish Digest*, November 1959, pp. 21–26. Reprinted in *Canadian Jewish Review* XLIV, no. 9 (1961), 4–5.

1960 "The Strange Blessing: A Modern Midrash on Genesis 27." *CCAR Journal* VIII, no. 2 (1960), 30–34.

"The Three Signs." *CCAR Journal*, October 1960, pp. 18–21.

"The Impossibility of Jewish History." *Menorah* (Dublin, Ireland) XIV (1960), 7–8.

1961 "News and Views" was the title of regular editorials in the *Bulletin* of Holy Blossom Temple, Toronto,

1961–1977. A selection appeared in 1971, in *Page Two* (see entry under "Books").

"Second Thoughts About Mordecai." *American Judaism* X, no. 3 (1961), 10ff.

"The Sin of the Brothers: A Commentary on Numbers 20." *CCAR Journal*, April 1961, pp. 18–24.

"The Pillar of Salt, A Commentary." *CCAR Journal*, June 1961, pp. 16–21.

"The Trace of Joseph—A Commentary on Genesis 47:13–27." *CCAR Journal*, October 1961, pp. 29ff.

1962 "The Wandering Aramaean: A Commentary on Deuteronomy 26:5." *CCAR Journal*, January 1962, pp. 18–21.

"A New Look at Mordecai." *Jewish Digest* VII, no. 5 (1962), 33–37.

"Victory of the Spirit." *GM*, March 31, 1962.

"Thou Art My Sister—A Commentary on Genesis, Chapters 12, 20, 26," *CCAR Journal*, April 1962, pp. 26–30; 51.

"The Ghost at Our Seder." *American Judaism* XI, no. 3 (1962), 9ff. Reprinted in *Jewish Digest*, March 1963, pp. 22ff.

"Illumination of a Shadowy Era." Review of N. N. Glatzer's *The Rest is Commentary*. *The American Rabbi*, April 1962, pp. 25ff.

"Fire of Faith Needs New Fuel." *GM*, May 5, 1962.

"Ruth Taught Individual Value." *GM*, June 9, 1962.

"Government and Prayers." *GM*, July 24, 1962.

"Star of Many Meanings." *GM*, August 18, 1962.

"A Dreadful and Dangerous Aberration From Democratic Principles." *GM*, September 20, 1962.

"The Year 5723 Arrives." *GM*, September 22, 1962.

Review of *The Failure of the American Rabbi*, by S. Michael Gelber. *Congress Bulletin* 16, no. 8 (1962), 5.

"Pharoah's Hardened Heart—A Commentary." *CCAR Journal*, October 1962, pp. 18–23.

"The Two Priceless Treasures of the Talmud." *GM*, October 27, 1962.

"Zionism in Germany Today." *Hadassah Reporter* XXVI, no. 3 (1962), 2.

"Morality and Baby Killing." *GM*, December 1, 1962.

1963 "A Fervent Wish for the New Year," *GM*, January 5, 1963.

"New Torah Translation Forthright, Fearless," *GM*, February 9, 1963.

"Toward a Higher Morality—The Emergence of Neo-Biblical Man." *Religious Education*, March–April 1963, pp. 160–65; also *The Reconstructionist* XXIX, no. 2 (1963), 6–11.

"Dialogue Opening Route to New Spiritual Frontier." *GM*, March 16, 1963.

"Rabbi Lauds Encyclical." *GM*, April 10, 1963.

"When Faith Alone is Not Enough." *GM*, May 25, 1963.

"Morality Notions Wrong." *GM*, June 29, 1963.

"Rabbi Lauds Encyclical." *Canadian World Federalist* 11 (1963), 5–6.

"The Punishment of Aaron—A Commentary on Numbers 12." *CCAR Journal*, June 1963, pp. 35–38.

"Rabbi's Authority Stems From Scholarship and Piety." *GM*, August 3, 1963.

"Courtesy's Challenge Arises in Every Human Being." *GM*, August 31, 1963.

"Jews' Day of Atonment." *GM*, September 28, 1963.

"The Shofar's Uncertain Call." *American Judaism* XIII, no. 1 (1963), 9ff.

"Bilingualism: A Chance to Set an Example." *GM*, November 23, 1963.

"The Curse of Literalism." *Canadian World Federalist* 13 (1963), 2–7.

"4 Chess Problems." *Canadian Chess*, 1963.

"I Am a Jew." *GM*, December 21, 1963.

"A Glow of Hope, A Staccato Flicker of Apprehension." *GM*, December 21, 1963.

1964 "Contrasts and Comparisons—Ruminations on Seven Pairs of Sidrahs." *CCAR Journal*, January 1964, pp. 23–26.

"Conspiracy of Living Deceit Often Surrounds Dying." *GM*.

"Adoption—The Child's Right in the Adoptive Process." *Osgoode Hall Law Journal*, March 16, 1964.

"The Deputy: Crisis in the Christian-Jewish Dialogue." *The Canadian Jewish News—Passover Magazine*, March 27, 1964, pp. VI–VII; also in the *Jewish Western Bulletin* XXXI, no. 43 (1964), 27ff.

"Why Pharaoh's Heart was Stiffened." *American Judaism* XIII, no. 3 (1964), 8ff.

"U.S.-Canadian Relations." *GM*, April 30, 1964.

"When Even the Good Are Silent." *GM*, May 16, 1964.

"The still small voice." *GM*, June 15, 1964.

"Must Doctors Be Perfect?" *Ontario Medical Review* 31, no. 6 (1964), 409–12.

"In Defense of the Erev Rav." *CCAR Journal*, June 1964, pp. 36–38.

"Open letter to Governor Wallace." *GM*, July 13, 1964.

"Israel molds dreams into reality." *GM*, November 23, 1964.

"Israel fulfils an ancient promise." *GM*, November 24, 1964.

"Israel shares education problems of the world." *GM*, November 25, 1964.

"The threat facing Israel." *GM*, November 26, 1964.

1965 "Jewish Colonies at Painted Woods and Devils Lake." Selections from *The Jews in Minnesota*. *North Dakota History* 32, no. 1 (1965), 59–70.

"The lesson that lies behind closing the old City Hall." *GM*, March 19, 1965.

"A fond glimpse of Hubert Humphrey." *Toronto Jewish Reporter*, February 24, 1965, p. 4.

"In the camps of death a man of love and courage."

GM, May 14, 1965.

"Voluntary or Forced Giving?" *CCAR Journal*, June 1965, pp. 51–53.

"Allan Garden riots." *GM*, June 5, 1965.

"The Un-public Relations of our National Bodies." *Viewpoints* (1965), pp. 40–44.

Review of R. B. Y. Scott's *Commentary on Proverbs and Ecclesiastes*. *CCAR Journal*, October 1965, pp. 89–92.

"A wish for peace and universal goodwill." *GM*, December 25, 1965.

1966   "Why Love a Stranger?" *CCAR Journal* XIII, no. 4, (1966), 31–34.

"Continuous Learning at Holy Blossom." *Religion and Adult Education*, York University, January 1966.

"Are There Standards in Art?" *St. Regis College Art Catalogue*, April 1966.

"When Does Gold Help the Oppressed?" *CCAR Journal*, April 1966, pp. 53–58.

"The Commentary" (on the projected Torah commentary). *GM*, June 1, 1966.

"Taking the measure of the census." *GM*, June 11, 1966.

"World government." *GM*, July 6, 1966.

"A people's hope." *GM*, July 23, 1966.

"Russia: an unseen hand rules." *GM*, August 27, 1966.

"Russia's religious irreligion." *GM*, August 29, 1966.

"In Russia the foot must fit the shoe." *GM*, August 30, 1966.

"How Russia guides the painter's brush." *GM*, August 31, 1966.

"Youth turns to the West in the Red satellites." *GM*, September 1, 1966.

"Russian Jews . . . fading memories." *GM*, September 2, 1966.

"Bar Mitzvah: an old custom." *GM*, September 10, 1966.

"The Spence report." *GM*, September 30, 1966.
"The first Thanksgiving." *GM*, October 1, 1966.
"After 21 years the UN still lacks the key to peace." *GM*, October 29, 1966.
"Hitler began the same way." *GM*, November 26, 1966.
"What Jesus would see if He returned." *GM*, December 24, 1966.

1967 "Can We Have Integration Without Assimilation?" *Congress Bulletin* 23, no. 1, (1967), 5ff.
"Kosher diet for body and soul." *GM*, January 21, 1967.
"Will the real Von Thadden please stand up?" *GM*, January 27, 1967.
"Neo-Nazis–How Neo, How Nazi?" *Congress Bulletin* 23, no. 3 (1967), 3ff.
"The three Popes and the Jews." *GM*, May 12, 1967.
"Christianity emerges the real culprit." *GM*, May 27, 1967.
"How old fears rallied Canadian Jews to Israel's cause." *GM*, June 13, 1967.
"The Jews and Russia." *GM*, July 5, 1967.
"Jerusalem: A living centre of Jewish faith." *GM*, July 13, 1967.
"The Sabbath and Reform Judaism." *Temple David Review*, Durban, South Africa, August 15, 1967.
"The Jews' uneasy home in Germany." *GM*, September 20, 1967.
"Germany's Neo-Nazis." *GM*, September 21, 1967.
"The Jews and Russia—A Dream that Took 50 Years to Die." *Canadian Zionist* XXXVI, no. 10, (1967), 14ff. Reprint of *GM*, article, July 5, 1967.
"The Yom Kippur that Never Was—A Pious Pictorial Fraud." *Jewish Digest* XII, no. 12 (1967), 25–28.
"The Report of the Special Committee on Hate Propaganda in Canada." *Osgoode Hall Law Journal* 5, no. 2 (1967), 313–17.
"Notes from a New Commentary on the Torah."

CCAR Journal, October 1967, pp. 64–69.

"Israel Wants Justice Too." *The United Church Observer*, November 15, 1967, pp. 21ff.

"A Stinging Rebuke." *Canadian Zionist* XXXVII, no. 3 (1967), p. 5.

"Who Should Control Jerusalem?" *Ferment* '67 1, no. 2 (1967), 4ff.

"Abortion in the light of religious thinking." *GM*, December 11, 1967.

1968   "Commentary on Passages from Genesis 8 and 9." *CCAR Journal*, January 1968, pp. 89–93.

"The new kind of Judaism." *GM*, March 21, 1968.

"Special courage." *GM*, April 4, 1968.

"Who Sold to Whom?" *CCAR Journal*, April 1968, pp. 63–67.

Excerpts from "Presidential Address." *Canadian World Federalist* 36 (1968), 4.

"The Mental Health of the Nation." *Golden Jubilee Book, Canadian Mental Health Association*, May 1968.

"Why Israel defied world opinion." *GM*, May 3, 1968.

"A new act that conjures the ghost of a dictator." *GM*, June 15, 1968, p. 9; translated "Ein Gesetz beschwört den Geist eines Diktators herauf." *Toronto Courier*, July 1968, p. 8.

"Is Nazism Again Only 3 Years from Power?" *Toronto Daily Star*, June 28, 1968, p. 7.

"Israel–Notes from a Diary." *CCAR Journal*, June 1968, pp. 44–49.

"Hubert H. Humphrey." *GM*, August 22, 1968.

"A day of retreat." *GM*, October 1, 1968.

"Bleating Hearts." *GM*, October 30, 1968.

1969   "South Africa: a disciplined land full of puzzling contradictions." *GM*, January 27, 1969, p. 7.

"John Vorster: prophet of a new order?" *GM*, January 28, 1969.

"On Authority." *Ferment* '69 2, no. 3 (1969), 3.

"Notes on the Akedah." *CCAR Journal*, January 1969, pp. 45–47.

"The church battle." *GM*, January 29, 1969.

"Why TV isn't beamed into South African homes." *GM*, January 30, 1969.

"The festival called Passover." *GM*, March 31, 1969.

"The vital link with sense." *GM*, April 15, 1969.

"Journey to Israel." *GM*, April 19, 1969.

"Isaiah would smile in peace. A birthday party with no war candles on the cake." *GM*, April 27, 1969.

"Media." *Toronto Daily Star*, April 25, 1969.

"Understanding Joseph." *CCAR Journal*, April 1969, pp. 20–23.

"A double anniversary—one day to remember and another to forget." *GM*, May 22, 1969.

"The Sciences of Judaism." *Jewish Spectator* XXXIV, no. 6 (1969), 11–13.

"Rabbi Replies." *Canadian Churchman*, June, 1969.

"Why a black revolutionary aims his hatred at Israel." *GM*, July 5, 1969.

"Germany." *GM*, July 1969.

"Roumania's role in the Middle-East." *GM*, August 6, 1969.

"The meaning of the Jewish New Year." *GM*, September 12, 1969.

"Yom Kippur." *GM*, September 22, 1969.

"Some Unanswered Questions About Torah." *CCAR Journal*, October 1969, pp. 74–78.

"God and the Moonshot." *Rosh Hashanah Annual* (Dublin, Ireland) V (1969), 22.

1970   "A dilemma." *GM*, January 3, 1970.

"Fashion prophecy?" *GM*, February 1970.

"The trouble that makes Canadian Jews uneasy." *GM*, March 20, 1970.

"Moscow Rumblings." *Toronto Jewish Reporter* 5, no. 3 (1970), 1–2.

"The Death of 30 Children." *Toronto Jewish Reporter* 5, no. 4 (1970), 1–2.

"Roumania." *GM*, May 11, 1970.

"Solving a riddle." *GM*, June 2, 1970.

"Do-nothingism." *GM*, June 23, 1970.

"New hope in the Middle East." *Jewish Chronicle Review*, September 1970, pp. 32ff.

"What Now? Pledging and Paying." *Toronto Jewish Reporter* 5, no. 5 (1970), 1-2.

"Spiritual junk." *GM*, July 10, 1970.

"Russia's anti-Israel campaign." *GM*, July 14, 1970.

"Beauty business." *GM*, July 16, 1970.

"Psalm 1970—dedicated to Bruce West." *GM*, July 30, 1970.

"A little fear please." *GM*, August 7, 1970.

1971   "Why Egyptian plane shot down in reconnaissance flight over Suez." *CJN*, September 24, 1971.

"The New Year." *GM*, September 20, 1971.

"Day of Atonement," *GM*, September 28, 1971.

"Jordan resolution passed at UN" *CJN*, October 1, 1971.

"Ben Gurion: personification of a state, its people." *GM*, October 6, 1971.

"Ben Gurion at 85." *CJN*, October 8, 1971.

"Kosygin, Canada and Israel." *CJN*, October 15, 1971.

"If I Were Premier for a Day." *Toronto Daily Star*, October 19, 1971.

"New Directions for Reform Rabbis." *CCAR Journal*, October 1971, pp. 24ff.

"Rückblick auf mein Leben." *Emuna Horizonte* (Frankfurt/Main, Germany) VI, November 5, 1971, 348ff.

"Looking back on 10 years in Toronto." *GM*, December 31, 1971.

1972   "Confrontation with Kosygin in Canada." *Midstream* XVIII, no. 1 (1972), 20ff.

"The sad plight of the Jews in Syria." *GM*, January 8, 1972.

"Why do spoilsports have to ruin the superbowl fun?" *GM*, January 14, 1972.

"A little Arizona store where honesty is the best policy." *GM*, February 23, 1972.

"Tennis, anyone?" *GM*, February 24, 1972.

"When Kosygin came to Canada." *Shema* (New York), February 25, 1972.

"A valiant man" (Dr. Koch). *GM*, February 28, 1972.

"In Rome, with love." *GM*, March 24, 1972.

"Passover." *GM*, March 29, 1972.

"Russian immigrant life in Israel." *GM*, March 31, 1972.

"Another world." *GM*, April 11, 1972.

"The non-believers." *GM*, April 14, 1972.

"A striking parallel." *GM*, May 5, 1972.

"The pollsters: loaded questions," *GM*, May 1972.

"Are there special reasons for Golda Meir's visit to Roumania?" *GM*, May 6, 1972.

Review of H. Pollack's *Jewish Folkways in Germanic Lands*. *CCAR Journal* XIX, no. 3 (1972), 98f.

"Chessmen." *GM*, July 12, 1972.

"Air most foul." *GM*, August 1, 1972.

"The battle to preserve Yiddish." *GM*, August 11, 1972.

"Where to find tantalizing clonks." *GM*, August 18, 1972.

"Munich mars the Jewish New Year." *GM*, September 8, 1972.

"A moveable feast with rigid laws." *GM*, September 15, 1972.

"Israel 5733." *Congress Bulletin*, September-October 1972.

"The Man from Pethor." *CCAR Journal*, Autumn 1972, pp. 29–32.

"Brandt's new role in Europe." *GM*, December 2, 1972.

"Impressions of resurgent West Germany." *GM*, December 13, 1972.

"German Jews find themselves 'strangers in a strange land.' " *CJN*, December 15, 1972.

1973 "Epitaph for a long-time friend who moved men's minds" (Heschel). *GM*, January 11, 1973.

"Old West comes alive in a cemetery." *GM*,

February 22, 1973.

"The dream machine." *GM*, March 9, 1973.

"Festive frolic." *GM*, March 23, 1973.

"Human chauvinism." *GM*, March 23, 1973.

"A fine record" (Fred Oberlander). *GM*, April 2, 1973.

"Over the hill?" *GM*, April 5, 1973.

"Actors' actions deserve our praise." Editorial. *CJN*, April 6, 1973.

"Passover." *GM*, April 16, 1973.

"Genealogy games." *GM*, April 23, 1973.

"Old grey language." *GM*, May 2, 1973.

"Why Israel parades in Jerusalem streets." *GM*, May 12, 1973.

"A confidence game." *GM*, May 24, 1973.

"Time to think." *GM*, June 8, 1973.

"Anxiety." *GM*, June 21, 1973.

"Stage magic." *GM*, July 2, 1973.

"Ventilationism." *GM*, July 10, 1973.

"Three mover." Chess problem composed for the *Jerusalem Post*, July 13, 1973, p. 31.

"Pet snoopers don't need help." *GM*, July 20, 1973.

"Squeeze play." *GM*, July 31, 1973.

"A time to listen." *GM*, August 15, 1973.

"Match without par." *GM*, August 21, 1973.

"World reaction, especially by UN, to Israeli action 'clearly immoral.' " *CJN*, August 24, 1973.

"Beautiful freaks." *GM*, August 28, 1973.

"Still carrying the torch." *GM*, September 3, 1973. (Reply September 17, 1973 letter to editor.)

"Tower of Babel?" *GM*, September 19, 1973.

"Must live each day as if Messiah were at hand." *CJN*, September 21, 1973.

"Happy New Year." *GM*, September 25, 1973.

"Lid comes off ancient Jerusalem." *GM*, September 27, 1973.

"The Rumpled Poet" (W. H. Auden). *GM*, October 3, 1973.

"And my people wept." *GM*, October 9, 1973.

Reprinted in *On the Fourth Day of the War.*

"Observance and Commitment—The How and Why of the *Tadrich l'Shabbat." CCAR Journal,* Autumn 1973, pp. 39–44.

"We Are Jews." *Congress Bulletin,* November 1973, pp. 4f. Address delivered at demonstration following outbreak of the Yom Kippur War; also published separately by B'nai Brith; also excerpted in *On the Fourth Day of the War.*

"POW problem." *GM,* November 1, 1973.

"Popularity." *GM,* November 13, 1973.

"Political rabbi" (Maurice N. Eisendrath). *GM,* November 23, 1973.

"National emotion?" *GM,* November 27, 1973.

"In mourning" (David Ben Gurion). *GM,* December 6, 1973.

"Cars and privacy." *GM,* December 18, 1973.

"In troubled times.'" *GM,* December 19, 1973.

1974   "Grandparents." *GM,* January 4, 1974.

"Awful offal." *GM,* January 9, 1974.

"Small is big." *GM,* January 15, 1974.

"Back to normal." *GM,* January 29, 1974.

"Flowers of science." *GM,* February 6, 1974.

"Two kinds of president." *GM,* February 8, 1974.

"Benefits of war." *GM,* February 13, 1974.

"Needed: ingenuity." *GM,* February 19, 1974.

"A universal code." *GM,* February 22, 1974.

"Long-hand with Buber." *Judaism,* Winter 1974, pp. 61–69.

"A Dialogue: Christian-Jewish Relations in Today's World," with Gregory Baum. *Religious Education* LXIX, no. 2 (1974), 32ff.

"Trusting the Bible." *GM,* March 12, 1974.

"Israel turns inward to reshape its future." *GM,* March 20, 1974.

"Mr. K." *GM,* March 27, 1974.

"Special behavior and attitudes are called for in these hard times." Unsigned editorial. *CJN,* March 31, 1974.

"Apolitical." *GM*, April 3, 1974.
"Going home." *GM*, April 5, 1974.
"A holy time." *GM*, April 11, 1974.
"Rule of thumb." *GM*, April 17, 1974.
"Scapegoat." *GM*, April 24, 1974.
"The right way." *GM*, April 30, 1974.
"Wireless chess." *GM*, May 7, 1974.
"No easy exit" (Richard Nixon). *GM*, May 14, 1974.
"An invocation." *GM*, May 17, 1974.
"A final pact." *GM*, May 24, 1974.
"A word to the wise." *GM*, June 4, 1974.
"A crucial claim." *GM*, June 11, 1974.
"Grapes of wrath." *GM*, June 18, 1974.
"At Yad Vashem." *GM*, June 21, 1974.
"Terminal illness." *GM*, July 1, 1974.
"A change of heart." *GM*, July 4, 1974.
"Balderdash?" *GM*, July 8, 1974.
"Good intentions." *GM*, July 11, 1974.
"A complex science." *GM*, July 15, 1974.
"Case of Nazi-hunter raises moral question." *GM*, July 18, 1974.
"Pseudo-science." *GM*, July 22, 1974.
"The gap narrows." *GM*, July 24, 1974.
"Mobile courtesty." *GM*, July 31, 1974.
Review of John Woodenson's *Mark Gertler*. *Canadian Forum*, August 1974.
"Tennis anyone?" *GM*, August 15, 1974.
"In gratitude." *GM*, August 22, 1974.
"Pill vs will." *GM*, August 27, 1974.
"A bitter blow." *GM*, September 10, 1974.
"New Year's wish." *GM*, September 17, 1974.
"Yom Kippur War." *CJN*, September 25, 1974.
"A culture gulf." *GM*, October 3, 1974.
"A pillar gone." *GM*, October 9, 1974.
"Piercing candor." *GM*, October 19, 1974.
"A little too much." *GM*, October 22, 1974.
"Khrushchev again." *GM*, October 25, 1974.
"Regeneration by repentance." *GM*, October 26, 1974.

"Is Reform Ambiguous?" *Reform Judaism* 3, no. 2, (1974).
"Chess Problem in honour of Joshua Plaut." *Jerusalem Post*, October 1974.
"The facts make Arafat speech mockery at best." *GM*, November 15, 1974.
"Poor bachelors." *GM*, December 5, 1974.
"The lost scrolls." *GM*, December 11, 1974.
"Numbers, please." *GM*, December 27, 1974.

1975 "Strictly speaking." *GM*, January 1, 1975.
"Institutions vs humanity." *GM*, January 8, 1975.
"The super bash." *GM*, January 10, 1975.
"Playing God." *GM*, January 15, 1975.
"Bound in the pit." *GM*, February 25, 1975.
"Striking out." *GM*, March 19, 1975.
"No rational matter" (death penalty). *GM*, March 24, 1975.
"A Seder meal in wartime." *GM*, March 26, 1975.
"Nine years away?" *GM*, April 1, 1975.
" 'There are only men in our army' " (said a boy in uniform). *GM*, April 28, 1975.
"The death penalty." *GM*, May 7, 1975.
"Elegy for us." *GM*, May 15, 1975.
"Let's bow out" (Olympics). *GM*, May 20, 1975.
"Bluegrass is back." *GM*, June 3, 1975.
"Computer talk." *GM*, June 10, 1975.
"Trial by whom? An urgent problem." *GM*, June 18, 1975.
"A simple approach." *GM*, July 1, 1975.
"Dear Shriners." *GM*, July 4, 1975.
"Females lose in the crunch." *GM*, July 9, 1975.
"The pros and cons of admitting the PLO." *GM*, July 15, 1975.
"Space detente." *GM*, July 18, 1975.
"Breaking point." *GM*, July 23, 1975.
"Did Turner know?" *GM*, July 29, 1975.
"Foes and Friends." *GM*, August 7, 1975.
"What serves the greater good?" *GM*, August 13, 1975.

"Tennis craze." *GM*, August 15, 1975.
" 'Not yet timely.' " *GM*, August 22, 1975.
"No sweat." *GM*, August 29, 1975.
"Do we need a 'new' year?" *GM*, September 5, 1975.
"Mind over body." *GM*, September 12, 1975.
"Four score" (John Diefenbaker). *GM*, September 17, 1975.
"Show me, please." *GM*, September 26, 1975.
"What sport?" *GM*, October 21, 1975.
"Decision!" *GM*, October 30, 1975.
"Whose Sabbath?" *GM*, November 4, 1975.
"Special section special movie." *GM*, November 6, 1975.
"Texas' Canada." *GM*, November 12, 1975.
"Zionism and racism, or black equals white." *GM*, November 14, 1975.
"Time to strike." *GM*, November 21, 1975.
"Candles of freedom." *GM*, December 3, 1975.
"At the Olympics." *GM*, December 8, 1975.
"Banality of evil." *GM*, December 30, 1975.

1976 "Plumber's progress." *GM*, January 1, 1976.
"A body of purists cleanses a tongue." *GM*, January 13, 1976.
"Misinterpretation lies in the eyes." *GM*, January 22, 1976.
"A breadless circus that must be fed." *GM*, February 4, 1976.
"We've arrived" (Canada in Florida perspective). *GM*, February 16, 1976.
"Heartbreak move" (Doctors' Hospital). *GM*, February 19, 1976.
"Dirt on the window to all the world" (on speech). *GM*, February 26, 1976.
"London still solid." *GM*, March 2, 1976.
"Reflections on Spain—progress being made but slowly." *GM*, March 18, 1976.
Review. *Religious Education* 71 (1976), 223.
"Four Points of Law. Notes on the Relationship of

Law and Religion." *Gazette* (published by the Law Society of Upper Canada) X, no. 1, 6–10.

Communication, *CCAR Journal*, Spring 1976, p. 72.

"No rational matter" (capital punishment). *GM*, March 24, 1976.

"Better man drunk." *GM*, March 31, 1976.

"The right to pray." *GM*, April 9, 1976. Reprinted, *GM*, May 10, 1976.

"Operetta awakens family memories." *GM*, April 12, 1976.

"The wonder of Passover." *GM*, April 14, 1976.

"Catholic support of United Way." *GM*, April 20, 1976.

"Odd alliance." *GM*, May 7, 1976.

"The rabbi's son" (Haim Herzog). *GM*, May 12, 1976.

"Happy landings." Letter to Otto Lang. *GM*, May 20, 1976.

"A sense of resignation." *GM*, May 22, 1976.

"HHHere's hoping." *GM*, May 28, 1976.

Review of Jacob Katz's *Out of the Ghetto. Queen's Quarterly* 83, no. 1 (1976), 142f.

"A tragic tale." *GM*, June 2, 1976.

"Thrift? Whazzat?" *GM*, June 15, 1976.

"Healing's price." *GM*, June 18, 1976.

"Evil dream revived warns of peril." *GM*, June 24, 1976.

"Alike and not alike" (Canada and U.S.). *GM*, July 2, 1976.

"Reason for rescue" (Entebbe). *GM*, July 6, 1976.

"A prolific state." *GM*, July 27, 1976.

"Lob, no; lobby, yes." *GM*, August 17, 1976.

"Savior of the alm still not in sight." *GM*, August 27, 1976.

"Blindness no bar to understanding." *GM*, September 1, 1976.

"Change of sex no laughing matter." *GM*, September 8, 1976.

"And to each their own . . . ." *GM*, September 13, 1976.

"A season for faith in search of hope." *GM*, September 24, 1976.

Symposium on Attitudes toward Halakah in the Reform Rabbinate. *Ammi*, October 1976.

"Gladiators get too great awards." *GM*, October 12, 1976.

"Plain honesty beats perfection." *GM*, October 20, 1976.

"A perilous proposal." *GM*, October 27, 1976.

"A gift of blood trips up disaster." *GM*, November 11, 1976.

"A Eulogy for the Israeli Martyrs of 1972 at Munich." *CCAR Journal*, Autumn 1976.

"The great need is for peace." *GM*, December 11, 1976.

"Release raises moral questions." *GM*, December 15, 1976.

"Message remains." *GM*, December 16, 1976.

"Banality of evil." *GM*, December 20, 1976.

"Karma." Letter to the editor. *GM*, December 29, 1976.

"Don't Stop at 65." *GM*, December 28, 1976.

"Woo the undecided for Canada's sake." *GM*, December 31, 1976.

"Creative thought." *Dharma World*, December 1976, pp. 13–14.

1977   "Revving up for a super time." *GM*, January 13, 1977.

"Let the elderly try lobby tactics." *GM*, January 26, 1977.

"Nuts to Big Brother—well, just once." *GM*, February 9, 1977.

"Sinister stuff (call it one-sided)." *GM*, February 18, 1977.

"A lesson for cities." *GM*, March 2, 1977.

Editorial challenging WGP to assume leadership of grey heads. *GM*, March 5, 1977.

"Heart trouble strains marriage." *GM*, March 3, 1977.

"Time to get on with metric." *GM*, March 17, 1977.

"Passover symbol denied in Russia." *GM*, April 6, 1977.

"Strong leadership likely if Peres is PM." *GM*, April 16, 1977.

"A heretical view of baseball." *GM*, April 11, 1977.

"Spanking: gap between ideal, real." *GM*, April 27, 1977.

"Being Oneself—Only More so." *Canadian Institute of Religion and Gerontology Newsletter* 4, no. 5 (1977).

"Election bill is money well spent." *GM*, May 6, 1977.

Russian reply to April 6, 1977. *GM*, May 25, 1977.

"Car racing at CNE: Put the brakes to it." *GM*, June 6, 1977.

"A tragic tale" (Martha Mitchell). *GM*, June 2, 1977.

"Likud policies under scrutiny." *GM*, June 4, 1977.

"Battling perverters of history." *GM*, June 28, 1977.

"A land in which thanksgiving isn't quaint." *GM*, July 1, 1977.

"Aftermath of terror." *GM*, July 2, 1977.

"Laughter dangerous in some lands." *GM*, July 15, 1977.

"Making it in School—Making it in Life." *The School Guidance Worker* (Toronto) 32, no. 6 (1977), 34–35.

"Morality and the neutron bomb." *GM*, August 17, 1977.

"Champs on the courts? First court the young." *GM*, August 20, 1977.

"Warning flags up on neo-Nazism." *GM*, August 30, 1977.

"Reform Judaism." Temple Israel, South Africa, September 1977.

"Jewish concern, but not gloom." *GM*, September 10, 1977.

"An infantile washout called 'Soap.'" *GM*,

September 15, 1977.

"Yom Kippur, a day of assurance." *GM*, September 21, 1977.

"Battle for the rights of the aged." *GM*, October 26, 1977.

"Flexible retirement: by biological age." *GM*, November 9, 1977.

"Man is slow to give love." *GM*, November 21, 1977.

"Who holds the key?" *GM*, December 3, 1977.

"A maker of peace." *GM*, December 7, 1977.

"Officially elderly—a new career." *GM*, December 13, 1977.

Letter to the editor. *CCAR Journal*, Winter 1977.

"A time to act." *GM*, December 28, 1977.

"An enlightening leap across generation gap." *GM*, December 31, 1977.

1978   "Hubert Humphrey: champion of the underdog fondly recalled." *GM*, January 16, 1978.

"Down with old is ugly—age must take a stand." *GM*, February 4, 1978.

"Television and violence." *GM*, February 8, 1978.

Guest Editorial, *Shalom* (Atlantic Jewish Council) 3, no. 4 (1978), 1.

"Nazi right to march? Not really" (Skokie). *GM*, February 25, 1978.

"Canadian, Russian aged compared." *GM*, March 22, 1978.

"Is criminal mind track unique?" *GM*, March 27, 1978.

"Reunion." *GM*, April 1, 1978. Reprinted from *Hanging Threads*.

"Annie leaves a lot to be desired." *GM*, April 4, 1978.

"The Middle East and the media." *GM*, April 15, 1978.

"Air Canada just like the Argos?" *GM*, April 21, 1978.

"Holocaust: it had to be told." *GM*, April 22, 1978.

"Ancient tablets hold out promise of fresh look at the Bible." *GM*, May 13, 1978.

"Optimism and pessimism." *GM*, June 18, 1978.

"Informality, suicide in the theatre." *GM*, July 5, 1978.

"For Pressure to Be Exercised Effectively, the First Step is to Define the Points." *Maclean's*, July 10, 1978, p. 8.

"Mangling of rights warning to Russian dissidents." *GM*, July 12, 1978.

"Summer in Toronto? Lovely." *GM*, July 14, 1978.

"Russian trials a show of strength by Stalinists." *GM*, July 17, 1978.

"Artificial birth raises questions that demand action." *GM*, August 1, 1978.

"Food for thought on human rights." *GM*, August 4, 1978.

"God not a universal policeman." *GM*, August 8, 1978.

"What about just playing game."*GM*, August 14, 1978.

"Crudity creeps into courtly game." *GM*, August 24, 1978.

"The urgent need is for talk but within certain limits." *GM*, September 2, 1978.

"When police are viewed as inquisitors." *GM*, September 20, 1978.

"A rare case for euphoria." *GM*, September 29, 1978.

"Think the unthinkable! Safety for cyclists." *GM*, October 5, 1978.

"Who needs all this protection?" *GM*, October 31, 1978.

"Assessing the Jewish Mind." *Queen's Quarterly* 85, no. 3 (1978), 464–68.

"The Israelites in Egypt—a Historical Reconstruction." *Judaism* 27, no. 1 (1978), 40–46.

"What kind of welcome?" (Begin's visit). *CJN*, November 3, 1978.

"Night of broken glass." *GM*, November 9, 1978.

"Begin's visit in retrospect." *CJN*, November 23, 1978.

"Death became the only way of life in Jonestown." *GM*, November 30, 1978.

"Holiday lights reassuring symbols." *GM*, December 16, 1978.

1979 "We remember you in fondness, Golda." *CJN*, January 4, 1979.

"CJC functions not easy, says current president." *CJN*, January 11, 1979.

"Society shows blind eye to football's flaws." *GM*, January 24, 1979.

"Violence (of both kinds) needs attending to." *GM*, February 9, 1979.

"Rise in suicides among young raises important questions." *GM*, March 7, 1979.

"The thrust of Einstein and his thoughts." *GM*, March 9, 1979.

"Purim, when sober adults laugh and pretend." *GM*, March 12, 1979.

"What the two religions share," with Professor Dan Donovan. *GM*, April 1979.

"Passover: For Jews, one symbol emphasized." *GM*, April 11, 1979.

"Canada the land the U.S. papers forgot." *GM*, May 1, 1979.

"A couple of suggestions for candidates. Any takers?" *GM*, May 18, 1979.

"The diary Anne Frank wasn't destined to write." *GM*, May 22, 1979.

"Senior 'Gleaners' waste not what others want not." *GM*, May 26, 1979.

"Fast's over, but lesson not lost on world" (Soviet Jews). *GM*, June 4, 1979.

"Cabinet lacks old people's wisdom." *GM*, June 14, 1979.

"Shutting the door of remembrance is risky" (West Germany). *GM*, June 26, 1979.

"Senseless syndrome hits aged." *GM*, July 4, 1979.

"Jewish leaders present views on embassy move." Joint letter with CIC leaders. *GM*, July 5, 1979.

"Time is key to West Bank case." *GM*, July 7, 1979.

"Boat people of '39 also awakened world." *GM*, July 13, 1979.

"Surviving a child's death." *GM*, July 27, 1979.

"The crux of Iran's music ban." *GM*, August 7, 1979.

"Watching tennis stars a tonic for buffs." *GM*, August 16, 1979.

"Where's Sir Rowland when we need him?" *GM*, August 30, 1979.

"Symbol of universal hope amid madness" (Elie Wiesel). *GM*, September 11, 1979.

"The world's full of troubles—and yet . . ." (Rosh Hashanah). *GM*, September 19, 1979.

"Aiding boat people." Joint letter to Editor. *GM*, September 26, 1979.

"Mr. Clark and the PLO." Unsigned editorial. *CJN*, October 18, 1979.

"Confused Thinking." Unsigned editorial. *CJN*, October 25, 1979.

"How one woman works to mend broken lives." *GM*, November 3, 1979.

"The day will come." Unsigned editorial. *CJN*, November 8, 1979.

"Breaktime may be the panacea many seek." *GM*, November 20, 1979.

"Religion and politics do mix." *GM*, November 28, 1979.

"Christmas and Hanukah different at heart." *GM*, December 14, 1979.

"Making history." Unsigned editorial. *CJN*, December 20, 1979.

1980   "1980: But will it be a happy year?" *GM*, January 2, 1980.

"Let's skip the Olympics as in '40 and '44." *GM*, February 6, 1980.

"Quebec's Jews: Diminished But Determined." *Reform Judaism*, February 19, 1980.

"Americans and Jews joint scapegoats." *GM*, February 25, 1980.

"Security still the major worry" (Israel). *GM*, March 8, 1980.

"On Israel's 32nd anniversary." *Shalom* (Atlantic Jewish Council) 5, no. 4 (1980), 3.

"The '60-you're out' roadblock." *GM*, March 18, 1980.

"It's Purim in Cairo—time of joy, sadness." *GM*, March 20, 1980.

"Egypt's peace process welcomed by the masses." *GM*, March 22, 1980.

"Passover is a unique gathering of the clan." *GM*, March 31, 1980.

"The big stumbling block for Israel: autonomy." *GM*, April 11, 1980.

"Raising of Jewish consciousness." *CJN*, May 1, 1980.

"Final Address as [Congress] President." Abridged. *CJN*, May 8, 1980.

"The inspiration of the young at heart" (on mother). *GM*, May 14, 1980.

"Cotler 'man of word and deed.' " *CJN*, May 15, 1980.

"Deep anxiety dominates pre-election scenario" (Germany). *GM*, May 31, 1980.

"Jews again in Germany—about 30,000 'registered.' " *CJN*, June 5, 1980.

"Jews give many reasons for returning to Germany." *CJN*, June 12, 1980.

"Future of Germany's Jews raises question mark." *CJN*, June 19, 1980.

"Berlin is blooming again." *GM*, June 23, 1980.

"Goldmann honoured by WJC executive." *CJN*, June 24, 1980.

"Discours." French extracts from presidential address at CJC convention. *Bulletin du Cercle Juif* (Montreal). 28th year, no. 191 (1980).

"Reform Judaism: Past, Present and Future." *CCAR Journal*, Summer 1980, pp. 1–11.

"Chosenness in Jewish Tradition, *Sidic* (Rome) XIII, no. 2 (1980), 4–8.

"Halichot l'halachah—Wege zur Halacha." *Tradition und Erneuerung* 46 (July 1980), 23–30, with commentary by L. O. Zwillenberg.

"The basic fear the Russians reveal." *GM*, July 15, 1980.

"An air of stability pervades Amsterdam." *GM*, July 30, 1980.

"The greats stir memories of Big Bill." *GM*, August 13, 1980.

"Self-persuasion a big factor in life." *GM*, August 20, 1980.

"A time to awaken spiritual potential." *GM*, September 8, 1980.

"Absurd casting in a first-rate show." *GM*, September 30, 1980.

"When police are viewed as inquisitors." *GM*, September 20, 1980.

"Has anything really changed?" *GM*, October 13, 1980.

"Disheartening prospect for voters." *GM*, October 29, 1980.

"The religious element in Reagan's win." *GM*, November 11, 1980.

"Mirabel is a Kafka-esque experience." *GM*, November 28, 1980.

"From Moncton to Squamish," *Moment* (Boston) 6 no. 1 (1980), 32–37.

"When racism ripens violence is plucked." *GM*, December 9, 1980.

"With Lennon's passing something died in all of us." *GM*, December 11, 1980.

1981 "Ontario's giant steps to protect human rights." *GM*, January 27, 1981.

Letter to the Editor. *Commentary*, February 1981, pp. 14f.

"Israel still a land of vigor and doubt." *GM*,

February 9, 1981.

"A rare and truly unforgettable man" (Heinz Warschauer). *GM*, March 1981.

"Monkey trial revives conflict." *GM*, April 7, 1981.

"Courage of black woman remembered" (Rosa Parks). *GM*, April 28, 1981.

"Germany's embrace of Arabs alarms Israel." *GM*, May 9, 1981.

"Reagan's welcome tone on Israel and PLO." *GM*, May 22, 1981.

"Can Begin maintain his hold and power?" *GM*, June 15, 1981.

"Strange trends emerge from Israeli election." *GM*, July 11, 1981 (Shortened and changed without W. Gunther Plaut's knowledge.)

Review of Elie Wiesel's *The Testament*. *GM*, July 18, 1981.

"Worries about basic rights in Canada." *GM*, July 28, 1981.

"Religion a factor in Begin cabinet." *GM*, August 12, 1981.

"Painful memories of government secrecy." *GM*, August 24, 1981.

"One may be elderly, not old." *GM*, September 2, 1981.

"The Righteous Gentile" (in memoriam Harry Crowe). *The Atkinsonian*, York University, Toronto, September 15, 1981.

"Surviving in a world of madness." Excerpt from *Unfinished Business*. *GM*, September 18, 1982.

"Jewish New Year marks anniversary of Babi Yar." *GM*, September 28, 1981.

"Intriguing area of human rights." *GM*, October 9, 1981.

"The death-camp liberators look back." *GM*, November 5, 1981.

"A milestone for a house of worship." (anniversary of Holy Blossom Temple). *GM*, November 13, 1981.

"De vier fasen." Dutch translation of address to

1980 convention of World Union for Progressive Judaism. *Nieuw Joodsch Leven* 28, no. 2 (1981), 29–35.

"Who decides what is acceptably human?" *GM*, November 23, 1981.

"Vichy France and the Jews." Review of Marrus-Paxton book. *GM*, November 28, 1981.

"A Plea for a new deal for the aged in Canada." *GM*, December 10, 1981.

"Freedom is at centre of Chanukah," *GM*, December 18, 1981.

"Once again Jews in Poland are scapegoats." *GM*, December 31, 1981.

WEEKLY COLUMN IN THE CANADIAN JEWISH NEWS

1980

July 31 We have the responsibility to warn endangered Jews.

Aug. 7 New study says family unit "out of the woods" at last.

14 Regan may be better for Israel than Carter.

21 "Leaders, watch what you say" is dictum which many ignore.

28 "Zionism is racism" now surfaces in Canada.

Sept. 4 Denying Holocaust is next in anti-Zionism procedures.

11 Let's not forget capacity for good.

18 Dispute emerges over Holocaust.

25 Soviets hold Wallenberg; we must help to save him.

Oct. 2 Jews also believe propaganda of Arab stand on Jerusalem.

9 Redgrave in role of Tania is salt on open wounds.

16 Anti-Semitism flourishing in the land of Dreyfus.

23 All who care about freedom should fight against the Klan.

30 Nov. 4—U.S. election day called "doomsday" for Israel.

Nov. 6 *Saturday Night* editor decries signs of rising anti-semitism.

13 Prime Minister will make long heralded Mideast trip.

20 Russian Jewish immigrants revitalize small Ontario city.

27 Rally expresses solidarity but more participants needed.

Dec. 4 Another side to Miami Beach: The elderly living in poverty.

11 A very complex problem: how to help the Falashas.

18 Dispute over Moral Majority divides communities in U.S.

25 (No newspaper)

1981

Jan. 1 The new year dawns on a variety of concerns.

8 Suggestions to make Russian Jews welcome.

15 Delegates will meet in Israel for World Jewish Congress.

22 Issuing Palestinian stamp not worth protest to UN.

29 Holocaust presents dilemma, critics say studies off-track.

Feb. 5 Israeli press neglects plenary, Bronfman subject of cartoon.

12 Number of reasons for growth of disease of anti-semitism.

19 WCJ suggests co-ordination of research on anti-semitism.

26 Archeologist thinks he found Hebrew tribes in West Africa.

Mar. 5 Giving Nazi TV time called "cheap shot."

12 Vacationers in Florida seem unwittingly close to reality.

19 Unpredictable Warschauer was a passionate educator.

26 ADL using legal machinery to insure security for Jews.

Apr. 2 A special event, every 28 years.

9 Jewish intellectual endorses latest form of anti-semitism.

16 Our own dedication to aliya would see yerida disappear.

23 Cloak of semi-respectability covers anti-semitic group.

30 Survivor formulates characteristic traits.

May 7 Praise for Romans in Masada—little admiration for zealots.

14 Freedom of information important in a democracy.

21 Statement by Helmut Schmidt "looked like studied neglect."

28 Influence of Pope restrains Russian army.

June 4 Criticized after Nazi rally CJC became more activist.

11 David Lewis, Harry Hyde: both worked hard for us.

18 Day-to-day survival prompted raid (Iraqi reactor).

25 Many critics of raid could soon change their attitudes.

July 2 Study shows W. Germans' strong democratic beliefs.

23 The election battle was a bitter one, too personalized.
PLO is a catalytic agent for Terrorist International.

30 Israel cast spell on one during 1935 Maccabiah.

Aug. 6 Our enemies will not succeed in splitting us from Israel.

13 The coalition—an analysis.
Critics quick to descend on outspoken Timerman.

20 Crowe's passion for justice focused on Jews and Israel.

27 A sense of abiding gratitude for 20 splendid years here.

Sept. 3   Maternity leave big issue in area of human rights.

         10   Diverse feelings are aroused by lengthy war crimes trial.

         17   Parallel problems found in ghetto and reserve.

         24   How Clark's promise almost split community (excerpt from *Unfinished Business*).
At Rosh Hashanah services we'll remember Babi Yar.

Oct.   1   CBC's choice of news items leaves a lot to be desired.

          8   W. German official recalls reactions of war criminals.

         15   Current revolution in Poland is conflicting for Jews.

         22   Ontario's Bill 7 (unsigned editorial)
Editorial poses questions on Evangelicals and Jews.

         29   Formerly interned in Canada, they now enrich our society.

Nov. 5   Liberators join survivors at emotional U.S. forum.
Divisive squabbles caused by irresponsible incitement.

Nov. 12   Liberators' meet sparks some personal reflections.

         19   Lack of protest in Austria invites ''spate of attacks.''

         26   Future of Jews in France seems to be quite clouded.

Dec. 3   UN resolutions have lost all of their credibility.

         10   Constitution promotes freedom only by will of people.

         17   Continuous vigilance needed to counteract revisionists.

         24   Seniors should be participating in planning by community.

         31   (No newspaper)

About the Contributors

Gregory Baum

Gregory Baum is professor of theology and sociology at St. Michael's College in the University of Toronto. He is editor of *The Ecumenist* and a member of the editorial committee of the international theological review *Conciliam*. He is the author of several books, the most recent of which is *Catholics and Canadian Socialism*. Many of his articles attempt to promote Jewish-Christian dialogue and cooperation.

Eugene B. Borowitz

Eugene B. Borowitz is professor of education and Jewish religious thought at the New York School of Hebrew Union College–Jewish Institute of Religion. In 1981–1982, he became the first Jewish president of the American Theological Society. He is the founder and editor of *Sh'ma*, a journal of Jewish responsibility. His most recent book is *Contemporary Christologies, A Jewish Response*.

June Callwood

June Callwood, social activist and journalist, is the author of more than fourteen books. Her most recent publication is *Portrait of Canada*. She was a broadcaster with the CBC and a committed community leader who has held many posts, most recently, the presidency of Jessie's. A champion of human rights and a recipient of numerous awards, she became in 1978 a member of the Order of Canada.

G. Emmett Carter

His Eminence, G. Emmett Cardinal Carter, has been pastor, educator, scholar, author, liturgist, and chaplain over the span of forty-five years of ministry. For twelve years he was bishop of the Diocese of London and is currently serving as archbishop of Toronto. He was appointed by Pope John Paul II to the secretariat for non-Christians as well as to the secretariat for Christian unity. He was reelected a member of the Permanent Council of the Synod of Bishops in Rome. He has received many honorary degrees.

The essay is based on an address given in Toronto, on September 15, 1979, to the Canadian Institute of Chartered Accountants.

IRWIN COTLER

Irwin Cotler is professor of law at McGill University in Montreal. The founder of Canadian Professors for Peace in the Middle East, he succeeded W. Gunther Plaut as national president of the Canadian Jewish Congress, in 1977. Active in many communal and civil-libertarian causes, he is the author (with M. Weinfeld and W. Shaffir) of *The Canadian Jewish Mosaic*.

NORMAN COUSINS

Norman Cousins is adjunct professor of the School of Medicine at UCLA and for thirty-five years was editor of the *Saturday Review*. He is the author of fifteen books, the most recent being *Human Options*. President of the World Federalists' Association, he is the recipient of more than forty-four honorary degrees. The Society of Authors and Journalists named him Author of the Year, and he received the Gold Medal of Literature from the National Arts Club.

HARRY S. CROWE

While this volume was being prepared, Harry Sherman Crowe died suddenly, on July 25, 1981, at the age of fifty-eight. At the time of his death he was dean of Atkinson College, York University (Metropolitan Toronto), editor of *Middle East Focus*, and a staunch civil-libertarian as well as a scholar of Canadian labor. W. Gunther Plaut was amongst those who spoke words of eulogy at the memorial observance and called him a true friend of the Jewish people and of Israel.

The article is based on a lecture delivered on October 29, 1978, in Toronto. The portion dealing with the Evian Conference appeared in *Middle East Focus* 1, no. 4 (1978), 17–19.

YORAM DINSTEIN

Yoram Dinstein is rector of Tel Aviv University. He is editor of the *Israel Yearbook on Human Rights* and professor of international law. He was a member of the Israel Mission to the United Nations and on numerous occasions represented Israel on various United Nations' commissions.

EMIL L. FACKENHEIM

Emil L. Fackenheim, philosopher and Jewish activist, is university professor at the University of Toronto, and holds a sabbatical appointment at Hebrew University in Jerusalem. One of the chief interpreters of the Holocaust, he has lectured in many countries. The latest of his books is *Encounters Between Judaism and Philosophy*.

The article first appeared in *Masada* (Toronto) 7, no. 3 (1976), 4.

HARVEY J. FIELDS

Harvey J. Fields was rabbi of Holy Blossom Temple in Toronto and is now at Wilshire Boulevard Temple in Los Angeles. The author of *Bechol Levavcha*, he is the chairman of the Joint Commission of the Union of American Hebrew Congregations–Central Conference of American Rabbis–American Conference of Cantors' Commission on Worship.

ROBERT GORDIS

Robert Gordis is professor emeritus in Bible and the Philosophies of Religion at Jewish Theological Seminary of America. He served for over three decades as rabbi of Temple Beth El of Rockaway Park, New York. He was the founder and is currently the editor of the quarterly journal *Judaism*. His latest major work is a commentary and new translation of the biblical Book of Job.

His article is based on an article in *Conservative Judaism* 35 (1982), 47–55.

ALFRED GOTTSCHALK

Alfred Gottschalk is the president of the Hebrew Union College–Jewish Institute of Religion, which has campuses in Cincinnati, New York, Los Angeles, and Jerusalem, and is professor of Bible and Jewish Religious Thought. He currently serves on the United States Holocaust Memorial Council.

The article first appeared in *Judaism* 29, no. 3 (1980), 286-94.

WILLIAM W. HALLO

William W. Hallo is the William M. Laffan Professor of Assyriology and Babylonian Literature at Yale University, as well as curator of the Babylonian Collection, the chairman of the Department of Near Eastern Languages and Literatures, and chairman of the Advisory Committee on Judaic Studies. He is the author of numerous books, the most recent being *Early Near Eastern Seals*. He contributed five introductory essays to *The Torah, a Modern Commentary*, ed. by W. Gunther Plaut (1981).

The article is a revised version of a lecture originally delivered at Temple Emanu-El, New York, March 5, 1978, for the series "Crisis Moments in Jewish History".

BORA LASKIN

The Right Honourable Bora Laskin, p.c., is chief justice of Canada. He was formerly a member of the Ontario Court of Appeal, Professor of law at the University of Toronto, and has been the recipient of many honorary degrees.

The article is based on a lecture given at Simon Fraser University, Burnaby, British Columbia, on May 24, 1974.

MALCOLM E. LEIN

Malcolm E. Lein was the director and president of the Minnesota Museum of Art in St. Paul, Minnesota. He is the president of the Design Consultants of Minnesota, and since his retirement from the museum, a partner with The Gallery St. Paul.

WALTER F. MONDALE

Walter F. Mondale is a Minnesotan by birth, a lawyer by education, and a long-time friend of our jubilar. He was attorney general of his state from 1960 to 1964, and then represented Minnesota as a United States' senator from 1964 to 1977. He served as vice-president of the United States from 1977 to 1981.

The article is based on a convocation address at Hebrew University, Jerusalem, July 1, 1981.

DAVID POLISH

David Polish is founding rabbi of Beth Emet, the Free Synagogue in Evanston, Illinois. He has taught at Northwestern University, Garrett Theological Seminary, and is currently a visiting-lecturer at the Hebrew Union College in Los Angeles. He is a past-president of the Central Conference of American Rabbis. The latest of his books is *Renew Our Days—The Zionist Issue in Reform Judaism*.

HERMAN E. SCHAALMAN

Herman E. Schaalman has been the rabbi of Emanuel Congregation in Chicago, Illinois, since 1955. In 1951 he founded at Oconomowoc, Wisconsin, the first camp for the Union of American Hebrew Congregations. He serves currently as president of the Central Conference of American Rabbis. He was one of the five students who, along with Gunther Plaut, came in the summer of 1935 to the Hebrew Union College in Cincinnati on a scholarship.

ALEXANDER M. SCHINDLER

Alexander M. Schindler is president of the Union of American Hebrew Congregations and the former chairman of the Conference of Presidents of Major American Jewish Organizations. He has been awarded the coveted Bublick Prize by the Hebrew University in 1978.

The article is based on a Founders' Day address at Hebrew Union College–Jewish Institute of Religion.

Lou H. Silberman

Lou H. Silberman is visiting-professor in the department of Oriental Studies at the University of Arizona, and is the president of the Society of Biblical Literature. He has been a visiting-professor at the University of Vienna, at the Divinity School of the University of Chicago, and visiting-scholar in the Postgraduate Centre for Hebrew Studies in Oxford. For many years he was professor of Jewish literature and thought at Vanderbilt University.

Bhausaheb Ubale

Bhausaheb Ubale holds a Ph.D. from the University of Manchester, England. He was named to the Ontario Human Rights' Commission in 1978, and in 1979 was appointed race relations' commissioner. He recently wrote a report entitled *Equal Opportunity and Public Policy*, which deals with the concern of the South Asian community and their place in the Canadian mosaic.

Elie Wiesel

Elie Wiesel, author and lecturer, university professor at Boston University, is more than anyone else responsible for placing the facts and implications of the Holocaust on the moral agenda of the world. President Jimmy Carter appointed him chairman of the United States' Holocaust Memorial Council. The first of his twenty-one published books was *Night*, an account of his sojourn in Auschwitz.

The story was translated by W. Gunther Plaut from the original French.

Walter S. Wurzburger

Walter S. Wurzburger is rabbi of Congregation Shaaray Tefila in Lawrence, New York, and the editor of *Tradition*. He is president of the Synagogue Council of America and past president of the Rabbinical Council of America. He is a member of the Department of Philosophy at Yeshiva University.